American Girls, Beer,
and Glenn Miller

The American Military Experience
John C. McManus, Series Editor

The books in this series portray and analyze the experience of Americans in military service during war and peacetime from the onset of the twentieth century to the present. The series emphasizes the profound impact wars have had on nearly every aspect of recent American history and considers the significant effects of modern conflict on combatants and noncombatants alike. Titles in the series include accounts of battles, campaigns, and wars; unit histories; biographical and autobiographical narratives; investigations of technology and warfare; studies of the social and economic consequences of war; and in general, the best recent scholarship on Americans in the modern armed forces. The books in the series are written and designed for a diverse audience that encompasses nonspecialists as well as expert readers.

American Girls, Beer, and Glenn Miller

GI Morale in World War II

James J. Cooke

University of Missouri Press

Columbia

Copyright © 2012 by
The Curators of the University of Missouri
University of Missouri Press, Columbia, Missouri 65211
Printed and bound in the United States of America
All rights reserved
First paperback printing, 2016

Cataloging-in-Publication data available from the Library of Congress.
ISBN 978-0-8262-2111-7

♾™ This paper meets the requirements of the
American National Standard for Permanence of Paper
for Printed Library Materials, Z39.48, 1984.

Interior design and composition: Jennifer Cropp
Cover design and art: Jordin Ruthstein
Typefaces: Minion, MS Reference, Blizzard

A half-century ago, a GI stationed in Europe walked into the post Service Club and saw a newly arrived Special Services hostess. Wanting to talk to a pretty young American girl, I decided to pass up the coffee and doughnuts; I introduced myself. A year later we were married in the post chapel with the post librarian as a bridesmaid, my company commander gave the bride away, and my platoon sergeant was my best man. So much time has passed, but she still serves as my comma and subject-verb agreement queen. Those fifty years have passed with four children, one war, and a comfortable home in Oxford, Mississippi. Now there are memories with those faint sounds of crying babies, bugle calls, crash of guns, and additions to the house.

Contents

Acknowledgments

A half century has passed since the guns of Europe and Asia fell silent, and the number of military veterans and civilian participants slowly shrinks. It has taken five decades for many of those who fought to speak about what they did. Those of us who as children gathered tin cans and newspapers and filled Red Cross boxes for the wounded look with some pride at having been a part of that great seminal event in the history of the United States. I give thanks for the many veterans who spent time talking with me. In my Veterans of Foreign Wars post, we have a few World War II GIs, and we say with awe that one was on Omaha Beach on June 6, 1944. Civilians such as Mary Ann Bowen and Maralyn Howell Bullion gave generously of their time to answer questions and recall emotions. I thank them all. I must give a special place for Tim Frank, who did research for me at the National Archives at College Park, Maryland. His knowledge of the archives is great, and this book is complete simply because of his work. I must also praise Betty Bradbury of Blooming-ton, Indiana, who took my often messy manuscript and turned it into usable material for the University of Missouri Press. I am indebted to Clair Willcox, Sara Davis, and Annette Wenda of the press, who have guided me through the process of producing a readable book. Fifty years ago my wife and I married. For five decades she has been my staunchest critic and checked every comma, semicolon, and the like. There would be no books without her.

American Girls, Beer, and Glenn Miller

Introduction

World War II was, of course, the seminal event of the twentieth century. The United States, and indeed the world, would never be the same again. American historians and commentators have written countless volumes describing the campaigns, battles, personalities, and complex allied diplomacy of the war that produced "the greatest generation." The United States' commitment to the war far exceeded any preceding military effort, including the First World War, often called the Great War.

American troops, on a limited scale, began combat operations in France during the spring and early summer of 1918. In early September General John J. Pershing launched the Saint-Mihiel offensive, the first truly American battle of the war, and this was followed by the Meuse-Argonne fight at the end of September that ended with the Armistice of November 11, 1918. Although casualties were heavy, the American Expeditionary Force was in combat much less than one year. There was no grace, no sophistication, in the AEF's fighting. Some poorly trained divisions fell apart at the start of the Meuse-Argonne battle. Troops who had thought they would conduct open or maneuver warfare too often were thrown against German defenses in bloody direct-frontal assaults. Every unit suffered morale problems in various degrees due to cold and wet weather, poor food, lack of supplies, and what appeared to the Doughboys of the AEF to be a lack of concern for their well-being by superior officers. When mail or packages reached the soldiers in France, it was clear that their families, friends, and communities were behind them, and that had a great bearing on the morale of the soldiers of 1918.

The Doughboys of the Great War did benefit from the efforts of a number of civilian organizations that were determined to bring some small comforts to the soldiers in France. The Young Men's Christian Association (YMCA), Catholic Knights of Columbus, Jewish Welfare Board, Salvation Army, and

American Red Cross sent volunteers to serve the troops of the American Expeditionary Force as best they could given the circumstances of the battlefields of 1918. Depending on the generosity of the American civilian population, those organizations went to the front, opened what were called huts, and gave cigarettes, candy, and the ever-popular coffee and doughnuts to any soldier regardless of faith or denomination. Their gifts from the American people depended on shipping space and, consequently, were uneven in quantity. The volunteers were constantly praised by the troops because the huts were close to the trenches or front lines. Often under shell fire, the representatives of the organizations performed under very difficult circumstances. A number were killed or wounded during operations. Many of the volunteers were women, who lived under the same miserable conditions of the western front. Some days a prayer, a doughnut, or a cigarette was just as good as a bayonet or a rifle bullet as far as morale was concerned.

Into this mix came three men who would have great impact on the issue of army morale. Frederick H. Osborn was a Princeton University intellectual who had been deemed unfit for military service. Being a patriotic American, Osborn joined the American Red Cross and went to France to serve the troops of the AEF. Two decades later, Osborn would become the father of army morale efforts during World War II. Osborn saw firsthand the confusion over supplying troops and knew that morale was critical for an army either in training or in combat. Serving on the western front was a recent West Point graduate, Captain Joseph W. Byron. Together these two men would use their Great War experiences to shape the course of morale during the next war. Raymond B. Fosdick was an experienced American police officer who had spent time in Paris studying the techniques and problems there. Secretary of War Newton Baker appointed Fosdick to investigate problems with the troops along the American-Mexican border in 1916.

During the First World War, Fosdick became the chairman of Training Camp Activities, the commission aimed at providing activities for the soldiers in camp. Alcohol consumption and a rising venereal disease (VD) rate were of great concern for President Woodrow Wilson, and Secretary Baker backed Fosdick's activities. After the war, Fosdick, along with Edward Frank Allen, published a book titled *Keeping Our Fighters Fit for War and After* (1918), which outlined what was needed for soldiers to maintain their morale when making that difficult transition from civilian to military life. Osborn used Fosdick's work as a basis for army morale in the next world war.

The history of the army in World War II is filled with dramatic events and personalities, from Normandy to Bastogne to the bloody fighting in New Guinea and the Philippine Islands. Generals Patton, MacArthur, Eisenhower, and Bradley quite rightly occupy a special place in the study of the war. While great battles were fought and great leaders emerged, there were countless others who worked tirelessly to see that final victory was achieved. When war was on the horizon, General George C. Marshall determined that the United States would not enter the conflict as unprepared as the nation had been in 1917. Getting the best advice, he brought to the army a number of civilians who were willing to put their businesses or research efforts on hold and serve the country. Among them were Osborn and Byron, who initially worked as "dollar-a-year men"; eventually, they were commissioned and worked tirelessly to enhance the morale of the troops. Osborn had an interwar academic career, whereas Byron had left the army in 1919 to become a successful businessman.

The soldiers who would fight World War II were very different from their fathers and uncles who manned the trenches on the western front. In 1917 the 82nd Division, which had 25,000 officers and men, conducted a survey of its enlisted men. More than 3,000 soldiers stated that they had some experience with motorcars, and 548 men claimed that they had "expert" experience with driving. Five thousand men, however, said that they had extensive experience with horses. At Camp Mills, New York, Private Everett Scott of the 163rd Infantry regiment wrote to his parents in 1917 that several military aircraft flew over the camp and all the troops turned out to see such an amazing sight. By 1940 most of the soldiers had experience with driving an automobile, and airmail service from coast to coast had been established in the 1920s.

The radio was a family's main source of entertainment, and there was a constant stream of weekly shows bringing big bands, comedians, dramas, and the popular soap operas into the home. Movies were now filled with sound, and many movies were in color. The soda fountain was a favorite gathering place for young men and women; the milk shake, hamburger, and hot dog were standard fare. Mass markets and mass consumerism of the 1920s went well into the 1930s. Magazines featured ad after ad for the best shirts, skirts, whiskey, cigarettes, and labor-saving devices, such as the newest Hoover vacuum cleaner or washing machine. Of course, the automobile—the Packard, the LaSalle, the Cord, the Ford, the Chevrolet—was sold in vast numbers. Much to the distress of some, the jitterbug became the dance of the day, and the big bands—those led by Glenn Miller, Tommy Dorsey, and Artie Shaw— blended the large orchestra sound with the great American contribution, jazz. This was a generation of expectations, and that fact could not be ignored by the army. To men like Osborn and Byron who came from the mainstream of American civilian life, one from the intellectual community and one from the world of business, the needs of those young men would have to be met if morale was to be maintained.

The whole question of morale is a complex one. Battlefield morale has been explored by many writers, such as Stephen Ambrose. Readers are already familiar with such terms as *unit cohesion* and *good leadership* and know that in combat men fight for each other, their buddies. But what was available for the incoming World War II soldier, whether volunteer or draftee, to ease his transition from being a civilian to a combat-ready, effective soldier? It is the basic premise of this study that the Special Services clubs, the well-stocked and inexpensive Post Exchange (PX), the on-post and off-post United Service Organizations (USO) club, the Red Cross, and the Salvation Army hostess serving freshly brewed coffee and hot doughnuts played a vital role in morale during that transition, and those institutions followed the troops into combat zones in Europe, the Pacific, and elsewhere.

Men like Generals Osborn and Byron knew that where there was a demand, a supply would follow, and follow the troops it did. As the war became more intense, the issue of morale became more complex. The direction of morale activities took on form and structure and became an important fixture in army life during World War II.

When the guns fell silent in 1945, the need for morale building did not end. For the United States, the involvement in world affairs did not mirror the policies of the post–World War I era. The United States committed troops under the Third US Army to the occupation of Germany from 1919 to 1923, while the American government preferred to return to isolation from European affairs. That there was not a return to the American policy that followed the end of the Great War is evident from the Marshall Plan, the commitment to the North Atlantic Treaty Organization (NATO), and other overseas activities, including the wars in Korea, Vietnam, Kosovo, Iraq, and Afghanistan.

The institutions that Osborn and Byron built have borne great fruit and continue as a vital part of the army's attempt to provide for the soldiers and their families into the twenty-first century. Post Exchanges look more like civilian shopping malls, athletic field houses have all of the equipment that one finds in off-post civilian gyms, and army commissaries offer everything that large grocery stores advertise but at a lower cost. At Fort Bliss, Texas, the army opened a massive complex featuring everything from a PX to restaurants to a multiplex theater. This is certainly different from the rude wooden buildings that housed Byron's exchanges or Osborn's Special Services clubs during World War II. Because those World War II institutions continue to exist in a greater form, it is wise to look at their genesis, forged in the second great world conflict of the twentieth century.

1

The Abnormal Communities

Corporal Elmer W. Sherwood had been in France for almost six months. His unit, the 150th Field Artillery Regiment, formally of the Indiana National Guard, was a part of the artillery brigade that served under the 42nd "Rainbow" Division. His unit, being trained by the French, was near the front to learn the ways of mortal combat on the western front. Like most of his Hoosier comrades, he was hungry and out of cigarettes, and Sherwood decided to find a source for food and tobacco. After a two-mile walk, he found a YMCA hut where he got a meager, but hot, meal and found the smokes he needed. In his diary, for March 3, 1918, he wrote, "The Y.M.C.A. [representative] said he didn't like the language the Huns were using but he was sticking to his post, tho shells were landing in his backyard."[1] Sherwood knew, as did so many of General John J. Pershing's Doughboys, that the army provided little hot food and no small comforts like cigarettes or a candy bar. To a soldier like Sherwood, such things as a hot meal or tobacco were important to the morale that all combat troops had to maintain.

The United States Army's attention to morale issues had been a problem for as long as there was an army. The old observation that war was a few moments of sheer terror and days of mind-numbing boredom was quite true. Up to World War I, little attention was paid to the morale of the soldier in the ranks. The men played cards, rolled dice, and had ball games if balls were available. When left for long periods in camp, soldiers tended to look for something to drink, and when they got into towns, too many were inclined "to take a ride" on local prostitutes. Commanders were inclined to try to ban alcoholic beverages, and venereal disease was viewed with great dismay as cases increased. The twin vices of strong drink and prostitution became a continual area of concern for all army commanders, but until the entry of America into the Great War, little was done to offer alternative diversions for the troops.

When President Abraham Lincoln issued his call for seventy-five thousand volunteers in the spring of 1861, the situation changed as far as the public perception of soldiers, because those were hometown regiments, filled with men who were well known. The first camps took on an atmosphere of a weekend in the woods. Some regiments even hired cooks from their hometowns to prepare meals, and rations were plentiful. Regiments were attired in colorful uniforms, such as the gray of New York regiments, red shirts for some, and re-creations of Revolutionary garb. War was snapping banners, stirring bands, and little drill, as it would all be over in six months, with the Union restored. Then they met the equally untrained and garishly uniformed Confederates along a meandering creek in northern Virginia called Bull Run. In June 1861, the United States Sanitary Commission was created to supply kitchens in the ever-growing Union camps, distribute supplies to the always filled hospitals, and provide rests for disabled soldiers. Collaborating with the Sanitary Commission was the United States Christian Commission, which was formed in 1861 to provide spiritual comfort for the troops. This commission began with the efforts of the YMCA National Committee, and it had the duty of working with Protestant army chaplains who would preach in the camps and follow their regiments into battle. Later in the war, the Ladies Auxiliary was formed to raise funds to support the growing spiritual needs of soldiers. In a time when faith was a vital part of American life, the Christian Commission performed an important, morale-raising role. It also provided an opportunity for those back home to contribute or actually work for the well-being of the troops. It would come as no surprise that the YMCA would be in the forefront of providing for the troops in both world wars in the next century.

The volunteers in both armies, and later the conscripts, looked for those small comforts that made life in the camps and on the march better. By 1861 most regiments, Union and Confederate, had added a civilian merchant called a sutler. The idea, as far as soldier morale was concerned, started out as a good one, but as the war went on, the regimental sutler became known as a "dog robber," a miserable profiteer who fleeced the soldiers. Sutlers often sold rancid meat pies, three-cent stamps for five cents, cheap and shoddy goods at high prices, and worse—cheap rot-gut whiskey disguised as canned peaches. Liquor for enlisted men was banned in the camps, but allowed for the officers. As long as there have been soldiers, there has been a thirst for the alcoholic beverage, and that was certainly true of the soldiers in blue and gray.

As the first year of the war ended, the sutler all but disappeared from the Confederate camps because of the Union blockade of Southern ports and a general shortage of salable goods. There were times when Union soldiers raided the sutlers' tents, stealing what merchandise they had, and happy were the Confederates when they caught sutlers' wagons. Generals U. S. Grant and William T. Sherman detested the sutlers and regarded them as no better than disloyal thieves. They tried to rid the camps of them, but there was not any group that could replace them as far as comfort items were concerned. After the war, the institution of soldiers' canteens, later named the Post Exchange, would grow out of the chaotic situation experienced during the Civil War.

The public became war weary as combat dragged on for four years, and although there were continual fairs and fund-raisers for the troops of the Civil War, attention focused on the "boom times" that the war produced. Noted Civil War historian Bruce Catton asserts that by 1862, many viewed it as a chance to make great sums of money.[2] What Catton cites in his works on the great American conflict of the 1860s sounds very much like the bitter words of Private David Kenyon Webster of E Company, 506th Parachute Infantry Regiment, in 1944, when he wrote to his parents, "I wonder if the civilians at home realize, for instance, what an airborne operation in Germany will mean? It means trench foot and frostbite. . . . I can see no glamour or glory in such an affair, but that's all the newspapers in the States will feature, that and heroes."[3] Maintaining morale for the soldier and the civilian would be a tricky matter when millions of men and women served in uniform during a great war that lasted almost five years for some.

The end of the war in 1865 meant a massive demobilization of men and new missions for the United States Army. After the war, the nation returned to peaceful pursuits, and the army shrank as Congress reduced military budgets. The army had to maintain the peace on the frontier and had too many missions for the number of cavalry and infantry regiments stationed in the West.

There were few units in the East, usually posted near large cities. Life on the western frontier was quite boring unless there was a campaign against Native Americans, and few operations garnered the interest of the civilian population unless it was something on the scale of General George A. Custer's fatal encounter on the Little Big Horn River in 1876. Slowly, the army began a system of instruction for officers at Fort Leavenworth, Kansas, but for the rest of the army, pay remained low and promotions took years to obtain. Unless an officer came from an affluent family, social contact with the nonmilitary population was difficult to maintain. For the enlisted men, the situation on the frontier and on the eastern posts was worse. Their pay was dismal, and their associations beyond the post were few unless they were in the tenderloin districts, where cheap whiskey could be bought for five cents a glass and a cheap, often diseased, prostitute could be had for twenty-five cents. Many of the posts had a soldiers' canteen where a soldier could go, but, as was typical of the post–Civil War army, there was a distressing lack of form and structure for the canteens. To remedy this, in 1895 the Office of the Chief of Staff issued a general order that permitted commanders to establish a Post Exchange that would purchase items at a low cost and sell them to soldiers at a small profit. Those profits would then be used for the benefit of the enlisted ranks.

The Office of the Quartermaster General in Washington did not like the order, arguing that they, not commanders in the field, should purchase the supplies. The officers who had to oversee their troops heartily approved, positing that they knew best what their soldiers wanted. The PX remained in the hands of the post commanders. The exchange was a place where only enlisted men could gather to smoke, play cards, drink some beer, have checkers matches, and simply relax away from the routine of military life and the watchful eyes of their officers.

Sergeants would oversee the conduct of the men in the exchange. Some town merchants saw their profits decline, especially after the monthly pay-day when a private's twenty dollars a month could be wasted on watered-down rot-gut rye whiskey or paid to painted women of the street (as they were called). Officers were excluded from the exchange for good reasons. A soldier, perhaps with a bit more beer than was wise, might say something or do something that could result in a court-martial. Prudence dictated that the exchange remain the domain of the enlisted soldiers and their noncommissioned officers. This was a good step forward in organizing an institution that would support individual and unit morale, but what would happen when the troops deployed to the field for extended periods of campaigning?

The Spanish-American War added nothing to the maintenance of army morale. In fact, that "Splendid Little War" showed that the army was not prepared to care for the troops in the field. Superior officers did not understand what had happened, from the chaotic conditions at the Tampa port of embarkation to the deteriorating sanitation situation in the camps. Food, so vital to soldier morale, was very poor, and soldiers complained about what they called embalmed beef and army hard crackers that were so old and weevil infested they could not be eaten. The story goes that boxes of stale, wormy crackers were issued to the troops, and marked on the sides of the boxes was "BC," which stood for "Brigade Commissary." The soldiers immediately claimed that "BC" stood for "Before Christ." The rising venereal disease rate troubled the War Department, which knew that the situation was due to boredom in the camps. The subsequent occupation of the Philippines meant that troops would be sent overseas for long periods of time. The exchange followed simply because it had become an army institution.

The question of morale did not surface again until President Woodrow Wilson dispatched General John J. Pershing to the American-Mexican border in 1916 following a raid on Columbus, New Mexico, by Mexican insurgents led by the legendary Poncho Villa. In addition to the Regular Army, units of the National Guard were also sent to the area of operations. Now citizen-soldiers were involved in a lengthy campaign.

In 1916 President Wilson nominated Cleveland, Ohio, lawyer Newton D. Baker to be the secretary of war, and there was shock in the halls of the War Department. Baker was a well-known pacifist with no experience with the American military. The pipe-smoking lawyer, however, tapped into the best military minds in the army, and it was Baker's decision to name John J. Pershing to command the expedition into Mexico and to send National Guard regiments to the border. In the summer of 1916, reports began to circulate about the conditions on the border, with stories from observers and journalists that the venereal disease rates were rising and bored troops were often drunk. Jerome D. Greene of the Rockefeller Foundation became so concerned about the continuing tide of firsthand reports that he sought out an appointment with Baker. There had to be an official inspection and report about the accusations of rampant prostitution and cheap whiskey causing public intoxication among the troops. During the meeting, Greene suggested that Raymond B. Fosdick, a noted investigator who had spent a year in Paris studying police techniques, be sent to investigate. Fosdick, a political progressive, was no stranger to the seamy side of life, having observed it in New York and in Paris.[4]

Fosdick found two problems when he arrived. The first was that the reports did not fully represent the extent of prostitution or the widespread overindulgence in cheap whiskey. The number of hastily constructed brothels had expanded tremendously, with prostitutes pouring into Texas and other border states from cities like New Orleans and New York. The second problem was that Fosdick was distrusted by the officers he was sent to assist.

Many officers were educating their soldiers in sexual matters and the new procedures of prophylaxis to combat, as best as possible, venereal disease, and they feared that this official sent by a pacifist secretary of war might very well declare that such classes and efforts were in reality an affront to morality because such a treatment could encourage the troops to engage in illicit sex. Fosdick was no prude, nor was he an agent of the many religious and reformist groups who opposed prophylaxis as an invitation to patronize prostitutes.[5] Driving around camp areas, he saw a massive number of troops walking toward the red-light districts.

Fosdick recalled that the problems arose from the fact that troops had nothing to do with their time off. Boredom became an enemy of army morale and the accepted morals to which the majority of Americans adhered. Of great interest to Fosdick was the observation that when the YMCA set up buildings where soldiers could visit, play games, read, and have a cup of coffee or a doughnut, the incidence of soldiers going off toward the beckoning red lights of the tenderloin districts lessened. This was a lesson that was learned and would have a great impact on the maintenance of army morale during the Great War and World War II. Fosdick recognized that young men had continual sexual urges and that many had not engaged in intercourse. Hormones (Fosdick did not use that term) and a natural curiosity influenced men in uniform, far from home and the restraints of society, to be drawn to the brothels and saloons.[6]

No one in the War Department knew that in just a few months, the lessons learned about troop morale on the border would have to be applied with a national mobilization of millions of America's young men to fight overseas. Fosdick did warn Baker that many senior army officers opposed the inclusion of civilian agencies operating with the troops in the camps. They, according to Fosdick, wanted only those in uniform to minister to the needs of the troops, but their efforts during the 1916 operation amounted to almost nothing, which resulted in soldiers frequenting the brothels and tawdry saloons that had sprung up all around the camps. What Fosdick, who had now become Baker's resident authority on soldier morale, proposed was a concentration of the agencies under one authority that would work with the commanding officers but have a certain autonomy in providing for the troops. Newton Baker was impressed with the report, and he was in a political position of great power and authority. This pacifist, now in charge of the nation's preparation for war, named Raymond B. Fosdick to head the Commission of Training Camp Activities in 1917. This was a shrewd move on Baker's part in that he could allow Fosdick and the commission to take on the burden of building morale as well as morals while he spent the majority of his time supporting the requirements of John J. Pershing, who had just been appointed to command the American Expeditionary Force in France now that the United States was at war with Germany.[7]

On April 2, 1917, President Woodrow Wilson went before a joint session of Congress and asked for a declaration of war against Imperial Germany, and on April 6 Congress obliged Wilson by passing the declaration after furious debate. It was confusing for many because in 1916 Wilson had campaigned for reelection on a platform that included a promise that the United States would not enter into the European war. As late as January 1917, Wilson had hoped for a "peace without victory" that would end the ghastly bloodshed in Europe. Of great concern was his secretary of war, a well-known pacifist, and many wondered if a person who had been opposed to war could lead an army into conflict. What was not clear was that Baker had thrown himself into the job, asking some key generals such as Tasker Bliss, chief of staff of the army, not only their advice but also to instruct him concerning areas in which he was totally unfamiliar. Baker brought to the War Department a concern for the troops who would have to go to France, especially now that many were drafted into the army and that National Guard units were called into federal service for overseas deployment. Newton Baker's area of influence exceeded that of Abraham Lincoln's secretary of war, Edwin M. Stanton.

The War Department faced an amazing array of problems in that the nation was unprepared for war, with few weapons or experienced trainers, and a logistics system that would try the patience of everyone involved in World War I. While the mountains of problems grew for the War Department, Baker did have Raymond B. Fosdick and the Commission of Training Camp Activities to assume a heavy burden, and despite the grumbling of some senior officers, civilians would be a part of the training camps and a fact of military life in France.

It did not take long for conditions in the camps being filled by National Guardsmen and conscripts to become a matter of concern for the army. Corporal Maurice Moser had enlisted in the 1st Arkansas Infantry, which was sent to Camp Beauregard, Louisiana, where it was redesignated as the 153rd Infantry Regiment of the 39th Division. He wrote to his parents in Little Rock, Arkansas, that the towns of Leesville and Pineville were placed off-limits to soldiers because of the rising number of brothels and saloons that had sprung up in those places. He related that in one day, there were thirty-one cases of venereal disease. As he wrote, any soldier caught in the towns would be court-martialed, and, as delicately as possible, he said that the disease they contracted was syphilis.[8] To complicate matters for the commanders at Camp Beauregard, the post and the surrounding towns were struck with several types of communicable diseases such as meningitis and measles. Fosdick had warned Newton Baker that unless steps were taken quickly, the situation could deteriorate and morale would suffer. The question was not how to take a mass of young healthy men and turn them into effective combat fighters. It was how to keep those troops "fit for the fight." Camp disease was inevitable when so many young men from differing backgrounds were brought together, but the problems with prostitution and alcohol could be dealt with in other ways.

The surgeon general of the army recognized the problem and asked the American Social Hygiene Association in New York to prepare a booklet, written in plain language, that would be given to all soldiers. The booklet, titled

Keeping Fit to Fight, stated, "This is a man-to-man talk, straight from the shoulder without gloves."[9] It warned that venereal disease was the greatest menace to the army and that contracting a disease was akin to a self-inflicted wound. Based on Medical Corps reports in 1916, for every one thousand soldiers, measles infected twenty enlisted men, while VD was contracted by ninety-one. The small booklet was distributed, and officers were enjoined to carry out instruction based on the material. Interestingly, the booklet did not mention the newly introduced prophylaxis, urging only abstinence. Obviously, from General Pershing to his subordinate commanders to the surgeon general of the army, there was a concern over how increased high levels of VD infection could adversely affect training in the United States and combat on the western front in France.

Fosdick reported that when groups such as the YMCA arrived on the scene on the border in 1916, many more soldiers remained in camp and enjoyed the games and treats that the Y offered. As a major representative of Newton Baker, Fosdick and his commission urged agencies, church groups, and the like to come into the camps. Raymond Fosdick regarded the training camps as "abnormal communities," full of young soldiers far from home and the restraints of home, community associations, and church, and where few women were seen and normal privacy was nonexistent.[10] Time was regulated: meals taken in mess halls by the troops, baths taken in the presence of other troops, lights turned on and out at prescribed times. Men from all walks of life and social groups were thrown together. To build an army of millions to fight in France, it was necessary to construct a highly disciplined way of life, subordinating the individual to the group. To assist in this process, it was vital, so Fosdick and the commission posited and Baker firmly agreed, for institutions to be constructed to maintain a high level of morale that would have to follow the troops overseas.

The YMCA, Knights of Columbus, Salvation Army, Jewish Welfare Board, American Red Cross, and American Library Association joined the effort, as did local church and social groups. There were differences between the groups. The YMCA gave away cigarettes, while the Salvation Army refused to handle tobacco. There was a tacit agreement that the huts maintained by religious groups would not deny service to soldiers of a different faith. At Camp Mills, New York, local church and social groups undertook a campaign to supply socks, mufflers, and sweaters, and they assembled fifteen thousand items for the men of the 42nd "Rainbow" Division training there. The ladies were thanked by Captain Oscar W. Underwood of Alabama, who then informed them that these greatly appreciated gifts had to be distributed by the Red Cross.[11]

Morale activities slowly took on a centralized form. All training camps had an alcohol- and prostitute-free zone around the posts, which reduced to some degree the problems caused by vices, and as more organizations appeared in the camps, the incidents caused by cheap saloons and brothels declined. Of great help to morale was the American Library Association, which opened libraries in almost every training camp in the United States and followed the troops to France and eventually Germany. Public solicitation of funds and books brought reading materials to the troops, and since many of the soldiers were educated, the demand was high.[12] This was a lesson learned that would surface again in the next world war.

While civilian agencies and local groups were building their efforts to help soldiers and to maintain morale (and morals), the army had difficulties in dealing with the unprecedented influx of troops into the camps. Soldiers, fresh from civilian life, wanted what would become known as "comfort items." The Post Exchange did not fit the massive mobilization of 1917–18, and items such as candy, cigarettes, smoking tobacco, razors, and the like were to be sold by the Quartermaster Sales Commissary in the camp. They never really kept up with the demand, and often their shelves went unstocked with popular items. For example, Private Eustace Fielder of Vicksburg, Mississippi, arrived for training at Camp Joseph E. Johnston in Florida, and for several weeks the camp, with thousands of soldiers, had no Sales Commissary. When it did open, it was hard-pressed to provide items such as cigarettes or candy for the troops. Fielder, who ironically was assigned to a Sales Commissary unit in the AEF, constantly asked his parents to send him cigarettes, candy, socks, and handkerchiefs.[13] When the commissary opened, it had an effect on soldiers' morale. Corporal Maurice Moser at Camp Beauregard wrote to his parents, "The government opened a canteen [Sales Commissary] here and sells things for cost. They have some chocolates that they sell two pounds for 47 cents and in the town they retail at $1.00 a pound."[14] When a Sales Commissary opened its doors or the YMCA or Salvation Army provided coffee and doughnuts, the soldier, who would have to bear the burden of combat, did not feel alone or forgotten in a system that, by its nature, could be impersonal.

To be fair, when the army could not provide weapons, accoutrements, ammunition, blankets, medical supplies, and even socks, shoes, and uniforms, a pound of chocolate did not seem to be of any importance. The United States went into the Great War unprepared and had to play catch-up quickly. Quartermaster General Henry G. Sharpe was overwhelmed by the tasks at hand and frustrated that the massive buildup of manpower often took precedence over supply needs. Food, or chow as the Doughboys and GIs ever after called it, was a vital part of morale building, and there Sharpe excelled. He established cooks' and bakers' schools, improved mass feeding in mess halls, expanded menus, and, as the number of camps opened, obtained the services of four thousand professional cooks to prepare food.[15] Senators, however, constantly grilled Sharpe about the slow process of getting supplies to the troops, and the quartermaster general pointed to red tape, lack of appropriations, and the inability of textile mills and heavy industry to rapidly adjust their production from peace to war. Most of the soldiers, on the other hand, who were drilling with wooden rifles or using stovepipes to simulate mortars, did not know or care about the great hearings going on in Washington.

General John J. Pershing arrived in France in June 1917 with a small staff, so small, in fact, that the British and French thought that the remainder would be in Europe soon. Pershing would create the first truly functional combat staff as the AEF grew in France. When Pershing left for France, he had a simple mission—to fight as an American army, under American commanders, in an American sector of the western front, and beyond that General Pershing had a remarkable freedom of action to do what he needed to do; Pershing had a military kingdom to rule over.[16] By the Christmas season of 1917, Black Jack Pershing had only four ill-trained, but highly motivated, divisions in France: the 1st, 2nd, 42nd, and 26th. The French army made available training areas and trainers and supplied many of the weapons and equipment needed to fight the Germans. When the American troops walked down the gangplank, they were greeted by enthusiastic civilians, civilians who had endured three years of horrific war marked by endless casualty lists. Bottles of wine, most welcomed by the ever-thirsty Doughboys, were given to the men, as were bread, sausages, vegetables, and the like. Morale was high as the regulars and National Guardsmen marched through French towns toward their designated training areas, but how long would that first blush of cheering crowds and the smiles of pretty French women last? How would Pershing and the AEF deal with the question of maintaining morale in the face of hard training and then deadly combat against a well-seasoned German army? There would be little difference between Maurice Moser and Elmer Sherwood, now in France, as far as those little comforts—the cigarette, a candy bar, stationery to write home on, and the like. It fell to Pershing to make decisions about how to maintain his army's morale and deal with such thorny questions as venereal disease and alcohol, and, of equal importance, what to do with the representatives of civilian agencies who were arriving in France fully expecting to serve the troops as they were doing in the United States.

Certainly, the focus of the AEF had to be training for combat and building a logistical system to support the troops at the front. Pershing had little time to deal with questions of morale or with representatives of the agencies that came to France to minister to the comfort and morale needs of the Doughboys. The discipline of West Point would be the standard for the AEF, Pershing stated, and he fully intended to initiate it. Early on, Black Jack stated that the soldiers of the AEF could enjoy light wine and beer, rejecting the demands of the politically strong prohibitionists that the AEF copy the rules that existed for camps in the United States. Camps were dry, and a ban on alcohol near the camps was enforced, as best as it could be. The Doughboys of the AEF had already been showered with wine as they arrived at the ports of debarkation. The question of candy bars, cigarettes, and comfort items was another matter indeed, and there was no tobacco ration for the army. Black Jack Pershing refused to consider French-style inspected and controlled houses of prostitution near the training areas where the incoming troops of the AEF were stationed. He knew that Newton Baker opposed it and that the American public would be outraged upon hearing of legalized brothels patronized by their sons.

There was a major meeting between Pershing and the representatives of the Red Cross and the YMCA in which the commanding general insisted that those two agencies charge for their goods. Edward C. Carter of the YMCA protested that the contributions from civilians would be enough to give the troops what they needed. Pershing was adamant, saying that his troops would not be the subject of charity; they were not paupers. The YMCA and the Red Cross had to agree, and it was a serious error on Pershing's part. Too often the paymaster was slow in reaching the troops, and the soldiers were aware that there were massive donations from the home front. They never really understood that the commander of the AEF caused their distress.[17]

There were many vocal complaints about "that damned Y," a name the organization did not deserve. The YMCA would not participate in selling goods again during the next world war. It was a lesson the Y learned the hard way. To confuse matters, the Salvation Army, Knights of Columbus, and Jewish Welfare Board were not participants in the agreement made between Pershing and the Red Cross and YMCA. Furthermore, as combat increased for the AEF, there was no control over field representatives of any agency, and they could do as they pleased, as far as the distribution of comfort items was concerned, despite the wishes of General Pershing.

Doughboys were angered over the confusion caused by the YMCA and Red Cross selling what appeared to be donated items. Private Albert M. Ettinger of New York served with the 165th Infantry Regiment on the western front. Years after the war, he recalled with some bitterness, "We had a YMCA barracks [hut] and a Red Cross hut, both of which charged for everything they dispensed. The only place you got anything free was the Knights of Columbus hut. Naturally, I gravitated there."[18] Regardless of policy, those at the front did everything they could for troops, often in the face of grave danger. Mary and Sunshine Sweeny of the YMCA set up their little hut near the front-line trenches, where they made hot coffee and chocolate for the soldiers of the 82nd Division. The two women carried hot drinks, packs of cigarettes, doughnuts, and coffee into the trenches under fire. Both sisters were cited by the 82nd Division's general orders for their gallantry under fire, and Mary Sweeny was awarded the French Croix de Guerre for her extraordinary courage. Bernetta Miller of the YMCA also served the 82nd Division at the front and carried small comforts as well to the troops of the All American Division under heavy German artillery and gas bombardment. The division honored her bravery with a mention in the general orders, as they had the Sweeny sisters.[19] These individual acts of devotion and courage were among countless others across the western front. While sharing the dangers of the battlefield, those men and women simply would not ask a Doughboy for the five cents for a candy bar or package of cigarettes. In the hospitals near the front, the Red Cross turned a blind eye to the requirements of selling cigarettes to a wounded soldier.

A valuable lesson about morale was therefore learned on a twentieth-century battlefield. The American soldier, the product of an emerging mass-consumer society, expected that the fruits of that industrial giant would be available to him, even in the midst of intense combat. A candy bar, a stick of chewing gum, or a cigarette became an integral part of what kept up a soldier's morale and, often, was as good to have as a bullet or a bayonet. Another lesson from the Great War was that the army had to improve the availability and quality of combat rations. Soldiers of the American Civil War remembered their rations with distaste and disdain. Hardtack, salt pork, and coffee constituted the mainstay of the troops, while those in Union blue saw dried apples and an attempt to desiccate vegetables for soup that the soldiers called desecrated vegetables. Rations for the soldiers of the Spanish-American War were just as bad. Quartermaster General Sharpe had made great improvements in the area of food for the training camps in the United States, but once overseas the Doughboys of the AEF faced great problems in the quantity and variety of combat rations. Almost every soldier of the Great War recalled the monotony of rations, mainly a corned beef, called "corned willie," and hardtack. When rations could be cooked by the Mess Section, it was made into a stew known as "slum," for "slumgullion." Rations were a constant major problem for the AEF at the front. Late in the summer of 1918, the army authorized a tobacco and candy ration for the troops, but it came too late for the Doughboys fighting at Saint-Mihiel or in the Meuse-Argonne campaigns.

What became painfully clear was that the AEF had to purchase more than half of the sinews of war locally because industrial output and shipping from the United States could not supply all that was needed for the army. Pershing put in place the General Purchasing Board under the capable civilian-turned-general Charles Gates Dawes, who coordinated purchasing for the supply departments as well as the YMCA and the Red Cross. Although this helped the civilian agencies continue their valuable morale work, it did little to end the food problems for the troops. There were attempts to grow gardens to supply fresh vegetables for the AEF, and the Garden Service Branch was established with the acquisition of three thousand acres for garden plots. By the end of the war, half of the acres were under cultivation. The gardens did help supplement rations in fixed locations, but did little for the troops in combat. The constant reliance on canned, cold rations took its toll on Doughboy health and morale. Cooks tried their best to prepare food for the men in battle, but poor means of delivery meant that once-hot rations were cold and unpalatable when served to the troops in the frontline trenches.[20]

The guns of the western front fell silent on November 11, 1918, and the bloodbath that had beset Europe since 1914 was over. General Pershing had agreed to send an American force into Germany to occupy a sector on the west side of the Rhine River with a headquarters in Koblenz. Corporal Maurice Moser of the 355th Infantry of the 89th Division had been in some of the heaviest fighting of the war, and he, like most of his buddies, hoped to be among the first Doughboys to return to the United States. The division remained in its postcombat assembly areas awaiting orders, and on November 20 they were informed that they would be part of the Third US Army on the Rhine River. Three days later, Moser began his long march toward the homeland of his former enemies and marched in rain and cold until December 21.

Rations were indeed slight, since the cook wagons could not keep up with the moving columns because of muddy roads and steep hills. Many of the Doughboys bought meals from the Belgian and Luxembourgian families they were billeted with. Army rations were meager; comfort items were nonexistent. When the division finally reached its area of responsibility, the YMCA and Red Cross went into action, and on Christmas Day the YMCA gave each soldier "two packs of Camels, a bar of chocolate, and a cigar . . . swell feed for the army to give us at dinner fresh pork, mashed potatoes, jam cake and dried apples."[21] Moser's experience was the same as that of many other Doughboys moving to the Third Army area of occupation. It would take a while for the Commissary Sales units to move into Germany, Luxembourg, and Belgium to support the troops. Morale would have to be maintained with troops, especially with the citizen-soldiers of the National Guard and draftee National Army divisions. Despite orders against fraternization, the YMCA and Red Cross organized chaperoned dances with local girls. It is interesting to note that with the presence of the YMCA and the Red Cross huts and the organized and well-chaperoned dances, the venereal disease rate fell in the Third Army area. This should have been a lesson learned for the next massive occupation of Germany in 1945, but it was not and had to be relearned.

When one looks at veterans' postwar memoirs and questionnaires, one finds that poor food and a lack of comfort items fill their list of complaints. These serious complaints would surface again as America saw war clouds gathering in the late 1930s. Meanwhile, a blueprint for soldier morale was handed to Congress and to Secretary of War Newton Baker in the form of a detailed report on the activities of the Commission of Training Camp Activities. Known as *The Fosdick Report,* it delved into every aspect of soldier life in the training camps and made serious recommendations to improve the morale and the fitness of the American soldier.

Many old-line officers were suspicious of Fosdick and his civilians roaming about the camps, and they made their doubts known to the newly installed chief of staff, Payton C. March, who called Fosdick to his office. March wanted to know if Fosdick would accept the rank of colonel and be in uniform. When Fosdick refused, March suggested that perhaps he would take the rank of brigadier general. In no uncertain terms, Fosdick refused, saying that more often than not, he had to deal with the soldier in the ranks and a colonel or a general could not get an honest response from a soldier faced by a very superior officer.[22]

The report began with the conditions that existed on the border during the 1916 operation and then turned its attention to the new situation that began when America entered the Great War. Working with Edward Frank Allen, Fosdick stated in the report that the foundation of attempts to implement what was needed for a new army was to understand that the training camps, and indeed the whole army, was an assembly of "abnormal communities," that is, young, healthy men thrown together, far away from home, church, and the prevailing restraints of the community.

The first objectives were to reduce alcohol consumption and to end the prevalence of prostitution near the camps. What was needed was a system of "club life" in the camps using civilian agencies such as the YMCA, Red Cross, American Library Association, and the like. Getting the troops interested in organized athletics would build morale and reinforce mandatory army physical training. Dr. Joseph E. Raycroft, professor of hygiene at Princeton University, became the director of athletics for the camps. Football games in the camps became so popular that civilians attended the matches and were charged admission. So good were two teams from western training camps that civilians flocked to the game between the two and generated forty thousand dollars in gate receipts that were plowed back into camp morale programs. Allen and Fosdick also placed great emphasis on the work of the American Library Association in the training camps. In 1917 the public had donated one and a half million dollars to stock camp libraries, which were greatly utilized by the troops. The most requested books were detective thrillers, a trend that would continue during World War II.[23]

The camps grew so quickly that what were called "private amusement enterprises" were allowed to open, and they were closely monitored to make sure that the entertainment was wholesome and moral. Civilian-owned theaters, movie houses, soda fountains, and even a pool hall were opened at Fort Riley, Kansas, and when the post commander was questioned about it, he responded that there was no town close to the post, which now had thousands of soldiers. His reasoning was sound, because the more entertainment offered to the troops, the less the desire to visit the saloons and houses of prostitution nearby.

The Young Women's Christian Association (YWCA) opened Hostess Houses, where wives, mothers, and sweethearts might visit their soldiers in a well-chaperoned and homelike atmosphere. The first of the houses opened at the Plattsburgh, New York, camp, despite the disapproval of some of the older officers, who really did not like so many women in camp. The houses featured nurseries, cafeterias, and comfortable rooms for females only. There would be no conjugal visits between husbands and wives in the Hostess Houses.

Allen and Fosdick also placed special emphasis on the expansion of the Post Exchanges to provide a continual supply of the comfort items that the soldiers wanted. The report ended with the observation that when troops had such things as camp entertainment, athletic competition, comfort items, and the presence of agencies such as the Red Cross, YMCA, Salvation Army, and Jewish Welfare Board, the tendency of soldiers to visit nearby saloons and houses of prostitution declined noticeably.

The report appeared in early 1918, and by May of that year it was made available to the public. *The Fosdick Report* would form the foundation for the operations of the Morale Branch, later known as the Special Services Division, of the United States Army in World War II.

Once the fighting was over on the western front, the AEF turned its attention toward what to do with soldiers who waited to return home to the United States. The troops of the Third Army on the west bank of the Rhine became tourists in what had been the land of the enemy. Other units had leave to visit places like Paris, and in the 82nd Division, which had a high percentage of Italian Americans, trains were rented to take soldiers to Italy to visit relatives. Corporal Harold J. Sherman of Kansas City, Missouri, served in the 140th Infantry Regiment of the 35th Division; he never got to Paris but spent a seven-day leave in the city of Grenoble, France. Sherman enjoyed the facilities and the hot meals offered by the YMCA and Red Cross.[24] On Thanksgiving Day, the officers and men of the 20th Aero Squadron played football against the 11th Aero Squadron. There were hundreds of Doughboy airmen in attendance because of the large number of well-known collegiate football players on both sides. The 11th Aero Squadron won 8 to 6.[25]

The troops of the AEF began their return to the United States, and they were in a high state of euphoria. They had not yet the time to reflect on their experiences in combat on the western front, but they would after their return to civilian life. Many of the veterans turned to inner feelings about death, deprivations, and momentary moments of pleasure, and it was then that they evaluated what had been done to keep their morale intact. All too often, they remembered the irritation and confusion they felt over having to pay for a package of cigarettes or a candy bar. The veterans had little good to say of the leadership of "that damned Y," and said so on many occasions. On the other hand, they remembered the generosity and care shown by the representatives of the Red Cross, YMCA, and Salvation Army in the field, where they shared the dangers and hardships of the Doughboys. The photograph of a smiling, pretty young woman of the Salvation Army, helmet on top of her brown curly hair, making coffee and doughnuts at the front for the soldiers was a popular remembrance of the war.

The troops in the training camps when the news came of the Armistice of November 1918 expressed the lowest state of morale, because they would not have the opportunity to go to France to do "their bit" for the war effort. A soldier at the Officer Training School at Camp Gordon, Georgia, expressed this sentiment in an officially published poem:

> The unlucky ones in this Great War
> Are not the men who are killed,
> Nor wounded ones, be they Allies or Huns.
> The most unfortunate man today
> Is the man who jumped at the chance
> To fight like hell from the tap of the bell,
> But who'll never see service in France.[26]

The soldiers in the camps in the United States had the greatest opportunity to see the great efforts to maintain morale, but their disappointment clouded their views of the effort. They would not wear the overseas chevrons or even the wound stripe of those who fought in France. To make matters even worse, the returning Doughboys had a distinctive unit insignia sewn to the left shoulder of their uniforms—the Red One of the 1st Division, the YD of the 26th Division, the rainbow of the 42nd Division, the double A of the 82nd Division, the SOS of the supply, and many others. That was a brotherhood in which there was a closed membership, a bond among combat veterans for the rest of their lives.

When the army had to address again the issue of morale, it fell to Frederick H. Osborn, who had seen extensive service with the Red Cross in France, and to Joseph W. Byron, who went to France with the 304th Tank Battalion. Ironically, neither men had any extensive experience with the efforts to bring to the soldiers in training such things as the libraries, athletic events, or exchanges, but both men would be instrumental in building a comprehensive and successful system to maintain soldier morale in World War II.

After the war, the government and the army began a process of assessing what had been done right and what had been done wrong. Newton Baker was, of course, concerned over the whole conduct of the war, from training camps to combat in Europe. The status of army morale was part of his considerations. In January 1919, Baker sent a message to General Pershing pointing out that many of those who fought in France had a resentment toward the army that they believed did little to provide for the troops. To remedy this situation, Baker suggested that an association of the civilian agencies such as the Red Cross, YMCA, Salvation Army, and Knights of Columbus with the army would be the best way to provide for the comfort and morale of the troops. In other words, the building and maintenance of soldier morale in training and in combat should not be left to the army alone. Baker suggested that Raymond Fosdick should head up such an association.[27]

Certainly, the army in 1919 had two major tasks: the demobilization of the army and the operations of the Third US Army along the Rhine River in Germany. The plan was basically that eventually only regular army troops would make up the occupation force, and those National Guard and US Army forces that were part of the occupation force would be sent back to the United States as quickly as possible. Such an association between the army and civilian agencies, as proposed by Baker, would be unnecessary, since the traditional efforts of the army along with a small Red Cross presence would be enough for the professional soldiers in Germany. The idea surfaced by Baker, however, would form the foundation for the building of the great civilian agency of the Second World War, the USO. The question of army morale in wartime was put on the shelf during the 1920s and 1930s, but as the specter of war again entered into the American political and military debate, the old question of how to maintain morale would resurface.

But the second great global conflict would not begin for two decades after the November 11 Armistice. In Germany Corporal Elmer Sherwood of the Rainbow Division prepared for the movement to a port of embarkation, to go home, back home to Indiana. He had been in every major battle where the Rainbow was sent—July, Saint-Mihiel, Meuse-Argonne, and then to Bad Neuenahr, Germany, but on this March 26, 1919, he was in a lukewarm shower. He recalled, "Everybody is anxious to keep clean for no one with cooties will be allowed to leave for the U.S. Same applies to venereal cases. Glad I have no occasion to worry."[28] The United States Army was through with war, at least for the next twenty-one years. Right now it was over Over There.

2

American Beer and American Girls

Brigadier General Frederick Osborn, a giant of a man at six foot seven, towered over the four small but beautiful young women in his office in Washington. They seemed to be somewhat thinner and a bit more haggard than when he had first seen them. Mitzi Mayfair, Martha Raye, Kay Francis, and Carole Landis had just completed an extended tour for Osborn, chief of the Special Services Division. In late 1942 into early 1943, those four well-known Hollywood stars toured England and North Africa, performing for the American soldiers serving overseas. They had survived army red tape that was not set up to transport four civilian women overseas; they had seen war up close in North Africa and found out what dangers the infantrymen and bomber crews of the Eighth United States Air Force flying from airfields in England faced. One of them had met, fallen in love with, and married a dashing bomber pilot. Did the experiment work? Osborn was delighted. Every report from the European and Mediterranean theaters of operations indicated that the soldiers loved those American girls, hollered and whistled as they danced and sang, and felt a great lift in their morale from having a respite from the grim realities of war. There would be a flood of American stars of screen and radio to every theater of the war, and countless thousands of GIs from England to New Guinea to India would see and cheer their favorite comedian, band leader, and, more important, American girls! To make things even better, if anything could be better in a world at war, they had a supply of real American beer, American candy bars, and American cigarettes.

The post–World War I army would have had a difficult time even envisioning the transportation of four movie stars across the Atlantic to sing and dance for the troops. Once the Great War was over, the army had to turn its attention to some serious problems, including the survival of the army as an effective fighting force. If indeed World War I was the "war to end all wars," then the army would be small, some elements serving overseas in places like the Philippine Islands and the Hawaiian Islands. In 1923 the Third Army left Germany. Efforts were continually made to locate and identify American battle dead if possible and, if requested by the family, make arrangements to return the remains. More than 30,000 American dead were buried in military cemeteries in Britain, France, and Belgium. The large depots and AEF installations were turned over to French authorities by the late summer of 1919. The United States was withdrawing from world affairs, and there were no plans to commit the nation to further military alliances.[1] The failure of the Senate to ratify the Versailles Treaty and refusal to join the League of Nations reinforced American isolationism.

The regular army remained small, basically hidden from public view. In 1920 Congress established the size of the army at a little more than 250,000 officers and men, but continually reduced the strength to about 120,000, a level that was maintained throughout the 1920s and 1930s. There were few advances in basic weapons or in training methods, but there were improvements in the US Army Air Corps. There were no funds for morale purposes in the army, and the enlisted men, woefully underpaid, relied on the Post Exchange for relaxation and inexpensive goods. As far as civilians were concerned, the active army was rarely seen, except in parades on national patriotic days. The veterans of the Great War celebrated their service through division associations and organizations such as the American Legion and the Veterans of Foreign Wars. Those Doughboys tended to discuss their combat service only among themselves.

On November 21, 1930, General Douglas MacArthur became the chief of staff of the United States, a post he would hold until October 1935. Before assuming the position, MacArthur had expressed his great concern over Japanese designs on East Asia and over the influence of the Soviet Union. He was aggressive in his thinking about the condition of the army, and he began a study about the future mechanization of the army's combat forces. He was also a supporter of expanded American airpower, but in 1933 military appropriations fell to its lowest point since 1923. As the Depression continued, MacArthur became more concerned with communist influence on a desperate public, a concern that came to a head with the suppression of the Veteran Bonus Marchers in Washington in 1932, using regular army forces. Despite advice from one of his subordinates, Major Dwight D. Eisenhower, a bemedaled MacArthur gave interviews painting the Bonus Army as fertile ground for communist agitators. In October 1935, MacArthur stepped down as chief of staff, and President Franklin Roosevelt appointed General Malin Craig to the post. Craig, who had an excellent World War I record, represented the army's interests by pointing out the serious state of its unpreparedness and began planning for mobilization in the case of war. On September 1, 1939, General George C. Marshall became the new army chief of staff. This was the day that German armed forces crossed the German-Polish border, beginning World War II, and two days later France and England declared war on Germany. The results of the German blitzkrieg and the subsequent division of defeated Poland between Nazi Germany and Soviet Russia were clear indicators that the world had entered a dangerous phase. Looking back over MacArthur's and Craig's tenures as chief of staff, it was clear that their warnings about America's lack of substantive preparedness had now become critical.

George Catlett Marshall came to the post with a tremendous breadth of experience. During the Great War, Marshall first attracted the attention of his superiors as an effective and insightful staff officer with the 1st Infantry Division. He was instrumental in planning the fight at Cantigny and then the operations at Saint-Mihiel and the Meuse-Argonne. From 1919 to 1924 he was an aide to John J. Pershing, and from 1924 to 1927 he commanded the US 15th Infantry Regiment in China. For the future chief of staff, this was invaluable experience in that Marshall came into direct contact with the troops and with all the problems that entailed. By 1936 he was assigned as the senior regular army adviser to the Illinois National Guard. It was here that he came to know the citizen-soldiers' discipline, capabilities, and expectations. This was a rare combination of having both regular troops and National Guardsmen to learn from, and these were lessons that George Marshall learned well.

The rapid defeat of Poland in September 1939 was a matter of deep concern to Marshall, President Roosevelt, and Secretary of War Henry L. Stimson, and that concern grew as the German army overran the Low Countries and then France in the spring of 1940. These three men would not allow America to enter into a war in the same unprepared state as that in 1917, but there were problems with an isolation-oriented population and a Congress that would be hard to manage. After a great debate, Congress passed the Selective Service Act in September 1940, followed by a call-up of selected National Guard units for intensive training. As Marshall knew, once the guard was called to duty, the civilian population quickly became involved. He also knew that the guardsmen and the newly drafted men carried with them certain expectations for homelike comforts. General Marshall was also well aware of *The Fosdick Report* and knew what was needed for the troops in training, and the question was basically who would be the man to resurrect and apply the ideas that Fosdick had in 1918.

With the nation drifting toward a buildup of the army in the case of war, a number of civilian academics, intellectuals, and businessmen came to the War Department as "dollar-a-year men" to add ideas and expertise to the growing efforts. One of those intellectuals was Frederick Henry Osborn, Princeton educated and founder of the Office of Population Research at his alma mater, who was in 1941 the chairman of the Joint Army and Navy Committee on Welfare and Recreation and a member of the Advisory Committee on Selective Service. He had definite ideas about the draft that came from his interest in eugenics. He advocated a system whereby what he called "defectives" would be kept from military service. Osborn proposed methods that would make the public health service a part of identifying those people. He believed that the "able human stocks" would be the best, most capable leaders and that when they were in charge, soldiers would be better fit for their combat missions. Consequently, the Morale Branch should be filled with capable officers and civilians who would construct a viable program that would be beneficial for the military efforts now under way.[2]

Osborn, an intellectual with much practical experience, was deemed in 1917 unfit for active military service, but he was not content to simply return to the quietude of the scholarly life. He joined the Red Cross and arrived in France to serve the AEF in the zone of advance, where the fighting was taking place. There he had ample opportunity to observe what the Doughboys at the front needed and what they expected. Osborn, while not a soldier, could speak with authority about combat conditions, on the one hand, and what built morale, on the other. After the Japanese attack on Pearl Harbor in December 1941, President Roosevelt named him to head the Morale Branch of the army. Political observers and some journalists questioned the wisdom of Roosevelt's appointment, given Osborn's lack of uniformed military experience. The dollar-a-year man could not serve in that capacity, and he was taken into the army with the rank of brigadier general. He would be an energetic one-star general armed with a copy of Fosdick's 1918 report, some specific ideas of his own, and a lot of real authority.

Marshall had several interviews with Osborn and noted his work in France during the Great War. Osborn observed that Marshall wanted him to coordinate the same type of work for the troops in training, but Osborn did not indicate at that time that his main interest focused on education and information rather than recreational activities. Later Osborn stated, "I felt very strongly that the biggest thing we could do for the troops was really to tell them what was going on, keep them informed, give them a larger view of the world."[3] That was not how Marshall saw the mission of the Morale Branch, and Osborn recalled, "At the beginning it [the Morale Branch, later the Special Services] was looked on purely as a recreational activity."[4] General Marshall had the benefit of practical experience with troops and knew that as soldiers entered the army from civilian life or through the National Guard, a basketball, football, or quiet Service Club was more important than educational lectures. As the war went on, there would be a need for troop information and education, but in 1940 and 1941 it was more important to ease the citizen-soldier into army life.

One of Fosdick's major recommendations was that the army's Post Exchange be expanded to serve the needs and expectations of the troops. The 1918 report called for an expansion of the PX to serve individual regimental needs, which was a holdover from the Civil War and frontier army experience. Quickly, Osborn realized that this would not work because of the technological expansion of warfare, which called for specialized units not organized into regiments. The PX had to be postwide and also able to supply troops overseas in many places around the world. The World War I Commissary Sales system did not meet the needs of the Doughboys, and it was realized that a hard-headed businessman was needed to direct the newly created Army Exchange System (AES). The army found such a man in Joseph W. Byron, who had been one of the dollar-a-year men who worked with the newly established War Production Board.

Joseph W. Byron was born in South Dakota in 1892 and graduated from West Point as a cavalry officer. He served in the 1916 Mexican operation, and when the United States entered World War I, Byron opted to train with tanks. It was during his training that he came to know Dwight David Eisenhower, an association that would later serve him well as the head of the AES. Upon his arrival in France, he was assigned to the 304th Tank Battalion, but saw no combat action. Captain Byron tried to find a staff position with the Third Army in Germany, but in July 1918 was ordered back to the United States to serve in the Surplus Property Division in the War Department. Byron later wrote, "In assisting with the disposal of surplus property, I became so discouraged with the centralization, and what we both called 'red tape' in the office of Purchase, Storage, and Traffic, that I resigned; as I knew I could never be happy in the field service after having seen the Washington picture."[5] This insight into Byron's experience is important in understanding how he would direct the AES. The responsibility for ordering goods for the PXs would be at the local or post level. It would make no sense for a centralized authority to dictate that fur-lined gloves be sent to Africa or to India. Byron left the army and entered into business, where he was highly successful. In 1940 he went to Washington as a dollar-a-year man on the General Staff working with the War Production Board, where his abhorrence of centralization came to the surface. In 1942 Byron was tapped to direct the AES with the rank of brigadier general.

In June 1941 the War Department decided to separate the Morale Branch from the PXs, but there had to be close coordination between Osborn and Byron. The two generals had quite different backgrounds, the intellectual and the businessman, but they were united in their efforts to maintain GI morale. Frankly, Osborn was quite happy not to have to worry about selling Coca-Colas, hot dogs, beer, wristwatches, souvenir pillows, and trinkets. Osborn and Byron complemented each other and clashed rarely during the war.

This relationship took a great burden off the shoulders of General Brehon Somervell, chief of the Army Service Forces, who had a massive task providing the sinews of war for the troops in the field. It also helped that President Roosevelt and General Marshall supported the efforts of Osborn and Byron because both men worked well together and caused few, if any, problems for those supplying the troops or planning operations.

The question of morale did not escape the interest of President Roosevelt. He had heard stories of the often contentious and often chaotic relationship between the civilian agencies that tried, with the best of patriotic motives, to provide for the troops in the training camps and in the AEF during World War I. There were the same concerns that soldiers, left to their own devices when not in training, could very well fall victim to the old nemeses of alcohol and prostitution. The Morale Branch, soon to be known as the Special Services Division, would provide a comprehensive program on posts, but what else could be done? On February 4, 1941, President Roosevelt announced the formation of the United Service Organizations, which brought together the YMCA, YWCA, Jewish Welfare Board, National Catholic Community Service, National Travelers Aid Association, and Salvation Army to provide for the troops and to offer opportunities for civilians to work for a directed and well-managed war effort. The USO mission was simple, to provide "a home away from home" for soldiers in a wholesome environment off post.

Alcohol would not be served, but hot coffee, doughnuts, sandwiches, and soft drinks would be standard fare for the soldiers. Dances were organized with carefully screened young women and legions of chaperones. No one in 1941 could have envisioned the impact of the USO on soldier morale, nor could one have foreseen the long-lasting impact of the USO on American society well into the twenty-first century. Historian Meghan K. Winchell points out that "by September, 1942 an average of 4.5 million [military personnel] visited the USO clubs on a monthly basis. . . . [I]n July 1944, 12,740,431 people visited USO clubs."[6] The USO offered the GIs a positive alternative to the bars and brothels that sprang up around military camps.

By the spring of 1941, the United States was still at peace, but the buildup of American armed forces was obvious. Civilian involvement in maintaining support for the troops through the USO and other groups such as local churches and fraternal and veterans' organizations grew at an increasing pace. After December 7, 1941, however, the speed of public support went from a stream to a tidal wave very difficult to control.

It was one thing to have Brigadier Generals Osborn and Byron appointed to head the Morale Branch and the Army Exchange System; it was another to get the two offices organized. There were turf battles within the Roosevelt administration to overcome. Osborn and Marshall were to meet with Roosevelt to give him a preliminary report on the progress of the Morale Branch. Osborn found out that Paul McNutt, the secretary of education and welfare, wanted control over troop recreation and education. Both Marshall and Osborn were highly irritated over the secretary's intrusion into what was a strictly military situation. Much to Marshall's relief, Osborn stood up to McNutt and said that their plan for morale activities was going to be given to the president. Once inside the president's office, Secretary McNutt tried to gain control over GI recreation by minimizing the role of the USO. Then McNutt made a serious error when he said that he had talked to Raymond Fosdick and that Fosdick agreed that Education and Welfare should handle it. Osborn immediately challenged the truthfulness of the claim because the day before he had a lengthy lunch with Fosdick, and the man who wrote the 1918 report was enthusiastic about the USO and the Morale Branch of the army handling what was necessary for the troops. President Roosevelt quickly pondered this battle between the army and a civilian department of government and decided in favor of George C. Marshall and Frederick Osborn.[7] Osborn did comment later that, in his opinion, McNutt was not an intelligent person.

Moving into the fall of 1941, it was time to organize the branch. All of the planning, however, would do no good if there were no funds to do what was necessary. The budget for the fiscal year 1939 allocated $38,459, and for the fiscal year 1940 morale activities were allocated $68,812. However, the fiscal year 1940 saw the amazing supplementary increase of nearly $4 million, and by the fiscal year 1945 the sum rose to $42 million. Once the National Guard had been called to duty and the sons of constituents were drafted, the situation changed for Congress. Discontent on Main Street could very well mean not being reelected to serve in the halls of Congress.[8] Unlike the AES, the Morale Branch, soon to be called the Special Services Division, was dependent on the generosity of Congress and the interest and goodwill of the House

Subcommittee on Appropriations, and General Osborn was a sympathetic figure in appearances before the congressmen. It certainly did not hurt that the USO and Red Cross raised their own funds and had masses of willing volunteers. Those two agencies would, however, ask for and receive exemptions from certain taxes such as the one on cigarettes.

With the areas of authority established, Osborn went to work to build what was now called the Special Services Division. General Osborn assembled a staff of civilians and military personnel. Many of the officers who came to the Special Services were soldiers who were deemed too old for overseas combat commands, and some were veterans of World War I. The role of Special Services was greater than Osborn had envisioned, and the division was divided into an Army Motion Picture Service with a plan of five hundred theaters on posts in the United States; an Athletic, Recreation, and Welfare Section; a research group; and a section devoted to education and information. The United States had to carry the war overseas, and Special Services had to prepare to serve troops in every area of the globe. A great deal of time was spent in preparing for overseas operations where the Special Services would be a critical factor in maintaining morale. It was then vitally important that trained Special Services officers (SSOs) be assigned to every army, corps, and division headquarters to advise the commander and to implement programs for the troops. This officer would have some definite problems in that commanders and their immediate staffs had to focus on combat training and operations. The heart and soul of the commander's immediate interests had to be with his chief of staff, the personnel officer (G1), intelligence officer (G2), operations officer (G3), and supply officer (G4). The Special Services officer had to be aware that the time of the commander must be guarded, and he would have to judge when to approach the commander with Special Services projects. The Special Services officer would have more access to the commander during a training phase in England or Australia than during combat in France in 1944 or in the Philippines in 1944–45.

Since the Special Services Division was new to the army, there needed to be a serious training program to prepare officers to assume duties that would require knowledge and some degree of diplomacy. To deal with this, a Special Services School was established at Fort George G. Meade, Maryland. Two hundred officers and enlisted men could attend the school for one month, where they would study such subjects as how to organize athletic events, put on GI plays, organize music events using army personnel with talents ranging from opera to small jazz bands, maintain libraries, and coordinate with civilian groups, such as the USO, to present entertainment events. There were lectures on how to be a Special Services officer on the staff of a combat unit.

As the scope of Special Services grew, it was envisioned that one senior officer would be assigned to an army, three Special Services officers to a division, and one to each regiment. It was made clear that these officers would "be available for combat duty as replacements." A handbook was prepared and was in use by the early spring of 1942, as were a number of draft technical manuals. While at Fort Meade, those in the Special Services School followed army training programs in the areas of physical training and rifle marksmanship and had to adhere strictly to military customs and discipline.

As the program developed, it was initially estimated that six to eight thousand soldiers would be needed to man the division in the United States and overseas.[9] Eventually, the school would be moved to Washington and Lee University in Virginia because of the expanding activities at Fort Meade.

Would the Special Services officer be dependent on the goodwill of the commanders and their staffs, or would he have his own troops at his disposal? Certainly, he could not beg soldiers from the staff to hand out basketballs, organize a play, or show a movie. In early 1942, the Special Services Division began a plan for a Special Services unit to be used in the United States and overseas. This would be a unit new to the army, and before the plan could be presented to the army, it had to be well thought out. First, what would be the mission of the company, and what would be its table of organization and equipment? The development of the Special Services unit had to occupy a good deal of time of the division's staff. One test unit was organized at Fort Meade. Called the 1st Special Services Unit, it began to take form in March 1942 with two officers and ninety-three enlisted men. First Lieutenant Garland W. Stone was transferred from the 176th Field Artillery Regiment of the 29th Infantry Division, then in training at Fort Meade, to assume command of the unit, and by the date of activation the unit had four officers, one for each platoon. The unit knew that upon completion of its training, it would be deployed to England in the European theater of operations (ETO).[10] Only time would tell if the concept of a Special Services unit would be workable and, if it did add to morale, how many more units could be formed.

The formation of the unit brought on another set of problems for the Special Services Division in the area of manpower. Lieutenant Stone had been transferred from an artillery regiment training for combat. Although Stone amassed a good war record, being promoted to the rank of captain and serving at a higher headquarters, the question remained as to why the 176th commander transferred a junior officer to the Special Services. Neither Osborn nor his staff wanted Special Services to become a dumping ground for inefficient or incompetent soldiers. An officer could make application to join the Special Services Division be transferred, and it would be hard to tell, in the confusion of the massive expansion of the army, what the reason would be. A number of older officers, especially those in reserve or National Guard, applied simply to be of active service. Many of these men did everything possible to get an overseas assignment. A soldier with special skills such as a jazz pianist or an athletic coach could, for example, be singled out for Special Services duty. It was possible that a transferred officer could resent leaving a combat unit. General Byron had the same problems in staffing the expanding Army Exchange System. Also, a Special Services officer or an exchange officer wearing the insignia of a combat arm (infantry, artillery, armor) could very well be looked down upon by soldiers facing combat and could become the subject of scorn.

Osborn wanted to have a conference to coordinate the expanding morale activities in mid-December 1941, but the events of December 7 forced a change of date until mid-January 1942. From January 19 to January 23, morale officers assembled in Washington with speakers from every section of the Morale Branch. The vast majority of attending officers came from posts, camps, and forts east of the Mississippi and represented the four army areas, every division in training, the Army Air Forces, Armored Forces, and the major replacement training centers.

The two major speakers were Osborn and his assistant chief, Colonel Livingston Watrous, who basically explained what the Special Services Division was and how it was to serve the needs of the troops. Since the Special Services was a new army agency, General Marshall opened the conference by stressing the need for a serious implementation of the entire program. With the ruins of the Pacific fleet still smoking in the waters of Pearl Harbor and the nation at war with Japan and Germany, it was hard to focus on athletic activities, plays, camp newspapers, comic radio programs, or the hiring of civilian hostesses for the Service Clubs that were yet to be built. The army would fight the war, and the United States had to have a combat force with the highest state of morale, morale that would be formed in the units in training and then supported by the exchange, Special Services, civilian agencies such as the Red Cross and the USO, and the generous support of church and civic groups.

On the second day, the conference got down to business, with sessions on combat morale and the role of a morale officer (soon to be designated as the Special Services officer) with combat troops. What was clear was that the army viewed the Special Services as a vital part of the overall combat mission, and the Special Services officer should not be confused with a recreation director at a Boy Scouts summer encampment. During the second day, there was a session titled "Special Consideration Affecting the Morale of Negro Troops," which caused a great deal of discussion, because the army had a policy of strict segregation of the races. It became evident that there would need to be separate Special Services facilities regardless of the section of the nation. It would be unthinkable that dances could be racially integrated, for example. What emerged was a policy of "separate but equal" in Special Services facilities, but as the war progressed, it became obvious that separate was not equal at all. What would be the policy in hiring hostesses for the Service Clubs? This would not be just an army problem; it presented difficulties for the Red Cross and the USO as well.

Of great concern for the attendees was the question of constructing Special Services facilities because every training center and army post was experiencing an amazing expansion of barracks, unit headquarters, warehouses, mess halls, dispensaries, hospitals, and railheads. Where once there were farm fields, there were now row upon row of two-story wooden barracks with sewage systems. Many troops lived in tents and some in small wooden buildings called hutments. How then could the Special Services convince post commanders to divert wood, nails, paint, windows, and the like for a Service Club? There was not a system in place to ensure coordination between post commanders and the Special Services. Also, the old question of alcohol and prostitution surfaced as a serious danger for the expanding military bases. By working with the Red Cross and the USO, the army could, by energetically supporting the Special Services, keep alcohol abuse and venereal disease at a low rate. A good Service Club cafeteria, a motion picture theater, a Service Club with a continual offering of activities, and a well-stocked Post Exchange with 3.2 beer, tobacco, candy, shaving cream, and the like would be major pillars of army morale. When the conference closed, the attendees departed for their camps and posts with a vast amount of information about what had to be done and how to do it.[11]

Within the Special Services Division, the most harried groups of officers and civilians were those who dealt with camp construction and those who dealt with supplies for athletics and materials for the various activities of the Service Clubs. On March 9, 1942, General Marshall reorganized the War Department, with three general officers reporting to him directly. General Leslie McNair became head of the Army Ground Forces, General Henry "Hap" Arnold commanded the Army Air Forces, and General Brehon Somervell was named head of the Army Service Forces. Brehon, a no-nonsense logistician from Tennessee, directed every aspect of supply and support for the growing army.[12] Osborn and Byron would be directly responsible to Somervell, who expected all of his subordinates to deal with their own problems and coordinate with his staff. Somervell expected that he would be informed of major events, and he did not want any controversy to reach the ears of General Marshall or President Roosevelt unless he brought up the matter.

The Supply Section of the Army Service Forces had to be concerned with obtaining the sinews of war, everything from tanks to mess kits, GI boots to blankets, steel helmets to jeeps, uniforms, underwear, socks, knives, forks, spoons, and ammunition pouches—in other words, absolutely everything. Into this mix came the Special Services Division with its special needs. One can only consider what was said when the division requested balls, bats, checkerboards, badminton rackets, ukuleles, theatrical paints, football bladders, and hundreds of other athletic and recreational items. The supply branch in the division's staff received requests from the field and would contract for such items at a fixed price. Once large army forces were overseas, there was a competition for shipping space. To complicate matters, Special Services dealt with every place GIs were stationed, and although the army expected to support troops in places like North Africa, England, India, and Australia, it was taken aback by requests for GIs stationed in Brazil, sub-Saharan Africa, Persia, and other places around the world.

While the Special Services Division grappled with its problems, the AES under General Byron was moving quickly to establish a PX wherever GIs were located. In late 1941, Byron, businessman-turned-general, secured a two-million-dollar line of credit from the Defense Supplies Corporation. Each PX was then loaned money to buy their own supplies, depending on the GIs' demands, which were, at first, Coca-Cola, popular brands of candy bars, cigarettes and cigars, and snack-bar items such as hamburgers, hot dogs, and milk shakes.

Since the AES was a business enterprise, the profits were used to pay back the loans from the AES, to buy new stock, and to give the remaining funds to soldier recreational facilities on post. Within a year, Byron could boast that the PX system was the world's largest chain store, operating in every area where there were GIs. Byron made an important decision when he stated that the PX on post would sell 3.2 beer (so named for its low alcohol content). Prohibitionists had demanded that the army camps of World War II be dry, as the camps of the Great War had been. The United States had repealed the constitutional amendment that enforced Prohibition country-wide, and Byron knew that soldiers wanted beer at a low cost. The Post Exchange maintained a beer hall, often selling beer in their snack bars, and the AES worked hard to see that American beer was shipped to GIs stationed overseas. When the army was deluged with complaints from prohibitionists, spokesmen stated that the alcohol content in what was becoming known as "army beer" was low and that the incidence of drunkenness was quite low. A soldier could visit the PX beer hall rather than go to the tenderloin districts of the towns near the post. Beer, candy, shaving items, and cigarette sales counted for a majority of PX income, and money made from those items made it possible to continually expand the offerings of the exchange. In the United States, civilians manned the exchanges, and as the army expanded overseas, GIs and foreign civilians staffed them.[13]

The Special Services Division would not sell beer or any other alcoholic beverages, nor would the USO or Red Cross. Other civilian and church groups joined in the ban, leaving the exchange system as the only on-post activity to sell "army beer." The PXs, like the Service Clubs, were maintained for enlisted men; food would be cheap and entertainment free.

The monthly pay of the soldier was low, and both the clubs and PXs aimed at attracting the enlisted personnel away from the less than wholesome places in the towns. But there were always those troops who would visit the saloons and red-light districts, many of which were notorious. One such town was Phenix City, Alabama, which was close to the large Fort Benning training base. There soldiers were fleeced and cheated, supplied with cheap liquor, and tempted by prostitutes, and they often clashed with the civilian law enforcement, such as it was. The situation became so bad that Major General George S. Patton, commander of the newly formed 2nd Armored Division, threatened to bring his tanks into the town and simply flatten the red-light district. Eventually, the state of Alabama cleaned up the red-light districts of the city.

By mid- to late 1942, the Special Services were operating in full force. The services operated about 500 movie theaters with a daily attendance of nearly 260,000 troops. The soldiers paid fifteen cents per visit to the theater, where first-run movies were shown. More than 400 civilian hostesses had been screened and employed for the Service Clubs, and 150 libraries were open for troop use. Five and a half million books were available for the troops in the libraries. One hundred and ninety-five guesthouses were either opened on post or in the process of being built. In addition to the obvious post facilities, the Special Services Research Branch was busy preparing special reports for the army. They covered such areas as attitudes toward "negro troops," satisfaction or dissatisfaction with job assignment, or the troops' evaluation of clothing and food.[14] The questionnaires completed by soldiers in the field concerning food and combat rations would be of great value to the subsistence branch of the Quartermaster Corps. These were tasks and efforts that far exceeded the recommendations made by Fosdick in his 1918 report.

Close to Osborn's heart was the issue of troop education, and by 1942 the Special Services developed a number of off-duty correspondence courses "to contribute to military efficiency." Contracts were made with colleges and universities for courses that would help a GI obtain a high school diploma or earn college credit. As the war dragged on, the educational focus became greater and exploded after VE and VJ Days. The army had established the Army Specialized Training Program (ASTP) at colleges and universities where soldiers with prior education or academic promise would be sent to further their education, with a view toward enhancing skills that would benefit the army. By 1943, however, as combat increased there was a need for more infantry, and the ASTP came to an end, with most of the troops being assigned to combat divisions slated for overseas deployment. The Special Services carried the educational torch for the army thereafter.

Going into the summer of 1942, Osborn and Byron had focused on developing their morale activities in the United States and serving the tens of thousands of troops pouring into the expanding training camps. Coordination between the Red Cross, the USO, and other civilian agencies seemed to be going well. USO clubs were open, and vast quantities of coffee and sandwiches, along with the ever-popular doughnuts, were in the hands of GIs. But this was a worldwide war, and American soldiers were yet to engage German or Japanese forces.

On June 15, 1942, the headquarters of the Eighth Air Force under the command of Major General Carl Spaatz opened near London. The first bombers flew from England against targets in Europe on August 17, 1942. The first American infantry regiment arrived in England in January 1942 to begin training. After fits and starts, and much coordination with the British military and political authorities, the European theater of operations came into being on June 8, 1942. American troops began to pour into England, prompting British civilians to say by 1944 that the island would sink into the sea under the weight of American soldiers and equipment. The Special Services and the PXs followed quickly to serve the needs of the GIs. George C. Marshall, Osborn, and Byron stated that the American soldier should get "his fair share" of all of the comfort items that he enjoyed as a civilian. First-run Hollywood movies, baseballs, footballs, hamburgers, hot dogs, cigarettes, and American beer would follow the flag overseas. Certainly, there were concerns that GIs, who were paid much better than their British counterparts and well supplied by the PXs, would soon irritate the reserved Englishmen. What would be the reaction of British girls to the brash, youthful, well-paid, and well-supplied GIs?

After Pearl Harbor, there was a massive outpouring of support for the war effort, and "Remember Pearl Harbor" became the nation's battle cry. For the military leadership who remembered the lean years following World War I, this public enthusiasm was welcome, but there was another side to the coin.

There were popular campaigns, well meaning to be sure, to raise money to send to the troops everything from cigarettes to knitted socks, and those campaigns ran counter to the army's efforts to supply the troops. For Osborn, reality set in as his Special Services Division had to deal diplomatically with all manner of public groups. The situation became clear in June 1942, when the well-known Hollywood star Gertrude Lawrence organized a group of popular stars of screen, radio, and movies to go to England to entertain the American troops arriving there. In a meeting with Osborn, Lawrence got the impression that his polite responses indicated a green light for her plan. She cabled a fellow actor in Hollywood that Osborn was enthusiastic and endorsed her ideas and added that they would have "complete control during [our] stay in England."[15]

The scheme reached the ears of the commanders in England and General Somervell in Washington. The commanders on the ground "are certainly unwilling to turn over to [them] complete control of entertainment or use of our stars if they should be sent to England." Somervell warned Osborn to be careful in dealing with civilian agencies and stressed that nothing could be done without the concurrence of the War Department and the commanders in England.[16] To complicate matters, British-born Lawrence was a member of the Entertainments National Service Association (ENSA), an English organization set up in 1939 to provide for British troops. What Osborn did not understand was that Lawrence believed that ENSA would have control over American entertainers, and that arrangement would have been unacceptable to the Americans. Osborn had stumbled into the course of wartime Anglo-American relations. The American Embassy in London would be involved when American stars came to England, but the complication of dealing with ENSA and British sensitivities would be difficult. To compound the situation, British troops were not especially complimentary when discussing ENSA activities and shows. Somervell and the War Department wanted nothing to do with ENSA having any control over American morale efforts. If anything would be done, and there was no guarantee that movie stars would ever be sent overseas, it would have to be coordinated through the USO and Special Services. Osborn certainly believed firmly that entertainers should be a vital part of the morale effort for GIs, especially overseas.

At this point, Osborn began to ponder what could be done within the restrictions of the War Department. One of his problems in the spring and summer of 1942 was that there was no Special Services presence in England, and it was decided that the 1st Special Services Unit would be sent as soon as possible, across the Atlantic to England, where the American military units were increasing with each boatload of troops. Once there were Special

Services officers in England, why not send stars there? There would be coordination with the commanding generals and with local commanders, and then Somervell and the War Department would be satisfied.

On July 20, 1942, the 1st Special Services Unit boarded a train for Camp Kilmer, New Jersey, where they would prepare to deploy to England. The unit now had four officers and ninety-two enlisted men and had been in training for four months. After waiting almost a month for their transport, the unit arrived in Britain on September 6, 1942, ready to work. The unit set up their headquarters at Cheltenham in Gloucestershire, where the unit was divided into four functional platoons. Unit headquarters remained close to the headquarters of the Service of Supply with a platoon; another platoon was sent to an American military hospital and another to a growing ordnance depot.[17] Immediately, some problems emerged when the unit found that their electrical equipment was incompatible with the British system, and when equipment was broken, spare parts were hard to obtain. This was critical because one of the first offerings of the unit was an ongoing movie schedule. Despite the problems, lessons were being learned, and it appeared to Osborn and the Special Services staff that the unit was a good idea.

From that point on, Special Services would begin fielding other units for US and overseas service. In training camps in various parts of the United States, Special Services units were being formed, but there was no formalized table of organization and equipment. At some point in 1943, the army would have to give form and structure to the increasing number of Special Services units, including making them actual companies. That would clarify their status with commanders used to dealing with the traditional formations such as companies, batteries, battalions, and the like.

With the rapid and successful expansion of the PX, there was a vital necessity to clarify the relationship of the Special Services and the Army Exchange System, especially because the Special Services unit had a mobile PX section to serve the troops in the field and had to rely on Byron's Exchange System for those items to be sold to the troops. It was also clear with this first effort that commanders would have to be briefed on the functions of the unit and advised on how to use it for the benefit of the troops. But overall, morale activities were going well in the United States, and Osborn's Special Services Division and Byron's PX system were expanding day by day, becoming an integral part of army life, providing everything from beer to USO sandwiches and shows for soldiers.

On November 7, 1942, American and British troops landed in Morocco and Algeria, two French colonies in North Africa. The scope of morale activities expanded, as the war was finally overseas. Osborn decided that what GIs

needed was a taste of home, and he planned to send American girls to entertain the soldiers in England and, if at all possible, North Africa. The first contingent consisted of the famous singer Al Jolson, movie star Merle Oberon,
and many other entertainers. Despite some problems in transportation, the
tour went well, and Osborn decided that a troop of four well-known and
lovely stars would go next. Carole Landis, Martha Raye, Mitzi Mayfair, and
Kay Francis would depart as the second group. On October 25, 1942, the four
women boarded a military air transport for England. Needless to say, there
were red-tape problems with the Army Air Force, hesitant to fly female civilians on an air force transport plane. Stranded in Bermuda for several days,
the four put on shows for American personnel there and waited for another
transport plane. Finally, they arrived in England and toured the many bases.
From there they went to North Africa, where they saw war for the first time.[18]
While in England Carole Landis met and then married an Army Air Force
bomber pilot.

Osborn felt the tour was a success, and from reports in the field, it was clear
that GIs wanted to see American girls as much as they wanted to drink American beer, even if it was 3.2 beer. The foundation for the Special Services had
been prepared well, and, despite some stumbling along the way, it was ready
to grow to meet the expanding requirements of a worldwide war.

3

1943

Consolidation

Private Keith Winston from Pennsylvania had been drafted into the army and would go into combat as a medic with the 100th Infantry Division in Europe. While in basic training at Camp Blanding, Florida, he found himself alone on Easter Day 1944. Somewhat homesick, he gravitated to the Service Club, and he wrote to his family, "I took a walk around and ended up here in the Service Club--a beautiful place with a balcony where the boys can write letters. Downstairs is a lounging room, cafeteria exchange etc."[1] Winston also found that the Service Club was the best place to try to telephone home. There were a number of telephone operators who took the soldier's name and the number he wished to call. Once a line was clear and the call was in process, the operator called the soldier to a bank of telephones where he could take his call. It had taken a year for Osborn's Special Services Division to construct clubs in every post in the United States. By 1943 Special Services not only had arranged the construction and staffing of the clubs, but also had a working relationship with Bell Telephone Company to install large banks of telephones and supply operators for each club. Within one year, the Special Services was established as a vital part of the American war effort.

By June 1942, the army formally addressed its own massive and rapid expansion with a regulation that stated the obvious: "Morale underlies all aspects of military life." The War Department published *MR 1-10 Morale*, which was a rewrite of a manual issued in 1939 before the outbreak of war in Europe. This new edition incorporated the Special Services Division and defined its mission for the army, dealing with the establishment of Service Clubs, libraries, publications, movie theaters, athletics, and nonmilitary education and with the relationship of the Army Exchange System and the Special Services Division. The document also provided for Service Club hostesses to oversee the maintenance of the clubs and their cafeterias as well as programs for enlisted men. They were also able to carefully screen all activities where "women participate." In other words, the clubs were to provide wholesome leisure and entertainment for the troops. Of importance was the recognition that the post movie theater was to be a vital part of the offerings for GIs simply because movies were a major part of the civilian entertainment that they had enjoyed before entering service. Armed with an official status by regulation, Osborn and the expanding Special Services Division could move forward aggressively to provide for the troops. What were not clearly addressed were the functions of the Special Services in overseas theaters of operations. The regulation did shield the Special Services from the chaotic conditions caused by thousands of civilian groups trying, with the best of motives, to provide the troops with everything from dances to sandwiches to cigarettes. The only coordination allowed for the Special Services was with the USO and the Red Cross, and this would make life much easier for Osborn and his staff.

One of the factors that contributed to the expansion and the successes of the Special Services Division and the Army Exchange System was the consistency of fundamental philosophies held by Osborn and Byron. The foundation of Osborn's thought was the report prepared by Fosdick and the Commission of Training Camp Activities. He recognized that the soldier of World War II was quite different from the Doughboy of 1917–18 because of technology such as the radio and talking and color motion pictures and the expectations he had about consumerism and advertising. Every soldier could see a first-run movie for fifteen cents or buy a lower-cost book of tickets, and the Motion Picture Service of the Special Services Division did not cost the taxpayer anything. It was self-supporting and made a profit that was then given to Special Services' expansion for the soldiers' benefit. The Hollywood moviemakers reached out to Osborn and promised that they would make first-run movies available to the Special Services theaters. Only soldiers, their dependents, or families visiting sons or husbands could attend the post theaters. The constant stream of first-run Hollywood movies was popular with the soldiers, and many were shown in the field, serving as a welcomed break for intensive training. Private Arthur Jacklewski, from Buffalo, New York, was in training with the Medical Detachment of the 4th Cavalry at the Desert Training Center in California. The days were extraordinarily hot, and at night the temperature plunged. He wrote to his sister Irene that the only break his unit got was the open-air showing of the movie *Somewhere I'll Find You,* with Clark Gable and Lana Turner. One night the movie projector failed, and Special Services promised the disappointed troops that the next night they would have a double feature.[2]

The post theaters came under the Information Section of the Special Services Division, which also included a full selection of popular civilian radio programs as well as army-produced programs. The radio had become a focal point of family life where everyone would gather around to hear Jack Benny, Fibber McGee and Molly, detective shows, and musical variety programs. It was only natural that GIs expected the same amusement, but what would be done once GIs were deployed to Europe, the Pacific, India, and elsewhere? The Special Services assembled "recreational kits" for the troops deploying overseas, and four medium RCA radios were included with electric plugs or batteries. Each kit served a company of a hundred or more soldiers.[3] Radio programs, selected by Armed Forces Radio, were recorded in the United States, a complex and cumbersome process, and then shipped overseas for broadcast.

The Special Services Division included army-produced programs with care taken that they were informative, but not overtly propagandistic. The Radio Section knew that the civilian soldiers of World War II would not be impressed by, nor would they appreciate, the bombastic, overpatriotic music and writings that their Doughboy fathers and uncles had been subjected to. "I'll Be Seeing You in All the Old Familiar Places" replaced songs like "Over There" or "How Ya Gonna Keep 'Em Down on the Farm after They've Seen Paree?"[4] The citizen-soldiers of World War II preferred the Andrews Sisters or Glenn Miller, and Osborn and his radio planners were wise enough to know that and act on it.

The more the division added to the opportunities of soldiers to attend events on post, or those sponsored by the USO or Red Cross for that matter, the less the possibility that soldiers would leave the post and visit the saloons and brothels near the camp. In this Osborn very much agreed with what Fosdick advocated in 1918.[5]

Byron's fundamental concept was to create a worldwide GI chain store that would offer a rapidly expanding menu of items at a low cost, producing a profit that would be put back into purchasing goods to be sold and to expand the Special Services Division even more. General Byron stated that the Post Exchange system was "one of the greatest morale-boosting organizations in the world." The PX was the subject of complaints from many local businessmen, however, who saw the exchange as an effective competitor, taking GI business away from them. These complaints were heard in the halls of Congress, but Byron was able to show that the exchange did not cost anything at a time when the war budget was growing year after year. Byron, the former army officer-turned-businessman, had cogent economic responses to the cries of local merchants, and, besides, to attack the popular GI exchange could very well be seen as not supporting the troops who were fighting the war.

Osborn's Special Services Division expanded its activities during 1942 into 1943. Congress was eager to support morale efforts, which, of course, they could claim to their credit during the next election. In 1942 morale activities received more than $9 million, and in 1943 the Special Services received a substantial increase to $16.25 million.[6] The Special Services Division was immune from much of the confusion that afflicted the War Department and the Army Exchange System over the public's support for the troops.

The War Department welcomed public, patriotic support for the soldiers who would soon be committed to combat, but citizens' zeal often worked at cross-purposes with the army's goal of using the PX, Special Services, the USO, and the Red Cross as the major agents of morale building. Without government funding, church and civic groups poured into train stations to give sandwiches and hot coffee to the troops, who were, by nature of being in uniform, always hungry. That was fine with the army, but when groups began major cigarette campaigns, the AES and the War Department became concerned. There were thousands of plans to send smokes to the troops by the pack and by the carton. The AES had a tax-exempt status as far as cigarettes were concerned and could sell two packs for twenty-five cents in the United States and five cents per pack overseas. Cigarettes sold for about fifteen cents per pack on the civilian market. Groups such as Smokes for Yanks, the 37th Divisions Veterans Association, Send 'Em Smokes, and the Overseas Cigarette Service, for example, tried the patience of Washington. One patriotic soul had on his own made small cardboard containers and placed them in restaurants, stores, and the like. He asked that when a person lit up a cigarette, he or she should place one in the box for a GI. How the army was to gather all of the loose cigarettes and package them for the troops was not considered.[7]

The vast number of offers of all kinds of support threatened to obstruct army efforts. To remedy the situation, the president established in July 1942 the President's War Relief Control Board to review the growing number of offers to aid the troops. The board had great authority to authorize or deny plans for supporting the troops, and it denied more plans than it approved. There was a real tightrope that the board had to navigate when it came to organizations like the American Legion, Veterans of Foreign Wars, labor unions, the American Library Association, and others with a high political profile. Mrs. Edward G. Robinson, wife of one of Hollywood's most important actors, proposed that when a civilian bought a pack of cigarettes, he or she should buy one for the USO to give to a soldier. Harper Sidney of the USO gave a firm no to the plan because the USO was able to buy, with the moneys donated, cigarettes in large quantity for their USO clubs, and dealing with massive numbers of individual packs was not possible. The major cigarette producers were having trouble filling orders for the army and maintaining supplies for civilians without being saddled with orders from various groups.

The Stage Door Canteen, an all-volunteer organization, went ahead with its plans to support the troops with or without board approval. Here was a special problem for the army in that the Stage Door Canteen was in direct competition with the USO, but no one could deny that the Canteen, with its free food, soft drinks, and Hollywood actresses, was wildly popular with GIs and sailors. Since Hollywood and the radio stars were so vital to the morale effort, it would be difficult for the board or the army to say anything negative about the Canteen. The Canteen usually just informed the board of activities and plans. In 1943 the chairwoman of the New York Canteen reported that over the Thanksgiving and Christmas seasons, they had served 3,500 pounds of turkey, 4,000 full holiday meals, 750,000 sandwiches, 1.5 million packages of cigarettes, and 1,000 crates of Florida oranges.[8] The board was also simply informed that the Canteen would open a branch in London for the growing number of troops in Europe.

Overseas, the board had no real authority over civilians. In 1942 American citizens and concerned Australians opened a canteen in Australia sponsored by the American Center. This center had sandwiches and coffee for the troops and special holiday meals. In 1943 their Christmas meals for GIs featured cold ham and turkey, potato salad, tomatoes, and apple pie. This was an all-volunteer organization that asked for no funding from either the American or the Australian government, but it was also impossible for those governments to either oppose or ignore it.[9]

Complicating matters for the AES were the numbers of prohibitionists who complained about the sale of beer in the exchanges. It did not matter that army beer had a much lower alcohol content. Congressmen who had a large prohibitionist constituency voiced their concern as well. The Office of War Information, working with the AES and the Special Services Division, conducted a comprehensive survey of all troop training camps, contacting commanders, chaplains, civilian agencies like the USO, and exchange and Special Services personnel. In December the OWI issued a lengthy report that concluded, "No American army in all history has been so orderly." The report also stated that 3.2 beer as sold by the exchanges added to sobriety and that most troops preferred soft drinks such as those offered by the Service Clubs or the

USO. The sale of 3.2 beer, curfews, intervention by commanders, chaplains' lectures and counseling, the availability of the Service Clubs, post theaters, athletic activities, and community-camp committees all aimed at control. For example, Phoenix City, Alabama, cleaned up its red-light district, and venereal disease rates dropped from thirty-four per week in January 1942 to three per week in June of the same year.[10] There were concerns about alcohol consumption once large numbers of American soldiers arrived in staging areas in Europe and in the Pacific. Most GIs found foreign beer not to their liking at all. Staff Sergeant Charles B. Linzy of the 459th Mobile Anti-Air Craft Battalion, who had arrived in England in mid-November 1943, wrote to his wife in Little Rock, Arkansas, "They do not have beer over here. They have what they call bitters. It is."[11] It was important to get American beer overseas as quickly as possible and get it into the offering of the exchanges. The combination of PXs and Special Services on American and overseas bases would have the effect of creating "an orderly army," which would train for combat and then take advantage of what the army had to offer in the area of recreation.

Of course, GIs wanted to see London or visit the sights in Australia, and it was important that the American soldier be seen as a positive force in the alliances to defeat Nazi Germany and Imperial Japan. How could the Special Services Division take the lead in preparing troops for their first exposure to foreign lands and culture? This was an area in which General Osborn had a special intellectual and academic interest.

The Special Services Division began a series of what it called pocket guides. The Information Section sought out academic authorities and civilians who had in-depth knowledge of every country and region GIs were to be stationed. The first of the guides focused on North Africa and was available after Operation Torch in November 1942. A brief history of North Africa began the guide, and then the writer discussed the people of Morocco, Algeria, and Tunisia, including a brief introduction to the Islamic faith. The role of Muslim North Africa could be to "either supply us water or poison the wells, guide us through mountains and desert or lead us astray." There was a warning that if the Muslim tribes of North Africa found American forces to be offensive, they could very well become informants for the Germans. Of special attention was the role of women in Islamic life and how Americans were to regard the wives and daughters of a Muslim family. The writer of the guide was quite blunt about the European exploitation of North Africa and wrote that North African Muslims' "experience has been that the European soldiers, officials, and colonists have often been domineering and unprincipled." Naturally, GIs were curious about this strange land where they landed and now fought. Young men from Vicksburg, St. Paul, Denver, or for that matter Philadelphia had never seen a mosque or an Arab bazaar before, and they were open and friendly toward North Africans. This openness would serve the United States well after World War II as the North African colonies became nation-states and remembered their experience with GIs. The pocket guide to North Africa consisted of forty-three compact pages with one map and was especially well written. It was basically a cultural exposition about Islamic North Africa.[12]

One of the first cooperations between Special Services and the units in North Africa was the publication of a guide to the Army Air Transport Command base at Casablanca, Morocco. One of the missions of the Information Section was to work with local commands, and in the case of Cazes Airbase, it prepared a detailed guide as to what was available on the base for soldiers— PX, Service Club, snack bar, movie theater, library, exchange barbershop, and the like.[13]

While many Americans had seen movies about North Africa such as *Algiers* (1938) or the classic *Beau Geste* (1939), little could have prepared GIs for service in West Africa. The pocket guide to West Africa began by telling GIs what and who they would see, and that would not be Tarzan of movie fame. "West Africans are not savages, nor are they naked," the author wrote. The guide discussed both French and British West Africa and how they became colonies. Like the North African guide, this booklet focused on how Americans were to deal with Africans. This was a touchy subject, given that many soldiers came from areas of the United States that practiced legalized segregation of the races.[14]

Likewise, American troops were moving into India to conduct the China-Burma-India campaign, and the writer for the Information Section had to take cognizance that there were political and racial conditions that had to be addressed. In August 1942, the United States State Department issued a statement to the effect that under no circumstances would American troops in India become involved in internal Indian political problems, and there were many.

The writer of the *Pocket Guide to India* was specific about the activities of the Indian National Party and its leaders, Mahatma Gandhi and Jawaharlal Nehru, which aimed for Indian independence from England. The United States and Britain were allies, and the guide warned that Americans could find themselves in a dangerous political minefield if they showed partiality toward Indians or the British government. The mission of the American troops in India was to defeat the Japanese and to assist China in its fight against Japan. There were also warnings about dealings with Indian women and comments on the caste system and hurting any cow.[15]

On the other hand, the guide for Australia stressed the affinity between the Americans and the Australian people and the democratic and optimistic nature of both peoples. Although the national drink was tea, the Australians had a lot of beer, something of great interest to the thousands of GIs pouring into the country. Australians, the guide stated, played football (by different rules) and also baseball.[16] Unlike the guide for India, this guide stressed the American and Australian sameness.

Did the guides really add anything to the morale effort for overseas-bound troops? There were thousands of these guides printed, and they were considered so important for American military personnel that the guides were sponsored by both the War and the Navy Departments. A large number of these used guides now turn up in the effects of the veterans of World War II.

General Osborn had made no secret of his interest in troop information and education, and this included a great effort to publish a camp newspaper for every post or camp where there were American soldiers. The Special Services officers with the camps were to immediately start a camp newspaper, which would have a great deal of GI input through articles and letters. Often the letters basically complained about the exchange rationing of brand-name cigarettes or not having enough crackers or Hershey bars. When a soldier with a journalism background or with a particular literary skill was identified, he was assigned to the camp Special Services officer's section to write for the newspaper.

At the January 1942 morale conference, Major Charles S. Hart of the information division presented an outline of what the division intended to do for the troops. By early 1942, Hart stated, there were 203 mimeographed and 100 printed camp newspapers with a wide range of clear writing and material, but they all were popular with the troops.[17]

General Osborn was especially interested in establishing an armywide newsmagazine and brought together a large number of enlisted men and officers to produce it. On June 15, 1942, he presented the first copy of the magazine *Yank* to General Somervell.[18] *Yank* was to become the official magazine of the army, containing articles about every aspect of the war and including a "pinup" picture of a beautiful, swimsuit-clad Hollywood star. *Yank* was to be sold to the GIs by either individual copy or subscription.

The information division designated official *Yank* correspondents to every theater of operations, and they in turn sent their articles back to the central office in Washington, where they were checked for any information that might compromise military operations. With the correspondents were teams of photographers and clerks. This was to be a well-written and well-produced magazine printed on good paper.

During the summer of 1942, a problem arose with the introduction of the daily GI newspaper *Stars and Stripes* published in England. The *Stars and Stripes* was started as a Doughboy newspaper at the urging of General John

Pershing, who wanted his Doughboys in the AEF to be informed soldiers. The World War II edition went on sale to GIs as they arrived in England and became more popular than *Yank* because it was a daily newspaper in a format familiar to the American soldiers. Unlike *Yank,* the *Stars and Stripes* carried short articles concerning daily developments in the war and carried news about exchanges, USO events and schedules, and movie presentations. One of the problems for the army was that the newspaper was sold rather than given to the troops.

In September 1942, the suggestion was made to General Marshall that army funds be used to subsidize *Stars and Stripes* to make it available free of charge to GIs. Marshall looked into the funding and was advised that army funds could not be used. *Stars and Stripes* was to be sold because it had to operate under nonappropriated funding and had to be self-sustaining by sales and subscriptions.

Marshall's advisers said that since *Yank* had begun to show a profit, it would be possible to use some of that income to subsidize the *Stars and Stripes.* Another suggestion was that combining subscriptions of *Yank* and the *Stars and Stripes* could save the soldiers money and build both news sources. General Marshall felt that this question was important enough to involve President Franklin D. Roosevelt, asking his agreement to institute the combined subscription.[19] It was agreed to promote both papers, and the *Stars and Stripes* became more popular than *Yank*. It had some of the best writers in the army. *Stars and Stripes* began a Mediterranean edition after Operation Torch in November 1942. There would be a Pacific edition, an Italian edition, and finally, in 1945, German editions that would be printed on many of the same presses in Germany that had turned out Nazi-controlled newspapers only a few weeks before.

One of the best-known and most recognized writers of *Stars and Stripes* was Sergeant Bill Mauldin, whose cartoon characters "Willie and Joe" captured the life and the miseries of the combat infantryman. In 1945 General George Patton threatened to confiscate the *Stars and Stripes* because of Mauldin's cartoons, which showed irreverent soldiers who violated Patton's strict dress code. Supreme Commander Dwight D. Eisenhower happened to like "Willie and Joe" and arranged a meeting between Patton and Mauldin that was quite frosty, but ended with Mauldin's "Willie and Joe" remaining in the *Stars and Stripes.* Eventually, Ike had to issue orders that Mauldin and his ragged soldiers would remain in the GI newspaper.[20]

There is no better example of the major effort that the army made to maintain soldier morale in the midst of the horrors of World War II. Overseas in Special Services clubs there were free copies, and the PXs that served GIs in every part of the world sold copies of both *Yank* and *Stars and Stripes*. Sergeant Bill Mauldin died in 2003 and was laid to rest at Arlington Cemetery, with full military honors befitting his contributions to the morale efforts during World War II.

From 1942 into the early months of 1943, the Special Services Division, including the Post Exchange System, had expanded beyond what either Osborn or Byron imagined in 1941. The time had come for several things to happen. First, there had to be clear-cut lines spelling out the relationship of the Special Services and the PX, and second, there needed to be a detailed inspection of the activities overseas. It was relatively easy to inspect facilities in the United States, but there was no clear picture of what was going on in Europe, the Pacific, and outlying areas. Osborn had requested that air force transportation make space for USO and Red Cross entertainers going overseas to perform for the troops. The chief of the transportation service complained directly to General Somervell that space was so critical that little room would be available for singers and the like. Of great concern for the air transportation chief were the special problems involved with female entertainers, because toilet facilities were limited and there was no privacy in the aircraft. Seating was crude and uncomfortable, the time spent in going to Europe was long, and the time and distance to the Pacific area were even longer. Osborn's arguments for space for entertainers was cogent because GI reaction to the first few overseas entertainment was positive. The trip made by Carole Landis and the other female performers showed that women could adjust to discomfort as well as male entertainers did. The first steps toward unlimited travel came when General Marshall authorized military travel for female USO and Red Cross workers. To exclude those volunteers would have created a political firestorm during the early years of the war. Marshall also indicated that what was done for the USO and Red Cross women should be extended to those working for Special Services overseas.[21]

General Brehon Somervell was not a soldier who hesitated when decisions had to be made. His burdens were indeed heavy, and when a dispute arose between Special Services and the Exchange System, he reacted quickly. There were complaints from those working in the Service Clubs in the United States over the difficulties in obtaining supplies for the clubs, especially candy, soft drinks, ice cream, and cigarettes. The Special Services Division was accorded the same tax-exempt status for cigarettes as was the Exchange System, but it appeared that Post Exchange officers were not working with the Service Clubs. Somervell's staff quickly resolved the issue by stating that it was the responsibility of the Service Clubs to order what items they needed and in what quantity, based on Service Club usage by the GIs. The requirements would then be submitted to the Exchange System, which would include them when they ordered supplies. The exchange officers and the Special Services officers would take care that there was no duplication of requests for a post. The supplies would go to the headquarters of the various service commands, and they in turn would send them to the requesting post clubs and exchanges. It was then the duty of the post commander to divide the items based on the requisitions.[22] This would avoid the possibility of either the Service Club or the PX having nothing, or, worse, two captains rolling in the mud with fists flying over cases of Hershey bars, gallons of vanilla ice cream, or cartons of Lucky Strike cigarettes. That would have been quite an interesting sight for the GIs training as combat infantrymen for the battlefields of Europe and the Pacific.

Another problem for both the Special Services Division and the Army Exchange System was overseas transportation. Ships left the United States in vast numbers filled with troops and massive amounts of supplies, from tanks to rifles and from boots to combat rations. The first priority had to be for the men who would fight and the equipment needed to sustain those troops in battle. At what point would there be a crisis caused by the need for men and the sinews of war and the extras that would contribute to the morale so vital to victory? Sergeant Robert D. Tuttle of Marion, Ohio, serving with the 499th Combat Engineers in New Guinea, summed up what those small comfort items could mean for a soldier serving so far from home when he wrote to his sister, "I am not any too tired tonite, we did get to a PX tonite and got me some things I was short on. I can get plenty of gum but no candy or soft drinks."[23] Disappointed at the lack of small things like his favorite candy bar or Coca-Cola, Tuttle just returned to his tent.

When the PX did not follow the troops, there were problems. Corporal Thomas R. St. George, serving in Australia, recalled, "Cigarettes were never a problem. A benevolent Uncle Sam (and the United States Army Service Forces) saw to it that we received one package a day (issue) until our own canteen [PX] opened."[24] Why did Somervell's Army Service Force issue cigarettes to the ever-growing number of troops training or staging in Australia? GIs, when out of cigarettes, bought Australian smokes, which were much more expensive than PX cigarettes, and for the GIs, they were akin to smoking dried grass and weeds. Australians, while open to the GIs, complained because their cigarette supplies were so short. Besides, American soldiers found out rather quickly that Australian girls really did prefer American cigarettes, and that was an important fact to know.

Byron was greatly pleased with the expansion of PXs and their offerings, which far exceeded the original concept of the AES. The AES offered to overseas troops a gift catalog so that troops could send things home. Since most

Americans were familiar with the mail-order catalog because many companies had used them since the late nineteenth century, an AES catalog would not be a novelty. Also, the exchange system dealt with American florists to take overseas orders, especially on Mother's Day and at Christmastime. The PXs in both the United States and the overseas theaters offered a full range of food stuffs, candy, cigarettes, watches, clothes, lighters, and gift items at a price the low-paid privates could afford. The exchange cafeterias sold hamburgers, hot dogs, milk shakes, soft drinks, and the ever-popular 3.2 beer. The post beer halls, away from the PXs, proved to be a popular meeting place for the enlisted men. Byron ended a discussion with his staff by saying that if the AES did not function well, "[General Somervell] will turn to me and tell me to go back to civilian life where I belong."

There was something new in the army, a movement that neither Osborn or Byron had foreseen—women in army uniforms in large numbers. Certainly, it was expected that women would become nurses and serve in the hospitals, and there was a rush of women to the factories to replace the men who were in the service. In July 1942, six young women left Albany, New York, for basic training in the Women's Army Auxiliary Corps, a part of the army soon to be known simply as the Women's Army Corps, or the WACs. Among the women leaving for training at Fort Des Moines, Iowa, was Margaret Hisgen, who had served in the Auxiliary Aircraft Warning Service, but decided that she could do more for the war effort. She went through the vigorous entrance examination, supported by letters of reference from persons of authority such as a pastor, mayor, and school principal. Women faced entrance requirements that were much more stringent than any man faced, and Private Hisgen passed every test and began her training. She arrived at Fort Des Moines and was introduced to the famed army truck, which seated eighteen women on hard wooden benches and bounced the new recruits over every pothole. She drew uniforms and study material and was assigned a bunk in a barracks where there was no privacy at all. Private Hisgen had her first experience with an army mess hall and then found out that the women were lined up and given the dreaded army inoculations, which all survived. She wrote to her mother, "They've given us a schedule of work to be covered in our course, and I don't expect to do anything much besides study, sleep, and study some more.... I've found out what an army foot locker is. It's just a good-sized trunk that stands at the foot of each cot."[25] Margaret Hisgen would serve as a lieutenant in the Far Eastern Air Forces and see service in the Philippines.

There were thousands of women volunteering for the WACs, and their presence would be felt. It was often difficult for older male officers to deal with the needs of the WACs. One AES colonel speaking about the WACs claimed,

"They [WACs and army nurses] make more noise than a hundred times that number of GIs. . . . We get gripes on cosmetics, toiletries, sanitary napkins, lipsticks, creams, and shampoos. Do not buy any girdles with stays in them."[26] By 1944 the Exchange Service and the Special Services would deal with the women in the service, but the road there would be rough indeed.

In March 1943, a WAC captain graduated from the Special Services school in Lexington, Virginia, and while willing to serve in any assignment, Camilla M. Frank had a novel idea. Since there were Special Services units training in the United States and one, the 1st Special Services Unit, was deployed to England and to North Africa, why not use WACs to form a unit for overseas service? Osborn was intrigued by the idea, but a number of the units in training were having difficulties with specialized requirements such as music, plays, and athletics. The War Department quickly pointed out that the all-male units would be expected to go to the combat divisions where they could very well be under fire from the enemy. What would the American public do if they saw their daughters and sisters on the casualty lists? The silence from the War Department was expected, but Captain Frank would not let her idea die. She found an ally in the person of another WAC captain, Ruby Jane Douglass, who was the chief of Special Services at the WAC Training Center at Daytona Beach, Florida. They continued to work on a paper unit with missions, organization, and equipment. In the fall of 1943, Frank was assigned to the European theater of operations' Special Services Division. While in England, Frank continued to lobby for an all-WAC unit, but with every effort being directed toward the eventual cross-Channel invasion of France, the idea received little support. But Captain Frank continued with her duties and continued to refine a plan for an all-WAC unit.[27]

Osborn and Byron found their domains expanding during 1943, with Service Clubs in operation on every army post and training center in the United States and almost everywhere an American soldier served. Overseas the Special Services became an important part of GI life in England and Australia. Often in conjunction with the Bell Telephone Company, the Special Services published hundreds of post guides. At Fort Lewis, Washington, the guide listed everything offered by Special Services, including a full athletic equipment program, a half-dozen Special Services–run Hostess Houses, a beach program, a field house, more than a dozen Service Clubs, and nine post movie theaters.[28] At the infantry replacement center at Camp Robinson, Arkansas, there were four Service Clubs, each offering dances, special events, and unlimited stationery; four libraries; twenty-six PXs; a guesthouse; and six movie theaters.[29] Camp Crowder, Missouri, placed the three Service Clubs, cafeterias, and libraries in the same location and had seventeen branch exchanges.[30] General Byron's AES had experienced such success that on every post there was the original main PX and growing numbers of branch exchanges serving the units in training.

What none foresaw, as old soldiers should have, was the power that American goods would have overseas. In Australia GIs found out quickly that American cigarettes and candy bars were highly prized and could mean a lot of money if they found their way into the growing black market. Master Sergeant Elmer Franzman of Cannelton, Indiana, was serving with the 329th Service Group. He observed, "There's one [Sicilian] boy who sweeps the [Special Services and USO] show place after each show. He saves the cigarette butts and sells them to the natives. Cigarettes here sell for 75 [cents] on the black market. We buy them in the PX for 5 [cents] per pack."[31] This was a problem that would haunt the exchanges and the Service Clubs overseas even after the end of the war. Staff Sergeant Wilbur Dunbar, of the 102nd Mechanized Cavalry serving in North Africa, complained about not being well supplied when he wrote to his girlfriend back in Westfield, New Jersey, "The beer over here is not as good as we have at home but it will have to do, I suppose . . . . These French gals go around with their dresses above their knees and some of them sure do have it. But don't worry kid."[32]

The needs of the troops overseas exceeded the abilities of the Special Services, and by 1943, Osborn and the army decided on a large expansion of the Special Services units, which had proven their value in England. Byron was equally determined that GIs, wherever they served, would have the American beer they wanted. In explaining why American beer should be sent overseas, Byron said that the American soldier "gets a lift just out of seeing his familiar American label."[33]

The year 1943 was a period of consolidation and finding out what would or would not work. The remainder of the year and well into 1944 would see expansion of both the AES and the Special Services working together to maintain GI morale, at a time when it was vital to have well-served troops who would carry the fight to the enemy.

Private Hugh Wiltshire of Memphis, Tennessee, would fight with the 351st Infantry Regiment in Italy. He was fairly typical of the civilian soldiers who would be the backbone of the infantry and would eventually see VE and VJ Days. Wiltshire was drafted and trained to be a replacement for those divisions who had seen heavy combat, and by late 1943, it was obvious that the most dangerous job in the army was a GI in a rifle company. From basic training, he went to Fort George G. Meade, Maryland, to await orders to go overseas. While at Fort Meade he made great use of the Service Clubs and the post theater. He wrote to a high school friend who was in basic training, "Boy, the PX here is just like a big department store. [C]okes, beer, socks, everything, clothes too."[34] Had Byron and Osborn been privy to Private Wiltshire's letter, they would have been pleased, feeling a boost to their morale as well.

4

Piccadilly Lilly

With the influx of soldiers into Fort Knox, Kentucky, the citizens of Louisville formed the Recreation Committee of the Louisville Defense Council to offer the new GIs places of wholesome and chaperoned entertainment. The committee published a weekly sheet, the *Entertainment News,* which indicated where the troops could go for a reduced price. The Louisville Colonels baseball team offered a ticket for fifteen cents, and dances were held on Friday and Saturday nights by the USO, De Molay, the YWCA, YMCA, and an off-post Service Club. GIs who liked professional wrestling could attend matches free of charge if they went in uniform. Every church and synagogue invited soldiers to attend services, and many of the places of worship offered the GIs free home-cooked breakfasts, a welcomed change from the mess halls of Fort Knox. Roller rinks, bowling alleys, and riding stables offered considerable discounts for the soldiers. To make it easier for the Fort Knox trainees, the city of Louisville offered free bus transportation to and from the post.[1]

The USO in the city of Boston, Massachusetts, in conjunction with the Greater Boston Soldiers and Sailors Committee, gave GIs and sailors a map and guide to Service Clubs, jam sessions, dances, historic points of interest, YMCAs, free meals, and even a "Glamour Bar" for women in service.[2] West Coast cities like Salem, Oregon, offered services to GIs at little or no cost. The Salem Defense Recreation Committee published a map and guide showing where the GIs could find sponsored dances, bowling alleys, Service Clubs, the YMCA, skating rinks, swimming pools, and movie theaters.[3]

After December 7, 1941, more civilians joined in the war effort to support the men and women in uniform. These efforts took a great deal of the pressure off the shoulders of General Osborn, and by 1943 the Special Services Division could focus on providing for troops in the United States and overseas where its services were most needed. The USO, which had emerged as the most important of civilian agencies, aimed at attracting women from diverse educational and economic backgrounds. Historian Meghan K. Winchell points out, "Local USO clubs usually staffed their canteens in shifts of several hours at a time, making volunteering most appealing to women who had large blocks of free time in the mornings, afternoons, or late evenings."[4]

The USO cooperated with local organizations to provide for GIs, offering a full range of entertainment aimed at maintaining the soldiers' morale. The soldiers, most of whom were draftees, found the transition to military life, with the real prospect of soon being in combat with battle-tested German or Japanese soldiers, bewildering at best. The army mess hall, though there had been great improvement in the preparation and variety of food, was certainly not home cooking. The hot coffee, doughnuts, sandwiches, and cakes offered by local groups, the Red Cross, and the USO helped in the transition for the GIs who entered the army with the expectations of civilian life left not far behind. Osborn and Byron both recognized the problem and welcomed all of the help they could get.

Private Raymond James Oblinger, a draftee from Pennsylvania, represented what most GIs felt when he recalled, "The USO . . . had two locations in Anniston [Alabama] where a GI could meet a 'nice' girl. [A]lthough the guys outnumbered the girls ten to one."[5] Oblinger, a small-town lad with strong moral convictions, spent a good deal of time in the Fort McClellan Special Services library and often visited the post's five movie theaters. Sergeant Charles Linzy, training at Camp Hulen, Texas, wrote to his wife in April 1943 that the USO had brought two shows to the camp. One show, titled *You Can't Take It with You,* had come directly from the New York stage, and the second show featured the popular music of 1943, with a number of lesser-known big bands.[6] Linzy moved to Camp Polk, Louisiana, where his unit would participate in large-scale maneuvers before being assigned to one of the theaters of war. Camp Polk was in a rural area of the state with few opportunities for entertainment in surrounding towns. Unfortunately, a large number of cheap saloons, widespread prostitution, and a criminal element moved into the area to prey on GIs. Special Services moved quickly to establish a Service Club and a Special Services presence there. Linzy wrote to his wife, "I have a good table, an easy chair, paper and pen, so what more besides you, could I want? This building covers about a block, coffee shop, library, pianos, cafeteria, dancing pavilions and all. It is not a USO but an army service club."[7] Linzy, who would see combat from Normandy to the Bulge to Germany, a soldier who enjoyed a beer, was typical of the many GIs who preferred to shun the red-light districts, and the Special Services met their needs for entertainment and leisure activities. Many of the new training camps were in rural areas with small towns. It was critical that Special Services establish clubs, cafeterias, and athletic programs, and the PX was pressed to get beer halls, with its 3.2 army beer, up and running as quickly as possible.

By early 1943, the PX system was worldwide, turning hefty profits that were used to enlarge the offerings of the exchange and to provide money for the troops' recreational needs. The farther away from the United States and major theaters of operations, the smaller the PX and the slower the restocking of the shelves. The Special Services overseas faced different problems in that the Special Services officers had to find space for Service Clubs and theaters.

Corporal Thomas R. St. George, assigned to Australia, recalled, "Our camp boasted one theater, in a tin building seating about five hundred or something less than ten percent of the available personnel, that insisted on showing double features. . . . Some of the movies we had seen; others were vaguely remembered by nobody except a couple of World War I veterans who were likewise playing a return engagement."[8] The movies had been borrowed from the Australians because first-run films had yet to arrive from the United States. St. George also complained that the PX had yet to stock enough American candy, cigarettes, or beer. In his words, a bottle of Coca-Cola was but a distant memory.

There were some major problems facing Osborn and the Special Services Division. The first difficulty was the space and time involved in getting Special Services supplies and troops across the vast Pacific Ocean. The need to ship large numbers of combat troops and supplies meant that space was limited for Special Services supplies. Eventually, Brisbane, Australia, would develop a large American army base with the necessary PX and Special Services facilities, but that would take time. As the war expanded across the Pacific, the problems of servicing large numbers of far-flung bases became acute. The climate and diseases also took their toll on Special Services personnel.

Early in the war, President Roosevelt and General Marshall agreed that the defeat of Nazi Germany would take priority over the Pacific theater, and, with American troops and supplies pouring into England, the need to maintain good relations between the GIs and the British population was critical. It was decided that the Army Exchange System and the Special Services Division place their greatest effort toward building facilities in England. Nothing was more important to American planners than a welcomed American presence. However, the situation rather quickly prompted the English to say, with some irritation, that the GIs were "Over paid, Oversexed, and Over Here." One of the tasks that Osborn's information branch had was to develop guides and lectures for the GIs that, it was hoped, would help ease the situation. The GIs were the possessors of first-class cigarettes and chocolate bars; they were the masters of the jitterbug; they could be generous, but also brash and confident; they were young, well nourished, and physically fit; and a GI was paid three times what a British Tommy was paid. They brought with them the music of Glenn Miller, Artie Shaw, and Tommy Dorsey—all of the popular dance tunes of the day. This could be a potent combination when the American soldier came into contact with the British population, especially with English girls.

The Special Services guides to North Africa, India, and Egypt worked fairly well, but would the same approach to England work in the same way? Pretty soon the term *Piccadilly Lilly* found its way into the GI vocabulary. While the Special Services was moving as much equipment and troops into England as possible, there were those soldiers who preferred to leave their bases, and London was a favorite city to visit. Sergeant William "Wild Bill" Guarnere, from Philadelphia, Pennsylvania, serving with Company E, 506th Parachute Infantry Regiment, recalled that when in London, "we went to pubs and threw our money away. We'd slap a ten [pound note] on the bar; we looked like big spenders and it impressed the girls. . . . We drank, danced. . . . A lot of sex. We raised Cain in London. Oh boy, did we have a ball."[9] This was what American authorities wanted to avoid, but many young GIs, away from home and the restraints of the society they knew, were drawn to the city.

There were, however, two sides to the coin in England. Britain had been at war since 1939, sustaining terrific air bombardment and thousands of civilian dead during the Battle of Britain. A severe rationing program was instituted that tried British resolve, and food was at a minimum, while comfort items almost disappeared from store shelves. Betty Swallow, a young woman from London, had an American pen pal with whom she corresponded during the war. A passage from one of her letters typified what many English felt when she wrote, "The clothes too, are a source of great envy to me. To see Betty Grable trailing about in yards and yards of chiffon, when I have to surrender five coupons for enough for a blouse, just isn't Cricket! I'd like to see la Grable look glamorous on a supply of 36 coupons a year."[10] Food, or rather the lack of it, and cosmetics were very much on her mind. Into England came the GIs, who were better paid, better equipped, and better uniformed than their British Tommy counterparts, and they seemed to have unlimited supplies of everything that had all but disappeared in British shops. Of course, the British could very well point out that except for fighting in North Africa, the brash Yanks pouring into Britain had yet to be tested in battle against the German army. Newly promoted technical sergeant Charles Linzy and his 459th Mobile Anti-Aircraft Battalion was stationed with British troops, and like most

Americans in similar circumstances, he complained about the quality and quantity of English mess hall food. Unlike his English counterparts, he was well supplied by the PX system. On one day he received fourteen packs of cigarettes, three candy bars, one package of chewing gum, and a pack of razor blades.[11] It was little wonder that the long-rationed Englishman looked on the GIs as well supplied and pampered. Linzy, however, was also aware of English privations and courage when he wrote to his wife that Britain was a gloomy land, but "I wonder sometimes if we would have stood up to the Blitz as this country has done."[12] Sergeant Don Malarkey of E Company, 506th Parachute Infantry Regiment, had never been out of his native Oregon and recalled, "We started hearing the people's stories of the bombings in London; even in the rural areas, where people weren't huddling in the subways, the British people were weary."[13] War was becoming real for a lot of GIs.

How, then, did the leadership balance the promise that the GI would get "his fair share" of what he or she enjoyed in civilian life with the danger that the American soldiers, highly paid and well supplied, could be seen as a threat to the fabric of a British society strained to the limit by war? British and Americans worked on both sides of the Atlantic to minimize the effects of the thousands of GIs pouring into the United Kingdom. Certainly, the huge number of American troops and equipment would be the critical factor in a successful cross-Channel operation.

This was certainly not lost on Osborn and his Information Section, which would begin a program of preparation for the incoming troops. Any program devised in Washington would be a waste in time, manpower, and money if the commanders, especially at the platoon, company, and battalion levels, where the troops were, did not make an effort to acquaint their soldiers with the country where they were to be deployed for training and eventual combat. The great majority of the noncommissioned and commissioned officers had never been out of the country before. They would have to learn and then teach and, more important, enforce the basics of good Anglo-American relations. It would also be foolish to think that the young, physically fit, and well-provisioned GIs would not come face-to-face with Englishmen and -women. London was a magnet for the GIs when they had the opportunity to visit, but almost every village and town across the country would have its share of GIs. Many of the troops had to be billeted in private homes because of the lack of facilities on bases and, when off duty and not in the PX-supplied beer hall, would visit local pubs and restaurants. There was an unwritten rule not to misbehave in local pubs, but once in London . . .

There were other pressing concerns that motivated Osborn to act quickly to prepare American soldiers arriving in England. The situation in Australia showed that soldiers were in definite need of those morale-raising facilities, which the Special Services were tasked with providing. When troops were left to their own devices, trouble could certainly ensue, and it did in Australia. The first GIs landed in Australia on December 22–23, 1941, to begin training, eventually moving to the area around Brisbane. On March 17, 1942, General Douglas MacArthur arrived in Australia and established the General Headquarters, Southwest Pacific Area (GHQ, SWPA), at Melbourne, but with more GIs moving into the Brisbane area, it became obvious that GHQ, SWPA, had to relocate, which it did on July 20. MacArthur learned of the surrender of American and Philippine troops on Bataan, an event that added urgency to the training of the troops.[14]

The 32nd Division (Michigan and Wisconsin National Guard), for example, called to the colors in 1940, was one of the units that arrived in Brisbane in May 1942. It had mastered the skills of the combat soldier and was ready for the hard, demanding training that would make it one of the first American divisions to engage the enemy in battle.[15] It was soon joined by the 41st Infantry Division and the Americal Division.

By the end of May 1942, there were more than one hundred thousand GIs in the Brisbane area, but little presence of the USO, PX, or the Special Services. A bad relationship grew between the better-paid GIs and Australian troops and townsfolk. Corporal Thomas R. St. George, who would become a well-known literary figure after the war and was an astute observer and chronicler of events, recalled that GI bands played popular music that attracted many of the local Brisbane girls to dances. Observing the interest manifested by the local girls, Australian males complained, "Thim bloody Yanks dance all over the plice." Nor would they call the music swing or jive. They persisted to the end in referring to it as "Yankee music. . . . [T]hey would mutter that our Yankee music sounded like 'what the black fellows played.'"[16]

This was an explosive mixture that did not bode well for Australian-American relations, and in fact there were violent clashes between GIs and Australians that included fatalities. Brisbane would eventually have more than a million American troops pass through to the front and would become a well-equipped rest area for combat troops. As quickly as Special Services could do so, Brisbane was supplied with the full range of Special Services and PX facilities, including a well-equipped beauty parlor for American servicewomen and Red Cross women. Osborn, Byron, and all of the Information and Athletic Sections of Special Services did not want a repeat of the sour relationship that developed around Brisbane to occur in England.

There were many GIs in England who were content to take advantage of being in a country that they had only read about, but had no real desire to leave their bases and go to pubs and drink or go to London to find the ever-present

Piccadilly Lillies. One such GI was Private First Class William E. George of the 415th Night Fighter Squadron, who found himself becoming a true Anglophile. He wrote to his mother and sister in Little Rock, Arkansas, "I sure do like this place [England] and you should see me on my bycicle [sic]." When not exploring English villages and learning about afternoon teas, he was happy to remain on base. The Special Services officer worked hard for his men, and George wrote to his kin, "The officer in charge of recreation really got some swell equipment for the squadron to use."[17]

There were constant baseball games between the officers and enlisted men, and it was not lost on Private George. Because of the athletic competition and the functioning of the PX, the morale of the 415th Night Fighter Squadron remained at a high level. It was imperative that the Special Services Division and the exchange system continue to do everything possible to maintain that level of morale and to keep GIs from incidents that could damage the precarious relationship of the Americans and the British population.

The Army Air Force in early 1942 issued a guide to Britain for its personnel being assigned to England. Unlike what Special Services would print a few months later, this guide dealt mainly with professional relationships with the Royal Air Force, with charts showing ranks, decorations, and a helpful dictionary of commonly used RAF and British military terms.[18]

There was no mention of British pubs or London nightlife, nor was there any description of American facilities such as those offered by the Red Cross or USO, because there were not any in England at that time. That type of professional publication was not what the GIs in the infantry and armored divisions needed. By late 1942, the Special Service's *Short Guide to Great Britain* went to press and directly addressed what military personnel needed to know about the English people and what they had endured. The guide began with a warning: "Hitler has given his propaganda chiefs [the mission] to separate Britain and America and spread distrust between them. If he can do that, his chance of winning *might* return." As the guide said, 1942–43 was not the time to fight old wars, an admonition for Irish American soldiers. Understand, the writers said, that the British people were reserved, but that did not mean that they were unfriendly; however, they could quickly become so if they thought the GIs were brash show-offs throwing their better pay and better supplies around without regard for the feelings of the strictly rationed English people. The guide also stated that the British army was issuing a similar guide titled *Meet the Americans* to British troops for better understanding of the GIs, and it reprinted sections of it. These were critical matters, and the guide ended with an admonition: "It is militarily stupid to criticize your allies."[19] Of the many guides prepared by the Information Section of the Special Services

Division, this one had a special sense of urgency. Others dealt with the land and people where GIs would go, such as India, North Africa, New Guinea, or Egypt, for example, but this one aimed directly at Anglo-American relations, which would be so critical if the cross-Channel invasion was to take place and succeed.

There were obvious stresses and strains appearing already in Anglo-American relations, such as the well-known Patton-Montgomery competition and the disagreements over the methods of carrying out the air bombardment over Germany. What was not needed were publicized fist-swinging brawls between American soldiers and the British military or civilians, like the situation that boiled over in Brisbane. No one, Osborn and Byron included, ever thought that GIs would monkishly refrain from meeting British girls (in 1942 or 1943, the term *war bride* was not yet in the lexicon) or enjoying the local pubs, sometimes with excessive indulgence in full-strength English beers. London would, of course, be a magnet for American soldiers, and nightlife, some not especially wholesome, would be a draw for many GIs. Once in London, GIs saw the sobering sights of rubble from the blitz. Tough paratrooper Sergeant Guarnere, a Philadelphian who could throw a punch with the best, recalled, "That place went through hell. The destruction in a place that was once beautiful, it was a bad scene. They did not like us to go on leave in London, because you never knew when the Germans were coming over."[20] Many GIs were like Linzy and George, who were content to enjoy what was offered by the PX and Special Services or would become tourists in GI olive drabs. The well-thought-out guide and the lectures prepared by the Information Section helped a great deal.

While the Information Section was working on the British and other guides, Special Services had to deal with other issues of great importance. In 1942 Congress appropriated $9.25 million for the Special Services, and for the fiscal year 1943, the sum was raised to $16.25 million.[21] The numbers of troops pouring into the training camps had grown to millions of men and women, and the need to supply them with recreational and athletic facilities, movie theaters, libraries, PXs, beer halls, and guesthouses was critical, with time always in short supply. The cost to the Special Services had grown as well, and the need for supplies grew daily. In addition, by early 1943 there were almost forty Special Services companies undergoing training in the United States for use there and overseas, where the needs were great. One concern not envisioned in early 1942 was the relationship of Special Services and the civilians who wanted to work for the troops but were not part of the USO or the Red Cross. Two months after Pearl Harbor, Henry L. Stimson, the secretary of war, established the Army Emergency Relief Fund to provide for the families of the draftees who found themselves in dire financial circumstances when the breadwinner suddenly found his monthly salary reduced to the $50 of a private. GIs would provide for their families through an allotment, but because of the massive amount of army paperwork, often months elapsed before the check could reach the family. Funds had to be available to assist in that time of hardship. John J. Pershing, Secretary Stimson, and other notables headed the fund, but the Special Services was tasked with receiving claims and forwarding them on to the proper army financial authorities. This was a duty that was vitally important for GI and home-front morale.

The funds involved would be considerable, and certainly Osborn did not want appropriated Special Services funds to be diverted. On the other hand, because Special Services was involved with attracting movie and radio stars to provide shows for troops in the United States and overseas, there was a good connection with show-business people. The famous entertainer Irving Berlin, who had provided shows for World War I troops, suggested to General Marshall that he would organize a Broadway show with all proceeds and contributions going to the Army Emergency Relief Fund. Marshall gave Berlin his support for a show titled *This Is the Army,* which would have about three hundred famous stars involved. "The show was corny and a bit dated even by 1942 standards," one historian has noted, and it mirrored a similar show put on by Irving Berlin in 1918.[22] The show was, despite its World War I origins, a great success and garnered $2 million in contributions. It went on to tour the United States and overseas theaters of operations, where it once came under Japanese sniper fire.

Since George C. Marshall viewed that type of show as a major military and civilian morale factor and a much-needed moneymaker, Osborn and his Special Services officers would be involved. With the well-known Ed Sullivan, chairman of the Theatrical Committee, a gala event was scheduled at New York's Madison Square Garden for September 30, 1942, featuring the best of Hollywood and Broadway performers. The Second Service Command designated Colonel H. Clay M. Supplee, the command's ranking Special Services officer, as the army's collector of funds and as the point of contact for GIs' families' requests for emergency funds. The Special Services Division became deeply involved with this type of star-studded show.

Members of Ed Sullivan's committee fanned out across New York and the East Coast, convincing companies, hotels, and activities to take out ads in the show's program, raising many millions of dollars. The show's title was *We're All in It, Let's Win It,* and it was much more current than Berlin's earlier presentation. Comedians Olson and Johnson opened the show-business extravaganza with a routine, followed by Ed Winn, Charles Laughton, Ethel

Merman, and Joe E. Lewis. Harry James's band began the musical section, followed by singers Kate Smith and Al Jolson and actress Joan Blondell. The stage was filled with more than three dozen of Hollywood's best-known actors and actresses, including GIs' pin-up favorites, like Dorothy Lamour. The Stage Door Canteen presented a major musical selection, the only act that had black entertainers, the popular Ink Spots. For the GIs in the Garden, there was a special treat when the well-known striptease dancer Gypsy Rose Lee did a routine titled "Heir to a G-String," with GIs whistling, clapping, and hollering their appreciation of her unique morale-raising talents.[23] By the end of 1942 and well into 1943, the Special Services Division under General Osborn had established its reputation as the premier morale-raising part of the army, and it did not hurt that Special Services displayed the talent to raise millions of civilian dollars for the Army Emergency Relief Fund to assist the dependents of the mass of newly drafted soldiers.

While the Special Services' Entertainment Section was raising money, the remainder of the division continued building the facilities needed for the troops wherever they were. To help the situation, the USO and the Red Cross underwent a massive program to open and staff clubs in every city in the United States, in England, and in Australia. Local church and civic organizations pitched in with clubs of their own as well. Civilian movie theaters, for example, had their ushers pass cans to their patrons for contributions for the war effort.

No one immediately after Pearl Harbor could have envisioned the scope of the worldwide commitment of Special Services and Exchange Services activities. Pressure to provide for the troops came from unexpected quarters. During the fall of 1942, for example, a fact-finding group led by Fiorello La Guardia, the dynamic mayor of New York, went to the Newfoundland Base Command, where there was a large buildup of American air assets. The group viewed the facilities for US Army Air Force pilots and crews in transit to England. They found that a major building program was under way to construct living quarters for the transit troops before the severe winter weather set in. Mayor La Guardia was troubled, however: "Recreation for the men [permanent troops and transit crews] is one of the difficult problems. There is absolutely nothing in the immediate vicinity. I strongly recommend more USO and more recreational equipment to be shipped in before freezing time."[24]

In Trinidad, which was also a transit base, the need for more Special Services and PX offerings was critical. Officially, the command warned troops that intestinal disorders and venereal diseases were serious problems on the island. Consequently, the Special Services and PX officers, in close cooperation with the USO and Red Cross, worked to build an athletic and leisure center for the troops. The PX offered "good American beer in clean surroundings, free from malaria and venereal disease." The USO opened a large facility in the capital of Port-of-Spain that offered tours, athletic equipment, and a clean cafeteria that sold ice cream, soft drinks, and sandwiches at low prices. Beer sales were left to the PX.[25] Would there a priority list be developed for the Special Services and the exchange system? Publicly, the answer had to be a resounding no.

By 1943 the Special Services Division had developed a good reputation for efficiency, cost-effectiveness, and response to the needs of the troops. As one could imagine, there were problem areas, and not every Special Services officer was effective, but the work of General Osborn and General Byron of the AES relieved a burden from the shoulders of General Somervell.

None of this could have happened had there not been a well-functioning and well-defined administrative structure for the Special Services Division, which comprised seven functional areas staffed by military and civilian personnel. The division had two thousand officers and four thousand enlisted men in the basic structure, and this number would grow as the Special Services companies were formed, trained, and committed to Stateside or overseas service. The Overseas Operations Section oversaw an allocation of eight million dollars' worth of radio, library, motion picture, and athletic equipment.[26] This section was also responsible for seeing that each unit overseas received two kits, named A and B. The A kit contained athletic equipment, mainly baseballs, footballs, boxing gloves, table-tennis balls and paddles, and horseshoes. Volleyballs were chemically treated for high heat and extreme humidity for tropical use, if the kit was scheduled for the Pacific theater of operations. A second part of the A kit contained checkers, chess, playing cards, poker chips, backgammon games, dominoes, and Parcheesi sets. The B kits contained radios, repair tubes and parts, as well as songbooks and harmonicas.[27]

One of the most important sections of the division was the Army Motion Picture Service, which maintained more than five hundred theaters drawing a staggering one hundred million soldiers in attendance in one year, both in the United States and overseas. This section oversaw the coordination for first-run Hollywood movies. The Athletics, Recreation, and Welfare Section coordinated the hiring of 400 Service Club hostesses, 150 librarians, and assorted drama coaches and song leaders; selected talented soldiers for GI camp shows; and coordinated with the USO for shows in the United States and overseas. The Welfare Section maintained more than fifty recreational camps and also coordinated with the Red Cross and USO. The Information to Troops Section was one of the largest functional areas of the Special Services Division. It dealt with motion pictures that oriented troops to their missions, indoctrinated troops about their Nazi and Japanese foes, and provided up-to-date newsreels. One of their most effective actors was an Army Air Force captain named Ronald Reagan. This section oversaw camp newspapers, produced the magazine *Yank,* and published the useful overseas guides.

The Education functional area coordinated correspondence schools that reached seventy-five thousand GI enrollees in 1943, with seventy-five colleges or universities involved. It participated in obtaining and distributing five and a half million books. General Osborn was especially interested in the field of education and would by 1944 oversee a massive expansion of education-al information and enrollment. The School for Special Services, which was first established at Fort George G. Meade near Baltimore, Maryland, and then moved to Washington and Lee University in Lexington, Virginia, trained two hundred student officers and enlisted men every month. Special attention was paid to those officers who would command the Special Services com-panies. The Research Section gained importance as it became an "operating research unit for all War Department agencies on problems of the soldier." It studied diverse topics such as "attitudes toward negroes," satisfaction or dissatisfaction with job assignment, and food. Food surveys were important for the Quartermaster Corps, which was constantly updating and improving combat rations.[28]

All of the organizational charts, the designation of heads of functional ar-eas, and the best intentions of the Special Services Division staff and workers did not mean much if it did not contribute to the war effort and to victory over Nazi Germany and Imperial Japan. The selections of Osborn and By-ron to head Special Services and the exchange system could not have been better. The best staff in Washington or the enthusiasm of the Special Ser-vices officers at the army, corps, or divisional level did not mean much if the troops were not well served. It became important to put well-organized and efficient Special Services companies into the field to serve the troops. This was a project that would eventually see more than forty companies in active service for the United States and all overseas theaters of operations. It was one thing to have plans in Washington; it was certainly another to see that those plans were actually put into action. By early 1943 it was clear that there needed to be an inspection of the overseas activities of the Special Services and the exchange system.

Osborn was not the person to conduct such a detailed inspection, but By-ron was because of his West Point ring, his service in the Great War, and his association with commanders such as General Eisenhower. Almost every in-spection began with the time-honored phrase "I'm not here to find fault, but to help," which no one really believes. Byron brought with him a certain mili-tary credibility and, frankly, a real desire to improve overseas activities. When

Osborn was in charge of education and information in 1944, he felt himself to be on more familiar ground to conduct an overseas inspection. In 1943 Byron was the best choice for what would become a thirty-six-thousand-mile trip that would have great implications for the future activities of the Special Services Division and the Army Exchange System.

After a trip spanning three continents, Byron submitted his report to Generals Somervell and Osborn. He viewed the inspection as an "initial step" for Special Services and the Exchange Service because it pointed out areas where things were going well and places where there needed to be improvement. For Byron, it was obvious that the major theaters got the lion's share of Special Services activities, while smaller areas were often overlooked.

One such problem area was Ascension Island, where the army and navy worked with British authorities to monitor antisubmarine operations. There he found morale so low that he made a supplementary report to the inspector general of the army. Officers and enlisted considered the assignment to "the Rock" as punishment for some offense. Byron reported that exchange supplies were plentiful, but that more Special Services equipment was needed to establish a program of athletics and games. In Byron's mind, the troops were bored and simply "decided to feel sorry for themselves." Once he left the volcanic island, Byron and his executive officer of the AES, Major Bernard Babcock, went to a different isolated post, Khartoum, in the Sudan. There it was a different story, with soldiers and nurses smoking and drinking cold American beer on a roof garden overlooking the historic and exotic city. In Cairo Byron discovered that the Special Services and exchange officers did not coordinate well, but mobile PXs went to troops in the field, and athletic equipment, radios, and books were available. In Persia he found that there were squabbles between army personnel and the diplomatic staff over who could use the PX. Pragmatic Byron instituted a ration-card system so that both groups could use the exchange. The facilities functioned fairly well in Teheran, but in an outpost in Gaya there was no exchange or Service Club or movie theater in evidence, and Byron had a rather lengthy discussion with the post commander as to what was available and what his responsibilities were in maintaining the morale of his troops.

In China Byron and Babcock met with the legendary general Claire Chennault, who had allocated twelve tons of shipping space for exchange and Special Services supplies, which was a real sacrifice that indicated the general's concern for the morale of his airmen. At Kumming Byron came face-to-face with a situation that would bedevil the exchange, Special Services, Red Cross, and USO. American cigarettes, candy, and other items found their way into the Chinese black market. A PX five-cent pack of American smokes sold for almost five dollars in gold! A strict rationing and oversight system had to be instituted in most areas in China. At Ling Ling, Chennault's airmen told Byron, "We are well fixed with cigarettes, General. What we want is gasoline and Japs." There was no question that morale was high, and there was a healthy baseball competition between units. After a satisfactory stop in India, Byron landed in Aden, which equaled Ascension Island for low morale, partially caused by having no effective PX or Special Services system. Morale was so low that the commander of American troops in Aden was relieved of his command, taking his ineffectual exchange officer with him.

In Algiers Byron met an old friend, General Dwight David Eisenhower, who fully supported AES and Special Services Division activities. Eisenhower sent Byron to see General Omar Bradley. Bradley, known as the GIs' general, briefed Byron about continual operations in North Africa, stating that combat action would soon be over, and then he fully expected to issue new clothing and serve better rations, and "also they will want exchange supplies." To ensure that the combat-weary GIs got everything that Bradley expected they would, Byron appointed an energetic colonel, O. W. Hoop, to be the theater exchange officer with the mission of seeing that Bradley's soldiers got what they needed and that Special Services would operate to provide morale-enhancing activities.

From North Africa Byron went to England, where the numbers of American combat and logistic forces were growing daily. Also, a Special Services company had been functioning for several months, the headquarters being located in Cheltenham. There he saw a need for more companies of that type to be sent to England. This was based on his observation that the Special Services company was a sound idea, if the commanders understood what they could do for GI morale. Also, Byron made the point that the army chaplains had to be part of morale planning and activities, simply because the army had listed faith and religious observances as a vital part of a soldier's morale and his effectiveness in combat.[29] There was much in this memorandum for Somervell to ponder, especially the availability of shipping space for exchange and Special Services supplies to every area of the world. This was certainly a far cry from the Great War, when the major areas of interest were the ports of France.

While in India Byron tried to find out why there were often shortages in both exchange and Special Services supplies. An exchange officer informed Byron that one ship carrying items for both groups had been sunk by a Japanese submarine and that they always faced grave dangers from the Japanese, who often targeted supply ships that were slower than regular navy troop carriers and surface-warfare ships. That only explained why there were brief periods when large numbers of cigarettes, shaving items, and beer were not on the shelves of the PX, or why there were not enough movies, baseballs, and checkerboards available for the troops to use.

Byron pointed out to General Somervell that too often commanders were not briefed by their staffs about the erratic nature of exchange and Special Services items. Those supplies were considered "filler cargo," and it was possible that a large shipment destined, for example, for the China-Burma-India theater was broken into smaller portions and shipped on several ships. At the theater-command level, the staff was concerned with reports from the field about shortages that affected morale. It was also fairly clear that Special Services officers at the command level had difficulties briefing the commanders and their staffs.[30]

General Byron anticipated future problems as American troops grew in number overseas. He informed Somervell that as the army looked to the great battles in late 1943 and 1944, it might be wise to curtail domestic exchange and Special Services activities while increasing shipments and personnel to the theaters of war. Typical of Byron, he urged that the purchase of supplies be decentralized, left to the exchange officers both in the United States and overseas.

Of course, the demand for American cigarettes, beer, and chewing gum and for baseballs, baseball gloves, footballs, checkers, and first-run Hollywood movies had to be filled in the United States. Looking into the future with victories in Europe, the Pacific, and the China-Burma-India theater, Byron stated that the exchange system would become a part of the regular army, as the Special Services Division was already.[31] Osborn profited from Byron's detailed report, and he informed the Overseas Operations Section that as many Special Services companies as needed be sent to the theaters of operations as quickly as possible. By late 1943 Osborn wanted more than four thousand troops trained, formed into companies, and embarked for overseas assignments. The Army Motion Picture Service, clearly one of the most popular offerings, had to expand its efforts to support overseas operations. Every effort had to be made to ensure that the Special Services companies maintained their unit integrity and their basic supplies, by having enough shipping space to get every private and every baseball in place, intact, and ready for use or service.

Inspections and observations become nothing but a paper drill unless there is corrective action, and that General Somervell demanded. General Marshall was not satisfied that troops were being used to the best benefit of the army, and he wanted every department and command to survey the troops under their authority, eliminating those personnel who were not absolutely necessary for the tasks assigned. Also by 1943 it was becoming clear that the army would need more infantry, armor, and artillery. A terse memo to Osborn from Major General W. D. Styer said that Marshall expected reductions in manpower and improvement in services offered.[32] Osborn and Byron did indeed make the necessary cuts, mainly in Stateside assignments Byron had envisioned. Construction was to be seriously considered, and when the Special Services Division requested funds for building five new athletic fields, one was denied at Fort Huachuca, which was the one post where large-scale training of combat troops was not taking place.[33] There could be no mistake; Somervell and Marshall were professional officers who would not tolerate failure. Marshall toured the European theater, and upon his return he made his displeasure known to Somervell over what he saw as a lack of recreational facilities for troops in North Africa. Since Somervell had charge over the Special Services Division, he made it clear that getting movies and projectors to North Africa without delay was a priority.[34]

On the other hand, Somervell was not a commander who would curry favor with superiors by laying blame on his subordinates. In a brief memo to Marshall, Somervell pointed out, "It appears that it [Special Services] has not been able to carry out its mission in theaters of operation because of the lack of appreciation on the part of theater commanders concerning their importance, and the dissipation of Special Service units and their equipment to other duties."[35] To be fair, many European theater commanders had seen the intensity of combat in North Africa, and they had to prepare for the invasion of Sicily. Infantry was needed to confront the enemy, which had proven itself to be capable, well commanded, and battle hardened.

During the American Civil War, a Confederate general saw a band playing, and, turning to an aide, he said, "What this army needs is more shooters and fewer tooters." It would be difficult for a division commander who had to count casualties and losses from the fighting in Tunisia not to wonder about GIs whose duties involved a movie projector or a box of baseballs and gloves. Special Services officers had to be efficient and know when to approach combat commanders with Special Services issues. Somervell counseled Osborn that he needed to get "top-notch" officers sent to the overseas theaters as quickly as possible.

As diligent as Osborn and Byron were, it would not be possible to meet all of the demands from every far-flung post. A good case in point was the situation on Kiska, an island in the Aleutian chain that was part of Alaska. On June 6, 1942, the Japanese landed troops on the island as a diversion at the beginning of a campaign that would result in their historic, tide-turning defeat at Midway. The presence of Japanese troops was basically meaningless in a military sense, but the news of Japanese forces on American soil, no matter how desolate and remote the site, could shake the public's morale at a critical juncture of the war. On August 15, 1943, American and Allied troops landed to expel the Japanese. As the Japanese threat receded, the US Navy announced a policy of rotating ships from the area, but army troops were basically stuck there as winter approached. General Marshall became involved when he was briefed by John J. McCloy, the assistant secretary of war, who had just returned from the area. Morale among the troops of the 7th Infantry Division was becoming low, as the soldiers had to contend with heavy fog, rain, and dropping temperatures.[36] Osborn received a memo from General W. D. Styer citing Marshall's concern for the troops on Kiska, stating, "It is believed that a special effort should be made to see that they [the 7th Division troops] are amply provided with all means at the disposal of the Special Services Division to keep up their morale."[37] Byron was made aware of the situation, and exchange and Special Services supplies were dispatched to ports in the American Northwest for shipment, along with Special Services personnel to administer the PX and the Special Services operations. Shipping the necessary equipment became a problem, because most of the shipping in the West was destined for the battlefields of the Pacific theater of operations. Try as they could, and with General George C. Marshall looking over their shoulders, their flow of supplies was haphazard at best, and morale among American troops remained low.

The morale situation on Ascension Island continued to be bleak, despite efforts to correct it. General Styer informed Osborn that the commanding officer on the island requested that batteries be sent there for portable radios, the only source of entertainment for troops on outpost duty. There was a dire need for more movies for the four movie theaters that Special Services operated. It was shown that the movie theaters were the most highly regarded form of diversion, but each theater could offer only two shows per week. The Special Services officer also requested a major increase in baseball equipment. The Special Services Division had a problem meeting all the needs because of the lack of consistent shipping to the island.[38]

Both the Special Services and the exchange faced the same difficulties. The same problems surfaced with American troops stationed in Georgetown, British Guiana, which was regarded as a backwater assignment, and morale there remained low. The US commander there complained about the quality of USO shows, and then requested that more current movies be sent to the command, because the GIs complained that they had seen those movies before they left the United States.[39] As to who in Osborn's Army Motion Picture Service Section could monitor who saw what and when in the United States,

General Styer offered no solution. The movie section had the massive task of copying large numbers of Hollywood movies and then shipping them to every area covered by the Special Services Division. It was obvious that there would be repeats of all movies. The same complaints from far-flung posts came to Byron's AES, but little could be done to see that Ascension Island and British Guiana got the same service as the troops in North Africa, England, India, Australia, or New Guinea.

On the other hand, General Marshall and his staff officers such as General Styer could not simply ignore complaints from overseas commands. However, when a high-profile civilian such as John J. McCloy said that there were problems with Special Services offerings in North Africa, action would be taken quickly. McCloy had taken note of the lack of athletic equipment and movies for the troops, especially those who had seen combat against the Germans. Osborn sent a dynamic officer, Lieutenant Colonel John M. Mitchell, to North Africa to work with the theater's commanding general and with Special Services officers there.[40] Of growing importance to the army was the Army Air Transport Command base at Casablanca, Morocco, where transports from five continents landed daily and where more than twelve million pounds of vital war cargo was processed every month. As the base expanded, there was a need for rapid, continual expansion of Special Services and PX facilities.

The base command was also concerned with the high rate of venereal disease, intestinal disorders from civilian off-base restaurants, assaults, robberies, and an active black market. The response by Osborn and Byron was quick, and by the spring of 1943, the Casablanca base expanded its movie theaters, Service Clubs, clubs for officers, and exchange beer halls. Five PXs, including a PX in the transit terminal, and an equal number of Service Clubs plus libraries were open for business.[41] Obviously, priorities for Osborn and Byron had to be based on the importance and size of the troop concentration. Shipping space to North Africa, for example, was much larger and more consistent than to Ascension Island or British Guiana.

Although there would be continual complaints from smaller posts and bases, the overall reaction to Special Services and the exchange system was good. Much had been learned by the first months of 1943, and much had been accomplished. Sergeant R. D. Tuttle, serving in the 499th Engineer Battalion on New Guinea, had seen some hard times from the heat, the rain, and the Japanese. He wrote to his sweetheart, May, back in Marion, Ohio, "There is a show tonite I am going to take it in. I just heard they are having a cowboy picture on Roy Rogers in King of the Cowboys. I am still going."[42] Private Arthur Jacklewski, training at the Desert Training Center in California with the Medical Detachment, 4th Cavalry, wrote to his parents about the intense heat, but he added that there was a double-feature movie that night. The Special Services showed a comedy and then *Blondie Plays Cupid,* based on the popular radio and comic strip characters.[43] The 28th Special Services Company at the Transportation Corps Unit Training Center at Indiantown Gap Military Reservation in Pennsylvania scored a real triumph for the 204th Port Company when they arranged a service-club dance with two hundred local girls, mainly from the town of Hershey, in attendance. That meant there was almost a ration of one GI to one dance partner, a rarity for service-club dances.[44]

Despite complaints and some experimentation by Osborn and his staff, the Special Services Division was proving its worth to the war effort. The remainder of 1943 into 1944 would see an expansion of both the Special Services and the exchange system wherever GIs were serving.

General Frederick Osborn, 1944. Courtesy of the National Archives.

General Joseph Byron, 1944. Courtesy of the National Archives.

Byron and Service Club hostesses, 1945. Courtesy of the National Archives.

GIs enjoy a belly-dance exhibition, Egypt, 1943. Courtesy of the National Archives.

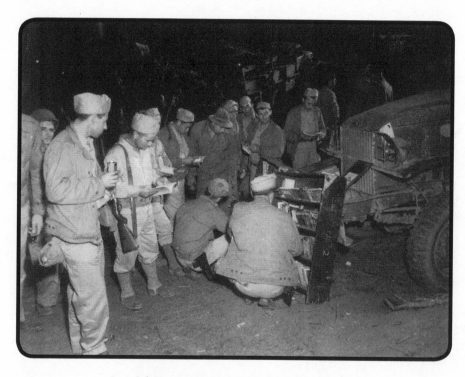

Special Services company Library Section,
Belgium, January 1945. Courtesy of the National Archives.

Special Services company Exchange Section for released
prisoners of war, Hollandia, 1945. Courtesy of the National Archives.

Service Club dance with volunteers,
Manila, 1945. Courtesy of the National Archives.

Service Club dance with volunteers,
California, 1944. Courtesy of the National Archives.

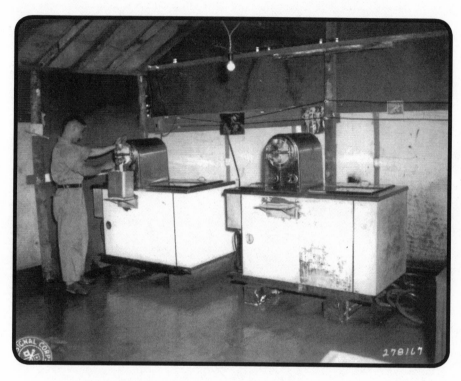

Preparation of ice cream by a Special Services company
Canteen Section, Burma, 1945. Courtesy of the National Archives.

Special Services company jazz band, Verviers,
Belgium, 1945. Courtesy of the National Archives.

GI enlisted men's club, Paris, 1945. Courtesy of the National Archives.

Special Services dance, Brisbane, Australia,
1942. Courtesy of the National Archives.

American female entertainers, Special Services–USO show, Australia, 1944. Courtesy of the National Archives.

Thatched-roof Special Services club,
Burma, 1944. Courtesy of the National Archives.

Typical Post Exchange beer hall in the United
States, 1943. Courtesy of the National Archives.

Red Cross–Special Services coffee and doughnut
truck, Belgium, 1945. Courtesy of the National Archives.

General Byron and Colonel Frank Kerr,
Washington, DC, 1945. Courtesy of the National Archives.

5

A One-Man Band

Camp McCain was built in a rural area of Mississippi near the town of Grenada and about a hundred miles from Memphis, Tennessee, over winding, two-lane roads. In the summer the heat and humidity were intense, but Camp McCain had large wooded areas in which to train the men of the 87th Infantry Division. Special Services came to the North Mississippi base and built heavily used Service Clubs, bowling alleys, exchanges, and beer halls and instituted a full schedule of athletic events. In August, however, the camp and the men of the Golden Acorn Division had a major event. For almost a week the beautiful Hollywood actress Carole Landis visited the camp and threw herself into a hectic round of entertainment, from singing to giving boxing championship awards. Landis had been working through the Special Services and USO to entertain the troops. She first went to England and North Africa, then to the Pacific, where she contracted a debilitating disease, and then to visit troops training in the United States. One morning she showed up at a company mess hall and helped two shocked GIs peel potatoes. According to the division command, morale for the 87th Division had never been higher.[1]

The Special Services officers worked to provide all they could for the men, and they formed a large group of local girls, called the "military maids," to attend dances and hold birthday parties for the troops at that isolated post. The 1943 Valentine's Day dance, organized by the Special Services and the town of Grenada, filled the large wooden Service Club, as the commanding general, his staff, and many local matrons, as chaperones, watched over the event. Music was provided by a GI band organized and equipped by Special Services.[2] With many troops being trained in remote areas, the Special Services was challenged, and every effort was made to provide those important morale-enhancing activities.

It was one thing to have a Hollywood star visit an army camp or open a PX beer hall; it was another to have a coherent program to extend Special Services offerings to units in training or engaged in combat overseas. Army units at the theater, army, or corps level were used to having units attached to them for operations in the process of building a force for combat, but this was quite different from having a Special Services officer attached to a commander's staff. To have Special Services personnel simply on site did not answer a commander's question as to exactly what they had and what their capabilities were. There was a need to have identifiable Special Services units that would become a part of the commander's assets. In 1942 Osborn's Special Services Division began a process of building the first Special Services unit at Fort George G. Meade, Maryland, with the purpose of deploying the unit to Britain as quickly as possible. The basic mission of the unit was as follows: "The Special Services [unit] is an independent, self-sustaining, semi-mobile organization, trained and equipped to provide recreational and informational services to troops serving in a theater of operations. It is able to provide forward echelons with services and facilities otherwise available only in base operations."[3] With a mission clearly defined and with plans to ship them to England by September 1942, there was a need to make the unit comprehensible to overseas commanders.

Consequently, by the end of 1942 the unit became a company, which did not change any of the activities or the tables of organization and equipment. Commanders and staffs would be happier now, having an identifiable army formation. By the end of the war in 1945, the Special Services Division had forty companies, with the vast majority serving overseas. By the very nature of the companies, they had to have a close working relationship with the Army Exchange System, the USO, and the Red Cross.

With the army in need of combat troops as the war progressed, the Special Services companies had to prove their worth. By the end of the war, there were more than four thousand soldiers involved in the Special Services companies. The soldiers assigned to the companies first completed basic combat training, giving them proficiency with the rifle and with the skills a combat soldier needed to function on the battlefield. Once that was done, the soldier was assigned to the company. Those who had special civilian skills such as musicians, actors, and the like were given first priority for assignment to a Special Services company. It was then that the soldier learned skills such as operating a 16mm movie projector, use of sound equipment, the basics of organizing GI shows, the rules of athletic events, dealing with the exchanges, operating soda fountains, and short-order cooking. At the same time, the company had to have a training schedule, which would reinforce the basic combat skills such as firing on the rifle ranges, marches, bivouacs, drills, and physical training. The army regarded every soldier as first an infantryman, and the members of the Special Services company were no different.

The army was used to standardization and having the documentation that would show what an army unit had as far as troops and equipment were concerned. Documentation for the companies would finally be available in draft form in 1943 and was finalized in January 1944 with the publication of the field manual *FM 28-105: The Special Services Company.* Special Services companies had been in operation in every major theater of war since late 1942, and there had been confusion as to exactly what their role was. There was, by 1943, a Special Services officer with a small number of subordinate officers and noncommissioned officers at every division corps and army headquarters. Along with the Special Services section, there was an exchange officer who oversaw the staffing of exchanges and the procurement of supplies for the PX. The First Special Services Company had done good service in England, and by early 1943, several companies were deployed to the Pacific and China-Burma-India theaters of operations. It was critical that the companies prove their value to the war effort. The army had good reason to watch the growth of Special Services and monitor its success in providing for the morale of the troops. A typical infantry regiment included 152 officers, 5 warrant officers, 3,100 enlisted men, and 4 men for a total of 3,261 men,[4] and Osborn's Special Services Division envisioned about 4,000 men in the Special Services companies. This was a little more than one regiment, and there were those in the War Department who wondered whether, when casualty lists were growing, there was a need for a large commitment to athletics, entertainment, cafeterias, jazz bands, dances, and mobile PXs. While the War Department was having second thoughts about some programs that drew manpower away from the combat divisions, there was a need for the Special Services Division to show results that really mattered to the war effort. By 1944 the budget for the division had grown to more than $30.5 million, and there were plans to increase the appropriation in 1945.[5] The concept of the company had better work.

At Camp Blanding, Florida, on May 15, 1942, the Second Special Services Company was activated, with 5 officers and 13 enlisted men. Blanding was a large training base, and the personnel section at camp headquarters began to comb records for soldiers with skills that the company might use. Those selected could be transferred to the unit only after they successfully completed basic combat training and qualified with the M1 rifle. At the end of July, the number of enlisted soldiers had grown to more than 100 men, and in early August the company, under command of a Captain C. P. Garbarini, left Camp Blanding for Fort Dix, New Jersey, to await transportation to England.[6] The Second Company arrived in England on September 12, 1942. As soon as the company and its equipment were operational, a platoon was detached and sent to the southern part of England to serve troops being assembled for the North African invasion, Operation Torch.

In May 1942 the 3rd Special Services Unit was activated at Camp Shelby, Mississippi, with 14 enlisted men and no officers. What those GIs were to do was not made clear, except to keep tents clean. There was a call from the Camp Shelby exchange officer for those GIs to help at the various branch exchanges since troops were pouring into this large army training base. Finally, by the end of the month 5 officers were assigned to the unit, and the number of enlisted men rose to 107. Training was sketchy because there were few authoritative documents, and some of the enlisted men had been transferred from the infantry training center before they had completed basic combat training. Before the Third could be a functional unit, the entire group of enlisted had to finish rifle-range training, the required combat infantry training, and a two-week bivouac.

As the units were formed, there was a basic outline as to how such a new specialty should be organized and function. As with most companies, there was a unit headquarters consisting of the company commander, first sergeant, clerks, a sergeant who served as a chief accountant who received and recorded reports and requisitions from the platoon, and assorted technicians. Under the headquarters there were four platoons, each divided into a Service Section and a Canteen and Exchange Section. In the Service Section there were athletic, library, music, motion picture, and theatrical specialists. The Canteen and Exchange Section consisted of a senior sergeant who worked as a store manager, with two corporals who actually worked with exchange goods. The canteen had three cooks who prepared sandwiches, hamburgers, and soft drinks. The exchange personnel could operate from modified trucks and sell their goods, while the Canteen Section had to have some sort of permanent site.

The problem for the 3rd Unit was that there was little direction, which was especially critical for defining the relationship of the unit and the Post Exchange officer. The situation at Camp Shelby was repeated with other units in the process of activation in 1942. What made the situation especially difficult for the unit being formed at Camp Shelby was the fact that the officers and men came from the infantry training replacement center, and many had not completed basic training. To compound the difficulties for the unit, they were scheduled for deployment to England in August. To bring the officers and men up to basic-training standards and have some practical work in being a Special Services unit, a two-week bivouac was conducted, and when the troops were not engaged in learning the basic combat skills, they provided special services such as cold soft drinks and candy bars to other troops on the rifle ranges.[7]

The 3rd Unit finally found themselves at Lambton Park, England, on August 31, 1942. But the trials and tribulations of the GIs were not over. Within two weeks a detachment of thirty men was sent to man the main PX near Lambton Park, a task normally handled by the Army Exchange System. Then orders arrived assigning the entire unit to Iceland, where it established facilities for a growing American presence. The Iceland Base Command was of increasing importance to the buildup of American forces in England, especially the US Army Air Force. The air force used Iceland as a stopover base for aircraft flying to England from the United States, and the navy had need of Iceland's many ports. The quantity of army matériel destined for England was continually expanding. There needed to be a large military contingent to maintain and refuel aircraft, and transient aircraft and crews often remained in Iceland for a number of days. Consequently, there was a need for a Special Services unit to deal with both permanent and transient troops.

When the 3rd Unit arrived, they found that there was almost no civilian entertainment for GIs except for an efficient group of American Red Cross volunteers in the capital city of Reykjavik. There had to be close coordination between the unit and the Red Cross, because there was a need to send platoons and detachments to outlying bases, and the 3rd Unit was simply too small to handle all of the recreational requirements. The 3rd Unit and the AES established a main exchange and Service Club with the Red Cross center in the capital. This was unusual because the exchange offered beer to the troops, which was something the Red Cross refused to do. Very quickly, the 3rd Unit opened two movie theaters in Reykjavik and formed a GI jazz and dance band by December 1942 for dances chaperoned by wary Icelanders and Red Cross volunteers. The record of the 3rd Unit was one of achievement, and in December 1943 the 3rd, now known as the 3rd Special Services Company, was ordered to deploy to Torquay in Devonshire, in southern England, to provide for the ever-growing number of American troops there. What arrived in Torquay was not the same group of green, minimally trained GIs that left Camp Shelby a little more than a year before. It had functioned in difficult circumstances in a barren area subject to great variations in climate and successfully coordinated with a civilian agency. This experience prepared them for the campaigns to come in France, Germany, and Czechoslovakia.[8]

In May 1942 at Camp Gordon, Georgia, the 4th Special Services Unit was activated with four officers and fourteen enlisted men, and on May 17 Captain Charles G. Wells assumed command of the unit. Unlike the 3rd Unit at

Camp Shelby, the core of this unit was trained and knew how to prepare for an overseas assignment. In one month the unit was up to full strength when more than ninety enlisted men were transferred from the Branch Immaterial Replacement Pool at Fort McClellan, Alabama. These GIs had completed basic training and had qualified with the infantry rifle, but had not received an assignment to a unit; they were a good addition to Captain Wells's command. Within one month, the 4th Unit was ordered to Fort Dix, New Jersey, to assemble all of their equipment and vehicles to prepare for deployment to England. The unit arrived in Scotland in early September 1942 and was transported to Boughton Park, Northants, where it was quickly put to work. The unit was scattered throughout England to support American operations and training. One platoon supported Bomber Command, Eighth Air Force, while another was sent to the London Base Command, with another directed to support the 11th US Corps' district engineers at Colchester. Designated as the 4th Special Services Company in early 1943, this unit remained the most scattered of all of the units in England until its deployment to France in 1944.[9]

The deployment of the first four fully formed units to the European theater of operations reflected the war plans of the United States. The priority for combat operations would be against Nazi Germany, which Roosevelt, Marshall, and others believed was the greater menace to the free world. Given the wartime alliance of the United States, Britain, and Russia, it was important to focus the major effort on Europe and the eventual cross-Channel invasion. England, of course, was the only staging area for what would become Operation Overlord in June 1944, but the massive buildup of American forces placed a strain on what England could provide for the GIs. The more the United States could provide for GI recreation, the better relations between Americans and the British population would be, or so it was hoped.

The work of the Special Services units in England was recognized as being greatly beneficial for troop morale and for Anglo-American relations, and commanders in England requested that more units be sent as quickly as possible. Consequently, the War Department devised a plan to get those units overseas to England rapidly, which also meant that specialized Special Services equipment such as the various kits—athletic, musical, canteen field ranges, pans, and the like—must be packaged and sent to ports of embarkation to then be shipped prior to the arrival of the troops. The officers and enlisted men would carry only their individual equipment, and the unit would carry files and necessary publications. In theory, the equipment would arrive before the units and be waiting to be unpacked and used as quickly as possible. Three units, now called by the more familiar army designation of company, were alerted to begin preparations for deployment despite protests from General

Osborn and his staff. Their concerns were based on conditions in the various ports of embarkation where supplies were loaded quickly, too often causing equipment for many troop units to arrive piecemeal at ports in England and Scotland. This had also occurred in West Coast ports.

The three companies assigned to England did indeed arrive before their equipment, and several weeks were lost as the GIs waited for their shipment.[10] Going into the critical year of 1944, the situation had to be reversed if the Special Services companies were to be of service to troops who knew that at some time they would cross the English Channel to land on French beaches well defended by German troops. The Pacific theater of operations could not be forgotten either, but combat operations against the Japanese proved to be quite different from the fighting in North Africa, Sicily, Italy, and eventually France and Germany. The first focus for the Pacific was to construct recreational, Special Services, and AES facilities in Australia, especially in the Brisbane area.

While the number of American forces was expanding in Australia, Special Services units were being activated for service in the Pacific. In June 1942 the 8th Company was activated at Fort Sam Houston, Texas, with fourteen draftees and no officers. This was one of the first units to be scheduled for overseas deployment to the Southwest Pacific area, but its organization moved slowly, with a high turnover in officer personnel. By late 1942 the unit finally received orders to move to a port of embarkation, with a final destination of the Fiji islands. As combat operations increased, the third and fourth platoons were formed into a single detachment for service of army troops in the New Hebrides. In March 1942 American forces landed in the New Hebrides, which became a major base for future operations against the Japanese. The climate and rainfall, coupled with severe health problems from hookworm, malaria, and dengue fever, together with basic boredom, were the main ingredients for serious morale problems. Consequently, the detachment moved quickly to establish a movie schedule of twenty presentations per week for the army units. The next step was to build recreational centers for each large command, which provided a full range of athletic events and theatrical and music shows using local GI talent, and finally open canteen and exchange facilities.

First Lieutenant William H. Power, an infantry officer commanding the 8th, established his headquarters on the island of Suva, where the unit oversaw the acquisition and distribution of a large amount of equipment such as balls, golf sets, boxing gloves, playing cards, horseshoes, and games such as checkers and cribbage. Through the Canteen and Exchange Sections of the platoons, several thousand magazines such as *Life, Reader's Digest, Time,* and *Newsweek* were sent to each recreational center, and the company edited, printed, and distributed the *Fiji Times and Herald.* The Special Services company also requisitioned or constructed a number of hotels for troops having a break from service in the New Hebrides area.[11] Despite its slow start at Fort Sam Houston, the 8th Special Services Company under Lieutenant Power became an effective unit doing exactly what the companies were charged to do: provide for GI morale under difficult circumstances.

Not everyone at the War Department was convinced that the Special Services Division or the companies were really necessary, and while some units were activated with few problems, some were not. On April 18, 1942, the War Department announced the activation of eight new units, complete with guidance for manning the units. The Office of the Adjutant General in Washington told area corps commanders, "Cadres will be furnished by [commanders] concerned from units under their control; overage personnel and personnel reported unsuited for duty with the field forces may be utilized. . . . The enlisted personnel will be equipped as infantry and designated as infantry. The officers will be furnished by the Chief, Special Services Division."[12] The main mission of the companies was to deploy overseas to service the troops serving in theaters of operations. How could the companies fulfill their basic mission with soldiers who were deemed unfit for overseas service? The directive not only opened the door for commanders to transfer unfit soldiers or their troublemaking malcontents; it also gave commanders the leeway to act slowly in filling the Special Services units. This was exactly what Osborn did not want, and it would take time and careful selection of personnel to overcome the apathy and hostility of some commanders. Eventually, by late 1942, enlisted men could apply for Special Services duty based on civilian skills, and officers could also request a branch transfer, but there was still the problem of a unit simply sending to the Special Services an officer deemed unfit for combat command or staff work.

What happened to the 9th Special Services Company was a good example of what could occur when there was little support from the corps area command. When it was activated on June 15, 1942, at Fort Sill, Oklahoma, there were 12 enlisted men present, and by the end of the month there were 3 officers present for duty. This was a ratio of 4 enlisted men to 1 officer, and the situation continued until late July, when 37 enlisted men reported for duty. When August ended, the 9th had 4 officers and 66 GIs present, which was a far cry from the 5 officers and 109 soldiers required for deployment overseas. Finally, by late October 1942 the 9th Company had the strength and training to be given orders to proceed to Fort Dix, New Jersey, for shipment to their assignment in Iran.

Certainly, the Persian Gulf Command was not considered to be a backwater of World War II given its strategic position, especially with the ports and transportation system that supplied the Russian armies, which were doing serious damage to the German military machine. By the time the 9th arrived in Iran, almost two million tons of military supplies had been shipped to the Red Army. In 1944 the amount of supplies reached more than five million tons.[13] The GIs of the 9th arrived at Khorramshar and prepared to supply all that a Special Services company could for the troops of the command. The Army Exchange System had established PXs at every base and paved the way for the 9th to begin work as quickly as possible. While the Iranian monarchy welcomed the Allied forces, the local population, mainly Shiite Muslim, was wary of the Western military presence. It was best that soldiers have recreational diversions rather than be let loose on Iranian towns, except for organized tours and occasional visits to local bazaars. While strictly a United States Army unit, the 9th allowed American Embassy personnel to attend shows and dances, which were few and far between because of the impossibility of finding local girls to attend.

The Persian Gulf Command presented problems for the Special Services because of the need to maintain good relations between the Muslim population and the Americans. The ground in Persia was fertile for Nazi, anti-Semitic propaganda and for espionage. Consequently, "all towns are 'Out of Bounds,' the men do not have any means of diversion." To deal with this, the 7th Special Services Company was dispatched to work with the command to provide recreation for the troops. The Army Exchange System had opened PXs and several beer halls on bases, and that had to be done with care, since Islam prohibited all alcoholic beverages. Captain C. M. Malley, commanding the company, was a graduate of the Special Services school at Fort Meade, Maryland, and he understood the need to cooperate with the 9th Special Services Company and the exchange personnel. Distances between American installations were great, and often the movie sections had to travel more than fifty miles over poor roads through inhospitable desert areas to show two movies on one day per week. The company instituted basewide athletic programs, and in one week alone there were volleyball and softball leagues as well as table-tennis and horseshoes competitions. A main library with more than twenty-five hundred books was opened and did a brisk business. The 9th had been activated at Fort Leonard Wood, Missouri, but nothing in their training could have prepared the unit for conducting ball games when the temperature reached a record of 140 degrees. A report stated, "Intense heat curtails our athletic program. This is one of the hottest spots in the world."[14]

Special Services companies were being deployed throughout 1942 and 1943 to every theater of operations, with the bulk allocated to the European theater, which included North Africa and Egypt. The 18th Special Services

Company was activated at Fort Meade, Maryland, in the spring of 1942 and was quickly allocated 5 officers and 109 enlisted men. At that time the Special Services maintained their school there, and consequently the 18th had the pick of officers and trained enlisted men. The company trained while they awaited orders, which came in June 1943, directing the company to proceed to Camp Shanks, New York. That indicated that the 18th would soon be on a troop transport to the European theater, but at Camp Shanks there was no indication that the company would be on any ship that would sail east. A few weeks went by, and then the 18th Company was ordered to board a large troop train bound for Camp Anza near Arlington, California, a train ride that would take seven days if all went well.

When the officers and noncommissioned officers of the 18th read their new orders, they learned that the company was designated to serve in the China-Burma-India theater. During the two-plus-week ocean trip to their assignment, the company took over the physical training of the ship's crew and other troops, providing, such as they could, athletic events, and organized theatrical and musical events. The Library Section organized and opened a lending library for the thousands of troops. At the end of the voyage, the commander of troops on the SS *Uruguay* sent an official letter of commendation to be placed in the permanent files of the company.[15] This was a good start for a company that would be considered one of the best Special Services companies during the war.

The 12th Special Services Company landed in New Guinea in early 1943 and immediately went to work providing for GIs who felt a different sort of isolation, not only fighting the enemy, but also coping with rain, intense heat and humidity, and an environment that was totally foreign to their experience in the United States. The climate and insects took their toll on the 12th's equipment within a few days, as mold affected movie films, rains caused malfunctions in electrical equipment, generators were unreliable, and food for the canteen services was in short supply. The supplies for both the PX and the Special Services did not arrive on time, and when they did, they had suffered from the long ocean voyage from the ports in the United States. It would take a year, but the 12th learned to improvise and overcome severe problems, becoming one of the most effective companies that the Special Services Division sent to the Pacific theater of operations. In 1944 the 11th Special Services Company arrived in New Guinea and quickly learned the lessons of providing for the troops in the jungle.

The initial allocation of Special Services companies for overseas service was forty, and the speed of getting them overseas was inconsistent due to a number of circumstances, not the least of which was the recruitment or transfer of qualified personnel. As the number of companies grew and the demand for Special Services units in the overseas theaters expanded, it was necessary to ensure that the units were indeed ready to accomplish their missions. This prompted a series of detailed inspections throughout 1943, carried out by the Training Branch at the War Department. No unit ever welcomed an inspection, especially when the inspector stated that he was there not to find fault, but to assist the unit in correcting problem areas. The inspectors were scheduled to visit units that were at the final stage of their training before deployment, and for certain companies the inspections revealed weaknesses that, if not addressed in the United States, could be fatal in combat areas. For example, Major Arthur W. Clevenger, an experienced officer in the Training Branch, arrived to inspect the 23rd Company stationed near Yuma, Arizona, carrying out practical training with the combat troops in the California-Arizona maneuver area. Major Clevenger's conclusions were not good for the company's capabilities for deployment, because almost 60 percent of the original company were soldiers who were classified as "limited service" due to disability or age. The army simply could not deploy that category of soldier to an active theater of operations. The company commander and three of his lieutenants were competent to serve. Of the other two, one had been transferred, while another was observed to be "immature . . . not particularly well qualified as a platoon leader."[16] A large number of enlisted men were in the process of requesting a discharge from the army, and seven GIs were in the hospital and would be discharged from the army. Observing the combat training of the 23rd Company, the inspector found that the unit had unsatisfactory instruction and practical experience with demolition of equipment and booby traps. Since Special Services companies were expected to occupy buildings in a combat zone, poor training in the area of traps could prove devastating. In the areas of athletics, entertainment, and motion pictures, the inspector rated the unit as very satisfactory, but the pending discharges of so many soldiers would quickly cause the unit to fall far below accepted standards. The Special Services company had as one of its basic missions the publication of camp or unit newspapers, but the inspector found that the 23rd could not publish any sort of newspapers because of incompetent soldiers. The canteen and PX service failed to account for supplies, due to a weak officer, but the cooks assigned to the Canteen Section were good, graduates of the army Cooks and Bakers School. The overall assessment was that the 23rd Company could not be assigned to any theater of operations or to any post in the United States. It would take a year to replace those soldiers deemed unfit for deployment, to retrain, and to add competent officers. This company never did recover from its problems.

Major Clevenger went on to inspect the 31st Special Services Company training at Camp Obispo, California, and found a very different situation in this unit, designated for deployment to an assignment in the Pacific. The G3 (operations officer) at the camp had been careful in assessing the readiness of the company, and he had already directed the 31st Company to extend their basic and mission training by two weeks. Consequently, when Clevenger arrived he found a unit well prepared to deploy. The officers and enlisted men of the unit had stabilized, and there were few soldiers deemed unfit for overseas service. The vast majority had qualified with the M1 rifle and were familiar with the M1 carbine.

With demands for Special Services companies to be deployed, the inspections continued, and the well-traveled Major Clevenger arrived at Camp Ellis, Illinois, to determine the status of the 27th Special Services Company, which had been activated in February 1943 at Fort Meade and completed basic and Special Services training at that post. The inspector noted that all but 6 of the 109 enlisted men had completed their basic training. By the time of the inspection, 75 percent of the company had qualified with the M1 rifle and familiarized themselves with the carbine. All had completed the infiltration course under live fire without incident. This company exceeded the qualifications being reached by infantry units, and this progress, Clevenger believed, was due to the work of First Lieutenant Henry F. Fields, the company commander, and his officer and enlisted noncommissioned officer subordinates. The commander at Camp Ellis had the highest praise for the 27th Company for providing the full range of Special Services company activities. Lieutenant Fields also arranged several GI shows to be given at the German prisoner-of-war camp located near Camp Ellis. Quite frankly, the Camp Ellis Special Services officer did not want to give up the 27th Company because, as he told the inspector, if the company deployed overseas, the Special Services activities would suffer greatly, even though the 22nd Special Services Company would replace the departing 27th. What was told the camp commander and his Special Services officer was that there would be a two-week transition period for the 22nd Company as they prepared to take over Special Services functions; the 27th was going overseas.[17] Go overseas it did, deploying to the Pacific theater of operations, where it landed at New Georgia and saw good service in the Solomon Islands campaign, offering the full range of Special Services activities to more than fifty thousand American troops.

The building of forty Special Services companies had taken a year, and the majority of the companies were either deployed or scheduled for overseas services in 1943. The task was so large it was decided that a second Special Services training center would be opened on the West Coast, at Camp Obispo, California. The actual classroom Special Services school would be moved from Fort Meade to Washington and Lee University, in western Virginia. The division made sense, because the West Coast saw major increases of army troops being sent to the Pacific theater.

While the majority of Special Services companies would be sent overseas, there were areas where a company would be needed in the United States. The greatest need was at the Desert Training Center in California, where heat reached more than one hundred degrees during the day and there were few, if any, opportunities to go off post because towns were small, with few facilities to entertain troops. This center saw countless numbers of troops train there because there were vast tracts of training areas where tanks and infantry could maneuver and fire with few restrictions. The environment toughened the troops, forcing them to live under trying circumstances. There was a real need to provide for the troops in the field and on the post, and a Special Services company was stationed there.

Since combat training was the goal, and units engaged in training there would deploy overseas as intact units, much depended on good relations with the commanding officer and his staff, and problems arose for the Special Services company. Some unit commanders saw this as an opportunity to sharpen combat skills and to operate as a complete unit as it would in combat, and they wanted no deliveries of Cokes, cigarettes, and the like. Their troops would train with what the army provided, such as combat rations. However, other commanders saw the arrival of the Special Services mobile exchange and canteen as a reward for hard training, a needed diversion from the harsh and demanding training regimen. One of those Special Services companies assigned was the 15th, a unit activated in 1942. The company commander of the 15th saw his time at the Desert Training Center as a great opportunity to function in hard, demanding conditions. What was needed was some understanding about what the role of the Special Services company was while at the center and how it could work with the post commander and the commanders of the units training there.

It was time to have a written policy regarding the functions and activities of the company and its relationship to the post and to the units training in the vast tracts of desert land. As the policy evolved, it stated that one company was designed to support forty-five thousand troops, including the post and the field. The Special Services company was a new formation, and to smooth the way for it to function, it was posited that it would come under the G3, or operations officer, for the permanent party on post. The G3 would be advised by the Special Services officer on the post staff, and the G3, in turn, would assign the company to divisional units, making each unit's commander and staff aware of what the company's mission was and how they could serve the troops. The commander and his staff would then become aware of what the Special Services could offer and that, once committed to battle in overseas theaters, they would again encounter Special Services companies.[18] At the center the company would provide the usual athletic and theatrical entertainment—the library, post movie theaters, and cafeterias. In the field the exchange and canteen services would go to "those isolated and scattered units to which normal exchange services is not available."[19]

It was the exchange and canteen services that in the long run greatly affected the troops in the desert. One section carried more than eleven thousand dollars' worth of cigarettes, shaving and cleaning material, cookies, candy, and the like. That section was welcomed by the commanding officer and certainly by the troops training in the desert. The desert sands and the extraordinary heat took their toll on equipment, especially the movie projectors in the desert and the pianos in the Service Clubs. One musician had his own violin that was quite valuable, and he had to house it in a service-club refrigerator to keep it from being damaged by the conditions. In a report, the company commander simply stated, "This heat and dust just can't be licked."

What was not welcomed in the field was beer. Most commanders told the Special Services company that the mobile exchange and canteen were welcomed at the end of the training day, if there were no night maneuvers, but even the 3.2 army beer should be left back at the PX-run beer halls. There were statements by the army that 3.2 beer would not cause inebriation, but after young men had trained in the desert heat, even 3.2 beer could cause a soldier to become drunk. Around tanks, armored vehicles, and live ammunition, soldiers without a clear head could very well cause a disaster. Cold beer was best left back at the beer hall and could be enjoyed when the troops were finished with their training. The beer, in one instance two hundred cases of it, was returned, and cases of Coca-Colas were sent in their stead. One platoon arrived at a regimental headquarters and asked where the PX tent could be pitched. The G3 laughed at the Special Services lieutenant and told him that the regiment would be moving to attack an enemy position. There could be no tent, and the G3 told the Special Services officer to load PX goods into vehicles and move with the regiment.[20]

The 15th Company had come a long way since its activation at Camp Blanding, Florida, as had the 22nd Company, activated at Camp Obispo, California, its replacement at the Desert Training Center. The 15th deployed to England, and the 22nd was sent to the Pacific. Both companies had been tested in a tough desert environment and had done well. Those companies knew how to service combat units, many of which would be in contact with the enemy.

In addition to the work that the Special Services companies were doing in preparation for overseas deployment, the Special Services officers serving on camp and post staffs oversaw the maintenance and operation of the Service Clubs and cafeterias. This involved screening and hiring civilians to serve as hostesses, food workers, and librarians. It was also important that the post facilities did not conflict with the training and work of the Special Services companies. The staff Special Services officers also coordinated with the USO for camp shows and visits from celebrities. It was vitally important that a good relationship existed between the Special Services and the USO. By 1943 the USO had grown into a national institution and raised its own funds. The Special Services Division was doing everything that Osborn and Byron had hoped it would.

With everything going well in 1943, the Special Services Division planned for the future as the war went on. In October 1943 a number of recommendations were made to increase the number of Special Services companies from the forty already in existence to seventy, with an increase of nine thousand men. This included an expansion of the Special Services training centers at Fort Meade and Camp Obispo, plus an expansion of the Special Services schools.[21] The problem for the authors of the plan of expansion was that General Somervell had already taken steps to halt the expansion of Special Services companies. In July 1943 Somervell had bluntly informed the commanding officer of Fort Huachuca, Arizona, that a new Special Services company could not be formed for service at that desert post.[22] Questions were raised about officers and enlisted men requesting transfer to Special Services. In a memorandum to the commanding general at Fort Jackson, South Carolina, enlisted men could apply, but they had to prove they had the skills or experiences that would enhance Special Services. The Special Services was not an alternative to combat service.[23]

The army faced a sobering situation as the casualty lists poured into the War Department from North Africa, Sicily, Italy, and the islands of the Pacific. The greatest losses were from the combat infantry platoons and companies. Contrary to the Hollywood versions of war, for every infantryman there were three to four GIs in support: providing rations, ammunition, fuel, medical support, air and ground transportation, air force ground crews, quartermaster and ordnance repair units, and, of course, Special Services. Without those support elements, an infantryman with his weapon, a tank crew, or an artillery battery could not confront and defeat the enemy. But by 1943 it was clear that programs that denied the army the infantry it needed had to be either curtailed or ended. No victory is ever easy or quick, and the War Department was finding that out. For example, in the Pacific the Americal Division committed to combat in New Caledonia in March 1942, the 25th Division landed on Guadalcanal in January 1943, the 32nd Division saw its first action on New Guinea in September 1942, the 27th Division went into action on the Marshall Islands in November 1943, and the 41st Division began combat operations on New Guinea in January 1943. Military planners knew that Japanese troops were fierce in battle, but no one in the War Department could have envisioned the intensity with which the Japanese fought. In North Africa combat had been lethal, but at the end, the Germans of the Afrika Korps surrendered. Fighting in Sicily had battered the 3rd Infantry Division, and subsequent fighting in Italy had taken its toll on American troops. At some point there would be a cross-Channel invasion of northern France, and it was becoming painfully clear that the army would need more combat infantry. This greatly influenced the decision not to enlarge the number of Special Services companies.

Not only was the Special Services Division affected by the War Department's concern over infantry losses; in September 1942 the army began the Army Specialized Training Program. After testing and interviews, soldiers accepted for the program were sent to colleges and universities for academic training. By the end of 1943 there were nearly 140,000 GIs enrolled in the program and attending classes in a myriad of subjects. In November 1943, the army ground forces reckoned that there were not enough soldiers in training and in the replacement depots to make up for losses in combat infantry divisions. It was no secret to anyone that in 1944 the Allies would mount the cross-Channel invasion of France, and given the proven abilities of the German army to fight, the need for combat infantry became something of a crisis. By February 1944, more than 100,000 GIs enrolled in the ASTP found themselves on orders to report to combat divisions. They could not transfer to Special Services companies; they were to become combat infantrymen.

To put the army's decision into perspective, one needs to look at what the decision to end the ASTP program meant regarding the shortage of infantry. Private Gerald Hirshberg of Patterson, New Jersey, was drafted in 1943. He was one semester short of graduation from Columbia University and was selected to attend the ASTP program at the University of Maine because of his education in business. By December 1943 the soldiers were told that the program would end, and Hirshberg was transferred to Company K, 104th Infantry Regiment, 26th Division, as an infantryman. He was twenty-two years old when he was mortally wounded in France, captured by the Germans, and died in an enemy hospital.[24]

Private Robert A. Molley of Minneapolis was also drafted in 1943, went to infantry basic training at Camp Fannin, Texas, and because he had some college education was ordered to the University of Cincinnati's ASTP program.

Molley also found that as the program ended, he would be transferred to the 14th Armored Division in training at Camp Campbell, Kentucky. He tried to get transferred to the air force but failed; he applied to the officer candidate school and was turned down. He wrote to a friend, "They usually take one look at my expert's record on the rifle and turn thumbs down."[25] He deployed with the division to France as a member of an armored infantry battalion.

The distress felt by the members of the ASTP would have meant little to Sergeant Robert Tuttle of the 499th Engineer Battalion, who celebrated Christmas Eve on New Guinea. Worn out by the jungle heat, Tuttle went to a movie shown by the Special Services company in his area.[26] A few weeks before, he had attended a USO show featuring the famous boxing champion Gene Tunney, but was disappointed that there were no American girls to entertain the troops.[27] Technical Sergeant Charles Linzy of the 459th Mobile Anti-Aircraft Battalion stationed in England would have echoed Tuttle's sentiments. On Christmas Eve he also went to a Special Services movie, starring Alan Ladd and Loretta Young.[28]

The army needed infantry, and because of that programs like the ASTP ended, transfers to the US Army Air Force were canceled, applications to officer candidate school were drastically reduced, and there would not be any large expansion of the Special Services companies.

The 13th Special Services Company was activated at Fort Meade in 1942, and it was the first of the Special Services units to have the designation of company. General Osborn observed the infantry and Special Services training of the company and called it "the parent organization of all special services companies." The company deployed to England with a number of platoons assigned to serve the troops of the Eighth Army Air Force, which was becoming an efficient bombing and fighting command. As troops and equipment poured into England to prepare for the invasion, shortages appeared, especially in movie projectors and radio equipment. In the area of entertainment, the 13th organized GI shows and comedy plays, and for a few weeks the all-soldier show had two American female USO entertainers as part of the cast. The company commander wrote in a report, "Though neither of the girls were musical comedy performers, they were both pulchritudinor [sic], excellent in the comedy sketches, and one of the them could sing sufficiently for a solo spot. Together they lent the spice ideal for a G.I. show. And at last the eternal query 'Any girls in the show?' could be answered in the affirmative." The GIs' great hopes of seeing American girls were at least satisfied for the men of the Eighth Air Force.[29]

Trying to satisfy the requirements of the Eighth Air Force was difficult. The senior music technician of one of the 13th's platoons had few real musicians, and much fell on his shoulders. The company commander wrote that the technician had "nary so much as a beer hall drummer." At one point he complained to his platoon leader, "Why wasn't I born a one-man band, why?"[30] For Special Services dances, the technician finally found some volunteer English civilians to provide dance music, some of it a bit strange to American ears.

Special Services companies like the 13th could expect few replacements, as the army left few stones unturned in its quest for more combat infantry, especially because the new year of 1944 promised to be the decisive year of the war. The Special Services Division was aware of the activities of the companies and their needs, but Special Services in the United States had expanded its scope of activities on every army post and training camp. Also, within Special Services the command structure was changing. General Osborn had become more and more involved with information and education as a vital part of morale, and soon he would move to head up a morale division with his promotion to major general. Brigadier General Byron would take command of the Special Services Division, with Colonel Frank Kerr moving into the directorship of the Army Exchange System. The budget for the Special Services Division for 1944 would be a little more than $30.5 million, a good increase over the 1943 budget, but the costs of maintaining all of the activities of the division had increased as the numbers of troops increased.

It would take care, and in some cases some belt tightening, to do all Osborn, and a little later Byron, wanted for the Special Services in the United States and overseas. The Special Services companies' funding came within the regular army budget, but the supplies in games, theatrical materials, printing, movies, and the like had to be paid for by the division. The Army Exchange System, on the other hand, was showing a considerable profit, and since the exchange system operated with nonappropriated funds, there was no need to discuss any assistance from the Special Services Division. In fact, the AES contributed greatly to morale activities from its profits, and 1944 promised an expansion of PX offerings in the United States and in the overseas theaters of operations. As the Special Services Division looked at the 1944 budget, Osborn and his staff knew that much would be possible because of the ever-expanding USO and the good relations between the division and that organization. American generosity and volunteerism would reach their high-water mark in 1944, and this would greatly benefit Special Services. Also, in 1944 Congress began debating legislation to assist the veterans who would return home after the defeat of Germany and Japan.

Budget discussions and decisions made by generals really did not mean much to the GIs in the field. They were concerned with the basics—combat, chow, something to drink, and what entertainment could be supplied. Master

Sergeant Elmer Franzman of the 329th Service Group was serving in North Africa in 1943 and was like most soldiers who endured days of heat and blowing sand. He wrote to his parents in Cannelton, Indiana, "I went to the show last night 'Lady Be Good' with Ann Southern and Robert Young. It was swell and full of good music. We've been having new and old shows every night recently. It's all the entertainment we have."[31] For the GIs, what the Special Services could provide was the difference between morale-lowering boredom and a slice of home. Corporal William E. George, serving in the 415th Fighter Squadron, was stationed in England, a far cry from the sands of North Africa. George, who was far from his Little Rock, Arkansas, home, wrote to his parents, "We have just finished playing badmington [sic] and we played tennis this afternoon and did we have fun. We worked some today but really had a swell time."[32] The Special Services company serving the base where the 415th was stationed provided the full range of athletic events, engaging the men who would fly against Germany.

From the Pacific theater of operations to the Mediterranean to England, the Special Services had established itself as the provider of recreation and entertainment for so many Americans so far from home. It remained to be seen what 1944 would mean to Special Services as the war grew in intensity.

6

1944

Invasions and Frustrations

There was no question that Marshall wanted something done about the state of morale activities in the Pacific theater, and General Osborn returned to the area to set a course for morale expansion. Generals fussed and ordered, and colonels scurried about to see that General Marshall or General Osborn did his great work to win the war. No one, however, could have been happier over the emphasis on morale and Special Services work than Corporal Thomas R. St. George, who was part of the American war effort on New Guinea. A writer of some note, St. George had published *C/o Postmaster,* an account of his arrival as a GI in Australia. The book became a best seller and was a Book of the Month Club selection in 1943. Here was a soldier who could fit in quite well with the emphasis on morale, and he was ordered to Australia to work on *Yank.* Sitting in an Australian pub, he recalled, "Practically speaking, we were out of the army. Out of the Army! My God."[1] Corporal St. George was happier than any general in the Pacific, or at the War Department for that matter. The year 1944 was a time of bloody invasions and battles as American forces aimed at the capture of the Philippine Islands. The campaigns in the Pacific area could be confusing for the American public and for GIs as well. England and Italy were clearly defined, but islands like New Guinea, Hollandia, New Britain, and the like were not well known. Soldiers with an affinity for clear and coherent writing could help in explaining the war in the Pacific, and soldiers like Corporal St. George were needed and well used.

Generals really did not matter much to Sergeant Robert D. Tuttle of the 499th Engineer Company, which was still struggling through the jungles and blazing heat and humidity of New Guinea. He wrote to his girlfriend back in Marion, Ohio, "Tonite is show nite and I think I will take it in. I suppose it will be some picture I have seen. The place here is now looking pretty good we now have horse shoe cortes [sic], volley ball cort [sic] and a soft ball diamond so it looks like we might have a little recreation. Right now I want some nice cool weather."[2] A half world away in Italy, Sergeant William E. George of the 415th Night Fighter Squadron watched a Special Services company set up a softball game on a playing field with concrete seats that had been constructed by the Fascist government. George and his friends had a good deal of fun "booing the umpire." After the game they attended the showing of the first-run movie *Arsenic and Old Lace*.[3] Despite the great differences between New Guinea and Italy, the presence of the Special Services contributed to the morale of the troops, many of whom were entering their third year away from their families and homeland.

As 1944 progressed, the stresses began to show themselves. There were forty Special Services companies formed and in the field; only two were retained in the United States. It was determined that the Desert Training Center in California needed a permanent company to serve the troops in training in the isolated, harsh desert conditions. Of importance were the four PX and Canteen Sections of the company. Three of the forty companies were designated as colored, staffed by African American GIs and a mix of black and white officers. The 17th Company was formed at Fort Huachuca, Arizona, in September 1942 to support African American troops, but in late 1943 it was deployed to the European theater to provide for the numbers of African American troops serving in England. The 29th Company, also formed at Fort Huachuca in 1943, was deployed to the South Pacific, and the 37th Company went to North Africa in 1944.[4] As the war moved into Italy, many of the Special Services companies were deployed from North Africa to the Italian campaign, especially after the occupation of Naples.

General Byron was a much more proactive director than was General Osborn, who tended to be more reflective. One situation that Byron had to deal with was the quality of the USO camp shows. By mid-1944 the number of shows had grown dramatically, and Byron determined that there had to be a better way of making sure civilian entertainers were suited for the rigors of overseas travel. Too many of the performers were falling ill, especially in the Pacific theater. Carole Landis, for example, had contracted an intestinal disease and fever that was life threatening. Some of the second- and third-level performers were not especially good and relied on stale jokes or old song-and-dance routines. Byron wanted some way to screen the entire show before it was sent overseas. There was a definite need for three- or four-person shows to entertain isolated units such as those who manned radar, antiair-craft, or smaller GI hospitals. Byron was especially concerned that as fighting increased, the three- or four-person camp-show groups be sent to the wards where there were GIs who had lost limbs, been blinded or paralyzed, and needed a real lift in their morale. The big, star-studded shows did not lend themselves well to the reality of the hospitals.[5]

Byron also knew that commanding generals would be amenable to having the big-name stars like Bob Hope, Frances Langford, Al Jolson, or Marlene Dietrich to shows for their troops. Generals would be more likely to provide space, equipment, and, most important, the time for their troops to attend the large shows if the well-known entertainers were there. Also, Byron warned his Special Services Division's Recreation Section that if a star was known to be difficult to deal with or was incapable of dealing with some of the hardships of being overseas, they should not be allowed to depart the United States. Byron stated that such a person would do "the USO and the Special Services more harm than good."[6]

Going into the spring of 1944, there was a distinct tension in the air, particularly in England, where troops trained and prepared for the cross-Channel invasion. Only a few top-ranking generals and politicians knew that the attack would come on the beaches and fields of Normandy. Meanwhile, the Italian campaign had a serious need for organized recreation, given the progress of the heavy fighting. In September 1943 Allied forces landed at Salerno, Italy, and began an agonizingly slow march through the mud and mountains of the region. The Fifth US Army under the command of General Mark W. Clark occupied the port city of Naples, and there problems abound-ed. GIs poured into the city, the rate of venereal disease rose dramatically, and GIs reported being the victim of thieves. A thriving black market flourished, as many GIs took advantage of the PX supplies of cigarettes, candy bars, soap, and other items that had all but disappeared from Italian stores. Private Ken-neth K. Gowen of Oxford, Mississippi, serving with the 69th Field Artillery, was shocked at what he saw in Naples. A girl he estimated to be sixteen years of age continued to invite GIs to her bedroom, and Gowen's disgust grew when he learned that her father was collecting money or, better yet, American PX supplies for the services of his daughter.[7] The Fifth Army learned a lesson in the early days of the occupation of Naples, and it was a lesson applied as the army prepared for the liberation and occupation of Rome. Soldiers needed the well-planned recreation and facilities offered by the Special Services, and they would be available once Rome was taken.

The year 1944 was one of expectations for the army. In the Pacific, with heavy fighting in New Guinea, Hollandia, and elsewhere, the 7th, 24th, 31st, 32nd, 77th, 96th, American, and 11th Airborne Divisions, plus other American combat units, were committed to battle, pushing the Japanese out of that area of the Southwest Pacific. General Douglas MacArthur had as his objective the ultimate prize, the invasion and liberation of the Philippine Islands. After much debate and high-level conferences, MacArthur got the green light to invade the Philippines, which he saw as a moral crusade, a national commitment to the people of the islands. In November 1944 American GIs landed at Leyte, followed by an amphibious landing of American troops at Lingayen in early 1945. MacArthur had his dramatic moment when he waded ashore at Leyte, proclaiming that he had returned to liberate the long-suffering people of the Philippines and to release the American prisoners of war who had existed under inhumane conditions imposed by their Japanese captors. Of course, the final objective of the campaign in the Philippines was the retaking of the capital of Manila. To achieve these objectives, the army supply-and-support system had been stretched to the limit, and the Special Services was hard-pressed to provide for the troops fighting under very difficult conditions.

In Italy, Rome was the prize for General Mark Clark's Fifth Army; Rome would be the first enemy capital to be taken. Of course, the Italians had left the war, and the Germans had sent more troops into Italy to stop the Allied advance. To break the German front, Allies landed troops at Anzio in January 1944, hoping to dislodge the Germans from their defensive positions and open the road to the Eternal City. It would take months to break out from the stalled Anzio beachhead, and no one really knew how determinedly the Germans would fight for Rome.

The tension was high in England, where American and Allied troops trained for the cross-Channel operation known as Operation Overlord. American units designated to make the airborne and seaborne assault on Hitler's Fortress Europe were the 4th Infantry Division, which had arrived in England in January 1944; the 29th Infantry Division, which had reached England in October 1942; and the 101st Airborne Division, which began training in Britain in September 1943. Other divisions and assorted units covered the British countryside in ever-increasing numbers. Special Services companies such as the 1st Company had four separate platoons serving as many combat units as possible. Most of the large units had PXs established, and the companies used their Canteen and Exchange Sections to serve units training in the field. Of vital importance was the establishment of ongoing recreational and athletic programs, with competition between regiments and divisions. The showing of first-run Hollywood films became a major source of morale activity for the troops preparing for the invasion.[8] The Army Exchange System opened as many PXs as it could, providing a place to drink an American beer, buy American cigarettes, or purchase American candy bars. The PXs offered a gift catalog for all overseas GIs, encouraging soldiers to send gifts and even flowers to their loved ones back home.[9]

The more the Special Services Division and the Army Exchange System provided for the GIs, and this was of great importance in England and in Australia, the less the possibility of tensions between American soldiers and the civilian population. Diversion for the troops who would either drop or land in France was the order of the day. There was therefore an increase in Special Services activities. Private Harry G. Wilson of Los Angeles, California, noticed that the army radio service increased the number of current American radio programs. Wilson, serving with an army weather station in England, wrote to his wife back home that he was surprised to hear a Jack Benny radio comedy show that was only a few days old. His wife had mentioned a dramatic program with the famous actress Barbara Stanwyck, and he replied that it had to be the same show he heard just a few days later.[10]

As the time drew near, those troops involved in Overlord were moved to ports of embarkation or airfields and restricted to their staging areas. It was imperative that soldiers not be allowed to leave the areas because possibly in pubs or clubs they might reveal the impending operation. The Special Services companies knew that they would not be deployed to France for six weeks to two months after the Allies gained a foothold. Once there, the companies would be under the Service of Supply and would work in what would be called the Communications Zone (COMZ), being sent where troops were in rest areas. Of course, all of these plans depended on successes on the beaches and fields of Normandy. Before the first ship departed or the first aircraft carrying American airborne divisions lifted off the runways, Special Services provided for troops who were under great stress and in need of diversion and recreation. The Special Services companies, who were under the same security restraints as the infantry, arrived with recreational materials such as basketballs, softballs, and games. One of the most popular items was decks of playing cards, and many troops took the dice from board games. The Canteen-Exchange Sections provided as many sandwiches and Coca-Colas as they could carry. The GIs were also advised to buy two cartons of cigarettes to carry with them, and the Special Services supply kept a continual flow of cigarettes going to the staging areas. The one thing missing from the offerings of the Special Services companies and exchanges was beer, the ever-popular American brands. The GIs who were waiting for their part in D-Day had no idea of the bargaining power a pack of American cigarettes would have, and soon they would add two new words to their vocabularies—*cognac* and *calvados*. The 1st Special Services Company, the oldest and most experienced of the companies, sent twelve Canteen-Exchange Sections to the staging areas and airfield. The other companies dispatched at least eight Canteen-Exchange Sections each to their areas of responsibility.

With the amphibious landings and air drops in Normandy, the duties of the Special Services companies became more complex. First, the companies had to provide for the follow-on troops who would reinforce the beachheads. Second, they had to complete plans for their own deployment to France, and third, the companies had to continue to train their own troops for combat service. There was a shift in the emphasis within the companies, as they would turn from being "static" to mobile units, ready to move from location to location as the combat troops did. The American troops in England prior to D-Day were in training and preparation, but in France, as combat increased in intensity, the Special Services companies would have to work in rest areas with "battle tired fighting men."[11] As plans for the companies developed, they were ordered to prepare GI rest areas, and as the Germans were driven from France, the Service of Supply envisioned four permanent Service Clubs in fully liberated towns. Of critical importance was the establishment of athletic recreation, including baseball, basketball, and football games. All of the companies that would serve in the COMZ were expected to provide movies as close to the front lines as possible.

The missions assigned to the Special Services companies were numerous and were seen as a safeguard against excessive alcohol consumption, a debilitating venereal disease rate, and incidents with the civilian population. At the same time, the officers and enlisted men of the Special Services companies were seen as trained infantry, GIs who could well defend themselves or be used as combat soldiers if necessary. There had to be a current certification that every man was familiarized with his basic weapon, which was either the M1 rifle or the M1 carbine. Combat gear had to be inspected and determined to be clean, serviceable, and ready for combat use, and steel helmets were fitted.

Before moving to the port of embarkation, the 1st Company estimated that while in England they had shown movies to more than eight hundred thousand GIs. Many of the soldiers would see three movies in a day. The unit had been successful in arranging well-chaperoned dances, but those activities were in the past as the company went to France six weeks after D-Day. At the same time, the 3rd Special Services Company would go to Utah Beach, Normandy, with the mission of being a highly mobile company, which would send seventeen movie sections to the troops. While in England the 3rd Company had established itself as a unit that could best handle the coordination with the USO for shows. In reports from the company, the most frequently asked question by the airmen was "Are there any [American] girls in the show?"[12] Upon their arrival in England, the 13th Company was assigned to support the Eighth Air Force, but as D-Day drew near, the company was assigned to support the 1st Infantry Division. In viewing the initial mission for the company in France, the commander began cross-training sections, using mainly men from the Canteen-Exchange Sections to become competent movie projectionists.[13]

When the Special Services companies were organized, it was envisioned that the Canteen-Exchange Sections would be busy moving from combat unit to combat unit. Vehicles assigned to the companies were modified into mobile exchanges or canteens that served what would later be known as "fast food." The nature of combat soon showed that the concept of the Canteen-Exchange Sections really did not accomplish what was initially planned. They could not serve the frontline troops in close contact with the Germans or Japanese. The soldiers who were assigned to the mobile services were trained as infantry and had, like any other soldier, qualified with their weapons and crawled the infiltration course under live fire, but they were not part of a combat infantry, armor company, or artillery battery. To expect a Special Services section to be on the front lines was not realistic unless there was a dire emergency.

By 1944 the army decided that small items such as soap, cigarettes, candy bars, and packaged cookies should be simply sent to those units that were under enemy fire. These items became known as "PX supplies," and they were distributed to the GIs free of charge. Also, the army began to include packages of cigarettes and candies in the unit and combat rations. Special Services company commanders began to question the need for a Canteen-Exchange Sections that had a mission of serving frontline troops. When those sections did serve combat units that were not in contact with the enemy, they served their purpose, especially in the rest areas. The Canteen and Exchange Sections received their supplies from the quartermaster stores and sold what an established PX offered, and that presented some problems. The Special Services and the Army Exchange System were bound by directives from the War Department, and no item caused as much trouble as did cigarettes.

During World War I the army did not include a tobacco ration for soldiers until late in the war, and when the United States entered the war in 1941, it was decided that there would be tobacco products distributed to soldiers at the front. The distribution expanded as troops operated in the European or Pacific theaters; this was a massive undertaking in the acquisition, shipment, and distribution of tobacco, mainly cigarettes. This was a good idea, but GIs, when they went to established PXs, bought what were known as the popular premium brands—Lucky Strike, Camels, Chesterfield, and Philip Morris. Civilian departments such as the War Production Board and the Office of Price Administration firmly pointed out that cigarettes were divided into premium and economy brands. The economy brands had such names as Spud, Wings, Sensation, Domino, and the much-disdained Chelsea, and, of course, they cost less than the premium brands.

The sale of economy brands was mandated by the civilian departments because those brands were produced by smaller companies, and the US government could not sell only premium brands, allowing the smaller companies to go out of business. When GIs bought their weekly allowed amount, only six packages out of ten could be premium, with the remaining four being economy. Complaints about the policy reached Congress and the press, and this in turn meant pressure on the War Department and, by extension, the Army Exchange System and the Special Services Division.[14] When the quartermaster organized cigarettes for the allocation of "PX supplies," the economy brands were included as well as the premium brands.

When General Byron became the director of Special Services, he altered the relationship of the division and the AES. Byron had run the PXs as a modern profit-making business, and he boasted that the Army Exchange System had become the world's largest, most successful chain store, with nearly twelve million GI customers. He had to be a leader who could fend off the many complaints that poured into the War Department and into Congress from manufacturers, business groups, and local distributors. The cheap prices of the PX, including the beer halls, cafeterias, barbers, and the like, attracted the GIs who earned little per month. The basic entry soldier made $50 a month and paid 12.5 cents per package of premium-brand cigarettes, sold normally at the PX at two packs for 25 cents. The smoking GIs saved 3 cents per pack, a considerable savings for the low-paid soldier. A soldier paid 15 cents to see a first-run movie and could buy a book of ten tickets for $1.20, which would give the soldier a savings of 30 cents per book of tickets. These savings ran the full gamut of PX and Special Services offerings.

Byron believed that the Special Services and AES needed to have a close working relationship because they served the soldier with the same things. The Special Services company, for example, had Canteen-Exchange Sections in each platoon. PXs and Service Clubs both operated cafeterias. Several months after General Byron took over the Special Services Division, he planned a joint conference to discuss mutual problems and plans as the war entered its critical phase in 1944. This conference was of vital importance because it marked the consolidation of the Special Services and the exchange system, something that General Osborn had not done. From that point on, the emphasis would be on entertainment, athletics, the items provided by the exchanges in their established locations, as well as the items carried by the Canteen-Exchange Sections of the Special Services companies. Also, the conference cited new areas where the Special Services and PXs could serve better, and this recognized the growing number of women serving in the Army Nurse Corps and the WACs.

Every area served by the Special Services Division had a chance to express its needs, problems, and expectations. Colonel S. Robertson from the staff of the Supreme Headquarters spoke first about conditions in North Africa, Sicily, and Italy, where Special Services were stretched to their limits. The Special Services companies were expected to provide entertainment, especially for the troops fighting toward Rome, but General Mark Clark's Fifth Army used many of the companies simply to maintain the canteen-exchange system. Frankly put, the Special Services had good, experienced officers and enlisted men, but there were too few of them for the missions assigned.[15] Then Robertson turned to another subject, what women in the whole of the ETO wanted. They wanted better lipstick, cosmetics, uniforms, and sanitary napkins, and Robertson added, "Do not buy girdles with stays in them." With some of the officers in attendance scratching their heads over what the colonel was talking about, Robertson stated, "They [the women in service] make more noise than a hundred times that number of GIs."[16]

Actually, the Army Exchange System was in the process of addressing the demands of the nurses and the WACs. General Byron understood that women in uniform were customers numbering more than 150,000 nurses and WACs, and no businessman worth his salt would ignore that. The situation for servicewomen in the United States was serious. The purchasing agents for the exchange were men, many of them from the regular army, where there had been no large female units. Second Lieutenant Margaret Hisgen of Albany, New York, had been selected to become an officer in the US Army Air Force and was stationed with the 513th WAC Headquarters Detachment in San Diego, California. In frustration she wrote to her parents that the exchange had nothing for women, and she asked her mother to send her old nylon hose, "if any thing is left of them." After searching the exchange she found that they carried no perfume and asked her mother to send some. The Service Club, however, had some good dances for her enlisted women, but of course officers were not allowed to attend.[17] Women in service were eager customers that the exchange could not ignore.

When Byron was selected to command the Special Services Division, Colonel Frank Kerr became director of the Army Exchange System. Kerr understood Byron's determination to consolidate the two units and to expand the offerings of the PXs. Like Byron, Kerr undertook a tour of exchange activities focusing on the ETO and the Mediterranean theater. When he returned in the spring of 1944, he briefed the AES staff and addressed women's needs. Kerr said, "Girdles are built for mature women, these girls are kids with figures corresponding. . . . [B]rassieres are like canvass hammocks—they don't need them. . . . The cheap lines of sanitary napkins they don't want."[18] It is not recorded if any officer at the AES headquarters commented on Colonel Kerr's specific inspection of the matter.

In keeping with the consolidation of the two units, Kerr also addressed the Special Services in the ETO and Mediterranean and said that there needed to be more emphasis on athletics and competition. He stated that when Special Services officers attended the school at Washington and Lee University, they should be taught the basics of "socker," which the Europeans loved and about which the Special Services knew nothing.

As the conference went along, problems for the Special Services surfaced. In every overseas theater of operations movies and recorded American popular music were enthusiastically enjoyed by the GIs. Jazz music, especially Glenn Miller, Harry James, and Benny Goodman, was played at makeshift rest areas. In Pacific areas like New Guinea, Hollandia, and elsewhere, movies and music were provided through the use of generators because of the lack of modern electrical systems. In Sicily, Corsica, Sardinia, and Italy, the electric service was erratic, and the flow of electrical current could not be counted on to keep movie projectors or record players operational.

Looking at the experiences of Special Services companies, it was urged that for every five projectors, there should be three workable generators available. The wild fluctuations of current blew out tubes, lamps, and photocells, and too often those parts were in short supply. In Italy, where the Fifth Army was moving on to Rome, the necessity of having generators to show movies to troops in the field was vital to maintaining morale. Consequently, the Special Services representative from that theater requested that two hundred more generators be sent to the Fifth Army as quickly as possible.

Byron ended the conference with a short speech that started with, "General Somervell does not believe in the impossible. I do not suppose we can turn a report into him to say that anything is impossible." General Byron had just returned from a visit to England and knew what so many of the participants did not, that the invasion aimed at Normandy was probably just a few days away. "Our policy for the overseas soldier is going to be aggressive, offensive. Morale is based on the little things the soldier wants and does not have. . . . The soldier is the judge of quality. He is entitled to the best."[19]

General Osborn had been a good director of Special Services, but his interests did not reside in the day-to-day support of the GIs in combat. The area and country guides had been an excellent idea, the GIs appreciated the emphasis on *Yank,* and the recreation and athletics had rendered good service for the soldiers. The Service Clubs had been a refuge for the enlisted soldier, a place where a letter could be written, a dance held, and an inexpensive cafeteria used, and Osborn was responsible for the growth of the clubs on American posts and overseas. Frederick Osborn, the intellectual and academician, could render the best service in the areas of information and education. Byron, the West Pointer–turned-businessman, was also where he could render the best service to the war effort. The Army Exchange System exceeded what Generals Marshall and Somervell had envisioned, and Byron was responsible for that growth.

Over four days there were speakers from every major theater of operation except the European theater in England. In late May 1955, the silence indicated that no one could be spared for a conference in Washington. As troops moved to their staging areas near airfields or to the docks, the Special Services companies and the exchanges were busy providing all that they could. Many commanders urged their smokers to buy two cartons of cigarettes, for example. Every movie projector and generator was in service. Sergeant Don Malarkey of the 506th Parachute Infantry Regiment was ready to jump into Normandy, but like the rest of his paratroop comrades, he was nervous. The night before the C-47 aircraft filled with the men of the regiment and lifted off the airfield, Malarkey saw a lighthearted movie, *Mr. Lucky,* with Cary Grant. It took his mind off what awaited him in Normandy.[20] Private Harry G. Wilson of the weather station in England had planned a leave in early June, but it was, to his surprise, canceled. He went to a Special Services movie, not knowing that by the next morning Normandy would be the scene of bloody fighting.[21] As General Eisenhower once wrote, "The eyes of the world are upon you."

To the men of Mark Clark's Fifth Army, the invasion and the Normandy fighting were of great importance and also matters of great frustration. They had been the liberators of Rome two days before the first paratrooper touched earth in calvados country or the first GI touched hell on the beach called Omaha. In April 1944 General Mark Wayne Clark returned to Washington to brief Marshall and Roosevelt on his plans to take Rome. Both General Marshall and President Roosevelt stressed that it was vital that Clark's GIs take Rome before Eisenhower's invasion troops hit Normandy. It was imperative to do so to raise the morale of the Normandy invasion force, to inspire the troops to greater efforts.[22] Clark, who had an oversized ego, agreed to be the modern-day conqueror of the Eternal City, and he could envision the photographs of himself entering his conquest. Clark was lucky because he would not enter a mass of smoking rubble; the Germans had decided not to defend Rome, to spare the city the destruction of street-to-street fighting. On June 5, 1944, Clark and his Fifth Army entered Rome to the delirium of liberation, but his great moment was overshadowed by the invasion, the Day of Days. Ironically, Marshall and Roosevelt saw the liberation of Rome as an inspiration for the D-Day troops, but most of the men in landing crafts or on the drop zones (most of them missed) cared little for the liberation of Rome, and many of them were unaware that their comrades were enjoying it with wines and kisses.

For the Special Services officers of the Fifth Army, a Rome taken with little destruction offered great possibilities of playing fields, a sports arena, buildings for movies, PXs, Service Clubs, and the like. One jeep-load of Special Services officers speeding through the city actually captured a number of German soldiers who were only happy to be out of the war.

When Colonel Frank Kerr visited the Fifth Army, he had the opportunity to meet with exchange and Special Services officers, stressing that plans had to be made for the occupation of Rome. The mess that was Naples could not be repeated in the Eternal City.[23] GIs were given *A Soldier's Guide to Rome,* published by the morale section of the North Africa theater of operations, which reflected Osborn's overall academic approach.[24] The Special Services officer with the Fifth Army joined the British Army Education Section and prepared a booklet titled *Rome: Allied Soldier's Souvenir Guide,* which, like the morale-section publication, was basically a guide to the historical sights in the ancient and, for many, most important religious city.[25] These guides did not touch on the major problems that the liberation brought about. There had to be major efforts to keep GIs from overindulging in alcohol and from contacting venereal disease. There was established quickly a US Army Rest Center, with the Special Services and exchanges playing a major role in maintaining the morale of troops who were enjoying a respite from the bloody battles north of Rome.

Private Kenneth Gowen of the 69th Mobile Field Artillery Battalion had been in combat for 140 days, and his unit was given a week, possibly more, in the rest camp. This young man from North Mississippi went into Rome to see places and historical monuments he had read about in his history texts. His first stop was at the Red Cross center that offered the standard GI coffee and fresh, hot doughnuts, and then, with guide in hand, he started out as a tourist. He was approached by many of the prostitutes who infested Rome, but simply said, "Thank you, but no thank you," and moved on to the Coliseum. Gowen returned to the rest center and spent the rest of his time sleeping and watching first-run American movies provided by Special Services. After nine days the rested 69th Battalion returned to combat.[26]

Many GIs had seen the aftermath of Naples and welcomed the recreational activities offered in Rome. Private First Class Hugh K. Wiltshire, serving in the 351st Infantry, 88th Infantry Division, saw the aftermath of Naples and the availability of houses of prostitution and wrote to his friend, "Houses are plentiful, but not for me. I'm staying clean as I plan on coming home and get married again. I don't want anything like Pogue got. It isn't worth it to me. I can get along without it, and you know me."[27] Wiltshire took advantage of the Rome rest area, overindulged in the local wine, watched movies, and stayed away from the possibility of a serious venereal disease. Many GIs did succumb to the temptations offered by the seamy side of Roman life, but the rise in venereal disease and incidents caused by alcohol consumption were far less than in Naples, and even Bella Napoli was being tamed a bit by the Special Services, the USO camp shows, and the PXs.

After the liberation of Rome and D-Day, Byron's Special Services Division was busy trying to provide for every theater, but the main focus was on the European and Mediterranean areas. General Byron surfaced the idea of joint army and navy activities to provide for all American service personnel, and a few weeks after D-Day Byron wrote to Somervell, urging Washington to support such recreational events, which would benefit soldier and sailor alike. If the secretaries of the army and navy agreed, the secretary of war should be approached to support joint activities.[28] There was immediate agreement, and the Special Services Division's officers serving in the theaters began to formulate plans.

In August the army and navy, through the Allied Sports Commission, sponsored a major swimming championship at the Stadio Nazionale in Rome. The commission had been formed to provide athletic competition among French, British, and American forces operating in North Africa and in Italy, and in April 1944 they sponsored an Allied basketball championship held in Oran, Algeria, with an estimated four hundred thousand Allied soldiers and sailors in attendance.

A few weeks after Rome had been liberated, the commission brought together track and field athletes in Rome, where there was a fine venue, a major facility for sporting events. The major figure in the planning and preparation for a swim meet was Colonel Leon T. David, the senior Special Services officer in the North African theater, who would coordinate with Fifth Army Special Services, the military police, and medical services. This was to be a major event, with free tickets available to the soldiers in the US Army Rest Center.[29] The turnout for the event was excellent, and the sports commission then planned for the Allied boxing championship meet to be held in December 1944.

In July American units began to move south of Rome to the Naples staging area for an upcoming operation called Anvil. The 3rd Infantry, 36th Infantry, 45th Infantry Division, and other combat units assembled, replaced lost equipment and weapons, received replacements, and repaired and waterproofed vehicles. They prepared for the invasion of southern France in mid-August. The troops, who had not been briefed on the invasion, would be allowed to visit Naples, and those veterans who had seen the city immediately after liberation were surprised that many of the prostitutes were gone, local gangsters who had preyed on GIs were reduced in numbers, and many of the bars that served cheap wine and watered-down liquor were closed. The Special Services orchestrated a continual supply of USO shows and organized tours, one of the most popular being a tour of the ruins of Roman Pompeii.[30] In mid-August the troops who landed on the beaches of southern France were armed with a Special Services–produced guide to that famous area of France second only to the city of Paris.

The GIs in the Pacific theater of operations read about the fighting in Europe in *Stars and Stripes, Yank,* or the Australian newspapers. But it was of little interest to the combat soldiers who fought in Guadalcanal or, more recently, in New Guinea. Typical of the GIs was Master Sergeant Elmer Franzman of the 329th Service Group, stationed in India, who wrote his parents in June 1944, "We received our monthly issue of beer today and were we surprised. Each man got one case (24 bottles). . . . It's a good brand too Pabst Blue Ribbon but some was Schlitz which is just as good. We get plenty of cigarettes, but little candy." This young soldier from Indiana enjoyed a first-run Bing Crosby movie, presented by a Special Services company's movie section. He also told his parents that he constantly received *Yank,* which was a major source of his war news.[31] It really did not matter where the GI served overseas; what mattered was winning a war and going home, and his focus was on his particular area of the war.

There were too many reports reaching Byron concerning the misuse of Special Services Division personnel and assets. The problem had been brewing for some time, and as combat increased in every theater of the war, there was a need to explain what the Special Services offered and how it could be used to maintain morale in the combat and support units. Byron directed his staff to prepare an explanatory booklet for overseas commanders that would tell the commanders and the staff, especially the GI (personnel), what was available. The Special Services officer on an army commander's staff had the rank of colonel, while the SSO at the divisional level held the rank of lieutenant colonel. The ranks would be equal to any staff officer and would give the SSO a voice in the process of maintaining the morale of the unit. The booklet, which was available before D-Day in Europe, began with a statement by General Byron. He wrote, "Special Services Division has only one mission—to help every commanding officer maintain the contentment and spirit of his command." He explained that the division offered not only the exchange services but also athletic and recreational services. The Special Services also worked closely with the US Signal Corps to keep showing movies, the favorite diversion of the GIs in the field, regardless of combat conditions.[32]

The booklet explained how the SSO would coordinate with USO camp shows for the troops. The shows, especially those with American girls, were well attended by the GIs in rest areas. Byron wrote that the SSO could be instrumental in keeping the troops physically fit. There was an emphasis on athletics, with organized football, baseball, and basketball games between units. Boxing matches were also popular, but Byron went one step further by stating that the SSO and his subordinates could organize the daily physical training required by the War Department Training Circular 87, which mandated twelve muscle-building and endurance exercises. Commanders knew that unfit troops did not survive long in combat, and tired soldiers made mistakes that could be fatal.

Every commander was aware of the armywide emphasis placed on keeping the venereal rate at a low level. As the booklet indicated, in a stabilized rest-camp area, the SSO would organize athletic events, and the exchange would open beer halls, with the aim of providing athletic events and inexpensive American beer and keeping GIs away from prostitutes and criminals who preyed on soldiers.[33] The Special Services and the army exchanges also increased offerings to the troops training in the United States. Somervell's decision to promote Osborn to direct troop information and education and to designate Byron to the director of the Special Services Division proved to be a wise one indeed.

Byron could be direct and to the point, often blunt. He had to appear before Congress to testify as to why there needed to be an increase in the Special Services budget for 1945. All of the optimistic predictions that the war in Europe would be over by Christmas 1944 proved false. The serious problems of supplying the fast-moving Allied armies, stiff German resistance as evidenced by the failed air-ground operation in Holland, and then the surprise and powerful German counterattack in the Ardennes in mid-December 1944 showed that it would be a hard fight in 1945 to end the war. More troops would be needed, and they had to be served by the exchange and the Special Services

Division. General Byron was promised that the appropriation for 1945 would be increased. Much to the relief of Byron and the division, funds were included to maintain service-club hostesses, librarians, and assistant librarians. (This was formalized by regulations AR 210-70 in 1945.)[34] Byron's appearance before Congress and the testimony of fiscal officers from the Quartermaster Services were successful. The appropriation for 1944 was $30.5 million and for 1945 $42.5 million. By 1944 and well into 1945 there were increasing calls for the Special Services Division to be more involved in morale-raising activities and providing expanded exchange offerings in the growing number of army hospitals in the United States. The Red Cross had been the most active presence in the army hospitals, but that organization did not have the funds or the trained personnel to serve the increasing number of wounded arriving in the United States.

The Special Services Division had forty companies in the field in Europe and the Pacific, and it also had to provide for the units and the replacements in the United States preparing for combat operations. For example, by the end of November 1944 the 69th Infantry Division had completed its training at Camp Shelby, Mississippi, and had orders to ship to Camp Kilmer, New Jersey, a staging area for the European theater. Before the division left Camp Shelby, each man was given a souvenir booklet to send home. Besides the usual pictures of combat training, there were several pages devoted to Special Services baseball, basketball, and boxing matches. Of special emphasis were the troops in the PX beer halls where they enjoyed "bottled beer, hand operated, model PX-caliber 3.2."[35] The "Fighting 69th" would arrive in England in December 1944, and one month later they debarked at Le Havre, France. Three weeks later they were in combat. Private First Class Keith Winston, thirty-two years old, was a medic in the 100th Infantry Division at Fort Bragg, North Carolina. An older man, a father of two children, he was typical of the state of manpower through the draft, but he went into training uncomplaining. Fort Bragg Special Services maintained a complete schedule of everything they had to offer, but Winston wrote, "One distasteful thing at camp is the constant waiting in line for everything you want to do. As was the case last night when I tried to go to the movies and couldn't get in—and to bowl—where I had to wait an hour.... There's a long wait even to buy a hot dog."[36] On October 20, 1944, the 100th Division landed at Marseilles, France, and on November 1 they were in combat against the German army.

As fighting raged across Europe and in the Philippine Islands, the Special Services Division and the Army Exchange System had to focus on 1945, the year everyone hoped would be the last year in the worldwide conflict. As army hospitals filled in every theater and in the United States, Special Services had to develop plans for morale-building programs for those who had suffered wounds and faced an uncertain future. Hospital operations had not been an area of emphasis from its organization up to 1944. Osborn, and later Byron, looked to the Red Cross to work with the troops and continue work with them they would, but by 1944 Marshall and Somervell directed that Special Services would have to be more involved in hospital activities.

Late 1944 and well into 1945 promised to be a year of challenges for the Special Services and the PXs in building and maintaining morale. For General Osborn the same time period offered a chance to expand troop information and education, especially since Congress had passed a major piece of legislation aimed at providing for the postwar GIs, best known as the GI Bill.

7

"Unnecessarily Unsatisfactory"

Bob Hope and Frances Langford were two of the most famous entertainers in the United States, and in 1943 they traveled to England and North Africa to entertain American soldiers and airmen. Their schedule of events had been coordinated by the Special Services officer and his staff in the American Supreme Headquarters and approved by General Eisenhower. It was obvious the troops enjoyed Hope and his one-line jokes and references to their service in England, but GIs being GIs, their loudest cheers were for the beautiful American girl Langford. Moved by the posting of casualties and missing aircrews, the entertainers also visited hospitals. From England, Hope, Langford, and their crew traveled to North Africa, where they experienced a German air raid. In North Africa were the combat troops who had engaged the Afrika Korps in battle and finally defeated them, but at a high cost. As in England, the two stars visited the hospitals and put on stage shows for the troops, and, again, the loudest cheers and whistles were for the real American girl with a great smile and upswept brunette hair. The tour was overseen by a Special Services lieutenant, who arranged every aspect of the shows, using the technicians of the Special Services company to ensure that microphones and speakers worked and that GI musicians were prepared to accompany Hope and Langford. One of the loudest crowds of appreciative GIs was at an airfield near Tunis, where fighters and bombers flew against the German army.[1]

In the audience that day was Corporal William E. George of the 415th Fighter Squadron, who was thrilled at seeing two famous stars. That night he wrote to his mother in Little Rock, "Well I saw Bob Hope and Francis [sic] Langford today in person, yep ain't that grand, this is a 'wonderful world.' I am telling you, you would have died to hear some of the jokes he pulled off, of course not knowing the army life and England as we do it would not be so funny."[2] Two days later George was promoted to the rank of sergeant, and he wrote to his parents to tell them the good news, but of equal length and enthusiasm was his recalling of the show put on by Bob Hope and Frances Langford.[3] Hope, Langford, and hundreds of other stars of radio and the movie screen would visit and entertain the troops in every theater of war, and their trips through the auspices of the USO would be made possible by the coordination of the Special Services in the United States and overseas. The number of overseas trips grew dramatically throughout 1944 and well into 1945 and became a major factor in maintaining GI morale.

The Special Services Division had come a long way since its founding, and the focus of Special Services activities had changed considerably as the war grew in intensity. One of the areas with which Special Services dealt in 1942 was the identification of artists among the incoming draftee soldiers. The project aimed at putting artists at work to "embellish mess halls, recreation rooms, Service Clubs, administration buildings, classrooms, etc., with appropriate mural decorations."[4] By 1943 and well into 1944 and 1945, Special Services and the Army Exchange System built clubs and PXs as quickly as possible out of wood or, if lucky, concrete, painted or paneled the walls, put in equipment or showcases, and opened for business. GIs were not particularly interested in artistic representations when they wanted a cold beer and a hamburger, to play pool, or attend a dance. Also, by 1944 the army needed more and more infantry, not mural painters.

The cooperation between the USO camp shows and the Special Services had grown as more and more shows went overseas. Problems had surfaced with some of the shows, and Special Services had to screen participants better as to health conditions, character, and actual skills such as singing, joke telling, and expertise with musical instruments. The director of Special Services, now General Joseph Byron, wanted Special Services personnel to hold auditions. The USO entertainers had to be questioned to make certain that there were no problems with air travel. Special Services had been informed that boat travel for entertainers was simply impossible. Army transportation was stretched to the limit as far as shipping space was concerned, and ships were needed for troops and necessary supplies. If an entertainer was, as Special Services put it, "allergic to air travel," they could not go. To save space, the entertainers were told to be prepared to buy GI clothing upon arrival in Europe or the Pacific, because a USO uniform made for wear in the United States could not stand up under the conditions imposed by being in active theaters of operation. As Special Services said, cleaning of civilian clothes was simply not possible.[5]

The large shows such as those featuring Bob Hope, Frances Langford, and other well-known Hollywood stars were fine for large gatherings of troops, and GIs flocked to those shows by the thousands. But what was being offered for smaller units such as antiaircraft battalions, radar units, or other far-flung troops? Basically, very little entertainment reached those isolated GIs. To remedy this, the Special Services advised that three or four entertainers be designated to those units unable to attend the large high-profile shows.[6]

Even with increasing appropriations, the Special Services Division could not have provided the entertainment that was so widespread and heavily attended without the USO. The USO opened its first "home away from home" show in Fayetteville, North Carolina, the town serving Fort Bragg. USO clubs sprang up all over the country, staffed by volunteers and funded by the USO. This took a great deal of pressure off the Special Services, allowing it to focus on building, maintaining, and staffing facilities on posts. In October 1941, Camp Shows, Inc., founded and funded by the USO parent company, began bringing together Hollywood and other entertainment entities with the purpose of providing big-name personalities for the troops in training in the United States. When the United States entered the war, the mission of the camp shows changed, and entertainers went overseas. The Special Services Division and Special Services personnel coordinated with the shows, providing transportation, sites for shows, billets and meals, and protection when near the battlefields of Europe, the Pacific, and elsewhere. Although there were disagreements and problems, the Special Services welcomed the camp shows, and frankly could not afford to offend or alienate those willing to entertain GIs and other military personnel. Nor did the Special Services have the funds to support the centers opened by the USO in the cities and towns near army posts.

The role of the Special Services officer at corps, army, or theater had changed since 1942. The arrival of the forty Special Services companies and the enlarging of the Special Services officers' staffs meant that the offerings of the Special Services had extended into areas that Osborn had not envisioned. By 1944 the Special Services recognized, "It has been necessary for Special Services Officers to foster and develop rest camps, beaches and sight-seeing tours to provide recreational facilities for troops off duty and on pass. The limited civilian facilities and transportation equipment, as well as language difficulties, have made this program mandatory, particularly as the average length of overseas service of the individual soldier has increased, and his need for rest and diversity of entertainment has progressed." There was a need to define where the Special Services officer and his subordinates belonged on the staff of a commanding general, be he in command of an army, corps, or division. The original assignment of the officer had been with the G3, or operations officer, because it was the G3 who knew what units were in training or in combat and would be available to take advantage of what Special Services had to offer. The G3 was a busy person, and his subordinates were constantly involved with writing orders, planning training or combat operations, and communicating with their subordinate commands. There was little time to deal with camp shows, PXs, libraries, and the like. Finally, in mid-1943, the army decided that the Special Services officer actually was part of the G1, or personnel officer's, staff, and should be regarded as "de facto an assistant to the personnel officer of a unit."[7] This made good sense, because the G1 could tell how many troops were available and where they were. No other officer on a staff had as much information, nor was the G1 involved in detailed tactical planning or execution of battle plans.

By late 1943 the majority of the Special Services companies had been deployed to overseas theaters, and the role of the Special Services officer had been defined as a part of the G1 organization. In Brisbane, Australia, the Special Services and the PX had expanded their activities to include a bowling alley, hamburger and Coke bars, beer halls, PXs, and even a beauty parlor for Red Cross, USO, and military personnel. England became an area of special interest because of the massive buildup of American combat and support units. Special plans for moving three Special Services companies to England were in place.[8] Overseas deployments of American troops reached a flood tide, but the offerings of the Special Services Division in the United States could not be ignored.

Special Services activities were divided into two distinct groups—those supplying activities in the United States and those overseas. By late 1943 General Somervell made it quite clear that the Special Services companies were strictly for overseas deployment and that "to fulfill this mission these companies must be ready on short notice for overseas assignments."[9] No post commander or his Special Services officer could rely on a company to serve the needs of the troops, and this came at a time when Service Clubs, libraries, PXs, and associated activities were expanding at a rapid rate. Every training base saw the need to establish branches of the main clubs, libraries, and PXs, normally with each regiment. These had to be staffed by either Special Services soldiers or civilian employees, and that could be expensive. The appropriation for the Special Services Division in 1944 was $30.5 million, but the requirements for the morale and welfare of the troops had greatly expanded. Despite the efforts of the division to continue to maintain morale activities, to save money Congress cut the amount of money available to pay service-club hostesses and librarians. The reason given for this congressional action was simply that masses of trained soldiers were moving overseas and fewer troops would be coming into the training camps. Congress had underestimated the numbers of draftees and new enlistments in 1944 into 1945. The intense fighting in Normandy and the subsequent breakout forced the German army to retreat into Belgium and Holland by the fall. Combat still raged in Italy, while in the Pacific theater fighting in the Philippines and on many islands increased. Every bloody battle moved American forces closer to the Japanese home islands. The need for combat replacements became critical, with casualty lists growing longer after each engagement in Europe and the Pacific. The number of service-club hostesses, Special Services personnel who ran the guesthouses, and assistant librarians had to be reduced to stay within the limits of the appropriated funds. General Joseph Byron, the director of the Special Services Division, began a campaign to retain what he saw as personnel vital for the morale and welfare of the troops and by 1945 saw a new regulation that would cover the employment of Special Services personnel. Post commanders and Special Services officers had to scramble to find some way to retain civilians who performed vital services, and most of them found that in nonappropriated funds for the welfare of the troops. Not every position could be saved, however, and a large number of assistant librarians were released.[10]

Pressure was building in the War Department to manage the amount of money being spent for every activity. By the spring of 1944, it was decided that the number of training installations needed to be reduced and consolidated at posts where there were large training areas for infantry, armor, or artillery. There were too many US Army Air Force bases by 1944, and the smaller ones needed to be eliminated. Troops attending courses at colleges and universities would be reassigned to military posts where training of equal effectiveness could be carried on. Every branch of the army felt this cost-reducing program, and this included the Special Services Division. In the plan, the Special Services' school at Washington and Lee University would be relocated to Edgewood Arsenal, Maryland. General Byron contacted the US Army Service Forces chief of staff's office, requesting that the school be retained at the university. His reasoning was sound, arguing that the university library, athletic fields, and gymnasium could not be replicated at the arsenal. With the need for Special Services at training bases and for qualified Special Services officers overseas, the disruption of instruction would throw the Special Services into confusion. Byron's arguments fell on receptive ears, and the Army Service Forces agreed with the retention of the school, which remained at Washington and Lee University at least while the United States was at war.[11]

At every training base that was designated to remain open, there were continual building programs for Special Services activities because the number of troops was scheduled to grow. Special Services and the exchanges had to expand to meet the influx, but funding for such expansion was limited. The Army Exchange System was in a better position to respond to the growth in demand. General Byron boasted that the PXs became the world's largest chain store, and profits could be plowed into opening new main and branch PXs. The service-club system was also limited by regulations, and according to MR (Mobilization Regulations) 1-10, dated 1943, one Service Club supervised by a hostess and her assistants was provided for every five thousand soldiers. The assistants were to manage the cafeteria, provide recreation and social activities, and maintain guesthouse facilities for visiting families.[12] By late 1943 and well into 1944, it was impossible to provide a complete Service Club for every five thousand GIs. This necessitated the opening of branch clubs that featured limited cafeteria offerings and recreational services such as athletic events, pool tables, areas to write letters, and, when the opportunity arose, dances. The branch Service Clubs were operated in conformity with the troops' training schedules. When soldiers were on the firing ranges or on marches and bivouacs, often lasting more than two weeks, the branch clubs were opened on a limited basis. Supervising the hostesses and her staff of assistants was the Special Services officer who served on the post commander's staff. The functioning of the system depended on the abilities and interests of the post commander, the Special Services officer, and the hostesses, and, as human nature would have it, some posts had better systems than others. The exchange branches fared much better because there a GI could buy his crackers, candy bars, chewing gum, shaving cream, shoe polish, cigarettes, and, of course, a glass, bottle, or pitcher of cold 3.2 beer.

As the army trained more replacements than complete units, certain posts expanded. For example, Fort Bragg, North Carolina, became a Field Artillery Replacement Center, taking recent draftees and volunteers. As the soldiers were told, "The main idea here is to teach you to be a soldier." Trainees were not encouraged to visit Fayetteville when off duty, as the newly inducted GIs had three movie theaters near the training center, and the pride of the post was the main Service Club, which also housed the library. It maintained a snack bar, a full cafeteria, recreational programs, and occasionally dances. There were two large Service Clubs at Fort Bragg, and like most army bases, one was for white soldiers and the other for "colored," or African American, soldiers. The Special Services maintained two guesthouses, racially segregated.[13] Whereas Fort Bragg maintained a centralized location for its Special Services activities, the post commander at Camp Crowder, Missouri, opted for a main PX, three Service Clubs (each with its own guesthouse), and five movie theaters. Unlike Fort Bragg, Camp Crowder maintained a good relationship with a USO in the town of Neosho.[14]

Since infantry was badly needed as combat increased in 1944, the infantry replacement centers received the most attention from both the Special Services and the exchange system. Camp Joseph T. Robinson near Little Rock, Arkansas, had been designated as a replacement center, and thousands of new GIs poured onto the base to be trained as quickly as possible and then deployed to replacement depots overseas. The Special Services officer and the camp commander established five main Service Clubs, each with its own snack bar and cafeteria. GI orchestras provided music for a continual round of dances, "with a selected group of charmers." There was one main library, but each Service Club had a reading room with newspapers, books, and reference materials, and the Special Services operated seven movie theaters. The soldiers in training were divided into five regiments, and clubs, theaters, and exchanges were located to serve each regiment. Special Services also provided for each regiment a full schedule of athletic and recreational activities. The PX system operated a main exchange and twenty-five branches throughout the camp and regimental areas, each with its own barbershop. The Special Services also published the *Camp Robinson News* on a weekly basis.[15] This was a carefully planned program involving the camp commander, camp training officer, Special Services, and exchange officers. Since the training was conducted by regiment, giving the novice soldier a sense of comradeship and competition, it was hoped that this cohesion would continue when the replacement joined a combat infantry unit overseas. It was common knowledge that the casualty rates among replacement soldiers was high, a fact not widely discussed in the regiments undergoing training. Whatever could be started at the infantry replacement centers, it was hoped, would give the soldier an edge, albeit slight, when he first went under fire. MR 1-10 stated that there should be one Service Club for every five thousand soldiers in training, but at Camp Robinson it worked out that there was one for every three thousand soldiers. Also, Camp Robinson encouraged the trainees not to visit Little Rock, but to remain on post and take advantage of what the army had to offer at a low price or for free. The USO in Little Rock maintained four clubs, but it was clear that at the infantry training center it was preferred that the new soldier immerse himself in the military life, with everything from a baseball game to a dance at the regiment's Service Club or to a movie or a cold beer at one of the PX beer halls available to him.

At some posts the Special Services had to deal with recreational facilities quite different from those at the majority of other military instillations. At Fort Lewis, Washington, for example, the Special Services officer and his subordinates had to manage four beaches set aside for enlisted personnel only. They had to oversee the maintenance of diving platforms, dressing rooms, the rental of rowboats at 10 cents per hour, and scheduling bus service from Fort Lewis to the four beaches at 10 cents per trip. In addition, Fort Lewis boasted a fine golf course where both enlisted men and officers could play. Enlisted men paid $1.11 per month, while officers paid $2.12 per month for a golf club membership, which could be obtained only at the Special Services office at Fort Lewis. In addition, the post Special Services and exchange system maintained a large number of Service Clubs, PXs, theaters, athletic fields, and guesthouses.[16]

The army of 1944 had a very different look from the army of 1942, and the same was true of both the Special Services Division and the Army Exchange System. The need for more infantry was critical, followed by the requirements for more armor, artillery, and combat engineers. The Special Services adjusted to meet the need, but it also made a contribution to the combat efficiency of infantry that went beyond dances at a Service Club or hamburgers in a snack bar. When the Special Services began functioning under General Osborn, there was an emphasis on areas like Service Clubs, movies, athletics, and the building of the Special Services companies for overseas service. That made sense as the army grew. Within the administrative structure of the Special Services was a section known simply as Research, and it was viewed as a preserve of academics. The Research Section was, simply, an "operating research unit for all War Department agencies on problems of the soldier." This was vague, but far-reaching in its implications. It was pretty well known that General Osborn came from a scholarly background and frankly was more at home with this type of activity than he was with the mundane day-to-day numbers of Service Clubs opened, the price of balls and athletic equipment, or how many troops saw a first-run movie in England, Italy, or New Guinea. The Research Section would delve into problems of soldiers in combat and in tactical units in the army and army air force. The first test of battle for the United States came in North Africa in late 1942 into 1943, and the campaign offered an opportunity for the Research Section to see exactly what the GIs thought about combat, their leaders, their equipment, and their morale. The researchers went into the combat companies and carefully avoided surveying senior commanders at the regimental level and above.

The researchers decided to focus on one infantry division that had seen heavy combat in Tunisia and in Sicily and questioned only infantrymen at the company, platoon, and squad levels. To further refine the questions, the Research Section divided the GIs into two distinct groups: those who had been awarded the Silver Star for gallantry and those who had not. To refine the surveys, there were two teams of researchers: those in the United States who dealt with trained infantry awaiting assignment overseas and those who were in the designated combat division, which was in a rest area after the campaign in Sicily. Among the veteran infantry there was a universal feeling that the infantry played the vital role in war, and there was little difference between the combat veterans and the untried soldiers in the conviction that what they were doing was worthwhile and vital to the war effort. When dealing with the realities of battle, the Silver Star and other combat veterans felt two to one that the Germans had better weapons and equipment, while those awaiting assignment overseas expressed the opposite view. The combat veterans had seen battle at Kasserine, El Guettar, and other places in North Africa and Sicily. The researchers found that the combat veterans, even those who had a comrade killed in battle, had little hatred for the German soldiers. In the final report to the G3s of the War Department and to the chief of staff, the researchers reported no such feeling of respect for the Japanese, and almost 70 percent of combat veterans felt that the United States should "wipe out the whole Japanese nation."

After combat in North Africa and Sicily, almost 70 percent of the veteran infantrymen felt that they were ready to be committed to the combat that was raging across Italy. More than two-thirds of the veterans felt comfortable with most of their officers, and this conclusion was reached after surveying ten rifle companies. A common complaint was that officers fresh from officer candidate school or ROTC needed more training and trust in their veteran non-commissioned officers. One private with a Purple Heart stated, "Some officers coming from the states with no combat experience are too proud to ask questions or follow advice from experienced men. I was led into a trap by a green platoon leader." A vast majority of veterans were highly critical of the quality of training the replacements received in the United States.[17]

As part of the Special Services Division, the researchers needed to find out how the frontline GIs felt about Special Services, and they were not disappointed with the response. The movies, the opening of beaches along the North African and Sicilian coasts, the exchange service offered by the Special Services platoons (although the troops had no idea that there was such a unit as a Special Services company), and the USO shows and other entertainment were highly rated. On the other hand, there were consistent complaints about mail delivery, the quality of rations, and the lack of cigarettes and fresh water. When combat infantry were interviewed, they rated Special Services highly, but when rear-echelon troops were queried, they were less complimentary, even though they had a consistent access to exchanges, Special Services, and the Red Cross.[18]

The final report was submitted to General Marshall's staff the day before Christmas Eve 1943, and it was assumed that the results would then be transmitted to the commander of the US Army Ground Forces for study. It was hoped that recommendations would be proposed to improve morale.

By the time the report was written, there had been a major change in the Special Services Division. In looking at the successes of Special Services, it was clear to Somervell and to Marshall that the investment, in the millions of dollars, was worth it. At the same time, Byron's Army Exchange System had exceeded all expectations both in the United States and overseas, and seldom was there a GI complaint about the PX system, despite nationwide shortages of cigarettes and beer. Complaints about the PXs came from local businesses that lost the soldier trade. Somervell decided that there needed to be a division of labor in the Special Services area, and a Morale Services Division, under the command of Osborn, was created. General Byron was designated to take over direction of the Special Services Division, with Colonel Frank Kerr, an energetic, competent officer, to take over the Army Exchange System. Osborn had done a good job with Special Services, but his interest had always been academic. Under the administrative structure of the Special Services Division there were Education, Research, and Information Sections. The Education Section dealt with correspondence courses, civilian and military lecturers, and the Army Library Service. The Research Section produced the infantry surveys and would work with more surveys in 1944 on combat rations, clothing, and equipment, while the Information Section oversaw the publication and distribution of *Yank*, news, maps, posters, and the well-used GI guides to the areas where soldiers served. The new division was formed under Somervell's Army Service Forces, and Osborn would be responsible for reporting to General Marshall for his guidance on army policies and to Somervell for everything else.[19] The new job and new title also carried with it a handsome prize, the two stars of a major general.

How did Osborn feel about the new position? Osborn had never been fully comfortable with the Special Services, because, as he said, "at the beginning it [the Special Services Division] was looked on purely as a recreational activity." The Princeton academic did begin the processes that resulted in the GI guides, *Yank*, camp newspapers, and the like, but he wanted to go further. As Osborn recalled, it was Somervell who felt that he would be better suited in the field of information and education, since Byron was obviously the officer to oversee important Special Services as the commitment of American troops to decisive battle would come in 1944. Finally, Osborn set about his task with intelligence and a vigor that would clash with some of the high-ranking traditional officers in the War Department.[20]

General Joseph Byron, a West Point graduate who had seen overseas service in the Great War, was better equipped to deal with the War Department. He was no-nonsense, but he realized that, despite entrenched groups, the gen-

erals in the War Department had one mission: the defeat and uncondition-
al surrender of Germany and Japan. Byron clearly had something to offer
through the PX system, and he could sell an expansion of the Special Services.

Osborn, to make his new organization work at maximum efficiency,
reached out to many in the academic community for expertise. He convinced
the head of Harvard's school of education to come to Washington, accept the
commission of a colonel, and be the director of education.[21] Other academics
were called upon by Osborn to work for him. Of course, these men were just
as dedicated to victory over Germany and Japan as any officer in the War Department, but their approaches were different. Many of the generals regarded
the influx of academics whose fields were psychology, sociology, and the like
as "long hairs," academic theorists, or "Hollywood goons."[22]

Osborn was now in a position that suited him, and he made the most of it.
Looking back from the perspective of a decade, he was amazed at what was
accomplished. "We ran all the army newspapers overseas. About three million
daily newspapers were going out. We had a hundred and twenty-seven radio
stations transmitting the news on the hour and recreational and musical programs the rest of the time.... We published *Yank*, which sold two and one half
million copies a week. . . . I got Frank Capra to come on from the west coast
and head up a motion picture division. He made a wonderful series of films
... 'Why We Fight' and 'Our Ally England.'"[23]

One of the areas that bothered Osborn was race relations, and as director
of Special Services, he had established Service Clubs, guesthouses, cafeterias,
and libraries that were segregated by race. The Research Section employed
Donald Young, a young African American, as a consultant, and Osborn said
that as a result, "The word Negro or black never appeared in our material, all were soldiers, fellow combatants in the war." Osborn followed army
policies in respect to racial separation despite his personal and professional
feelings that the policy was wrong.

With the critical election of 1944 drawing near, Osborn had to be careful
that all of the publications, movies, and radio broadcasts had no political
content. Osborn's education and information branch was directly involved
in every aspect of the dissemination of information, and the War Department and General Marshall were very much concerned that the army in a
time of total war would be seen as neutral. Certainly, soldiers were encouraged to get absentee ballots wherever practical, but beyond that the army
maintained neutrality. In August 1944 the army established a review board
to see that there was no political content in any film, and it was clear that
any production that had a political view would be censored. Osborn was to
select a member of his new morale services to serve as chairman.[24]

General Somervell had been concerned for some time about the possibility of surveys and informational materials going beyond the limits of what the army was trying to accomplish. In 1943 he had informed General Osborn that under no circumstances were there to be surveys of the civilian population. What Osborn did was to send military personnel to gauge the attitude of the soldiers toward the civilian home front. Somervell was upset and told Osborn to stop the survey because he was "convinced that any such investigation or sampling is highly dangerous."[25] Going into the politically charged year of 1944, no one wanted the army embroiled in any controversy. Osborn recalled that there were charges that the Roosevelt administration was "trying to influence troops for their votes." This was such a serious problem that Secretary of War Henry Stimson appointed a general as his personal representative to work with Osborn to ensure that all army information and education remained politically neutral.[26]

General George C. Marshall became involved with the changes taking place in the area of morale activities in the army. Common sense dictated that after three years of war, lengthy overseas deployments, and growing casualty lists, the stress on the army was considerable, and there was heavy fighting ahead. The planning for the cross-Channel invasion of "Fortress Europe" in the spring of 1944 loomed large as American divisions and support troops poured into Britain. While there was a rapidly expanding exchange and Special Services presence in England and Italy, there were disturbing reports coming into the War Department, and eventually onto Marshall's desk, of morale problems in the Pacific theater of operations. Australia was a mecca for GIs fortunate enough to get a leave, and there was a constantly growing American army morale base in the Brisbane area, with other smaller recreational activities in Sydney and Melbourne. But how many fighting troops could be spared even for a short time?

Upon assuming his new duties, Osborn decided to visit the European theater of operations to see for himself how to proceed with his information and educational mission. General Marshall thought otherwise and directed Osborn to turn his attention to the Pacific, where, as Marshall termed it, morale services were "most unnecessarily unsatisfactory."[27] Osborn had made an earlier trip to the Pacific and was not pleased with what he saw. As he formulated plans for the new Morale Services Division, Osborn felt that more had to be done in that area. Marshall then turned the problem over to his energetic, well-respected deputy chief of staff, Joseph T. McNarney, who met with Osborn and indicated that rather than visiting Italy and England, he should again tour the Pacific area. Osborn was informed that the Office of the Chief of Staff would give the new Morale Services Division all the support possible. To back this up, acting with the full authority of General Marshall, McNarney sought an extra allocation of funds to get officers trained in education and information to the Pacific area. Osborn indicated that he had the necessary personnel ready to go, and McNarney stated, "Transportation will be furnished in a high priority."[28]

General Somervell was directed to take immediate action to get Morale Services Division officers on their way to the Pacific by air transportation. All theater headquarters, bases, departments, and installations were to get an officer as quickly as possible.[29] A few days later there was a conference with the Morale Services, the Operations Division in the War Department, and the director of personnel to identify officers by name and rank and then inform the commanding general of US Forces in the Southwest Pacific, South Pacific, and Central Pacific who was coming to the staff and what they were to accomplish.[30] It remained to be seen just how General Douglas MacArthur and his staff would utilize this new addition and what impact the Morale Services Division would have.

Any dealing with General MacArthur could indeed be thorny, and Marshall sent a message to MacArthur stating why he was about to receive a staff officer from a newly formed organization. Marshall cabled MacArthur:

> I consider this program of great importance in maintaining the morale of troops and desire that you give it such personal attention as is necessary to produce satisfactory results. The organization of small staffs required to prepare and direct the program is authorized for theater commands. If positions of appropriate grade cannot be provided for within existing allotment for your theater, favorable consideration will be given to increasing your allotment accordingly. Steps are being taken here to send you qualified officers. . . . Advise immediately any necessary increase in allotment and any further needs to effectuate this program.[31]

Word had reached Washington that there were two major morale problems for the army in the Pacific. First, even with the deployment of Special Services companies to the area of operations, there was a lack of morale-enhancing programs because the troops were scattered over a series of islands, and not every unit could be consistently serviced. Second, there were continual incidents between American troops and Australian troops and civilians. The increase in Special Services and facilities in the Brisbane area helped, but there was more to be done to hold confrontations to a minimum. Also, with the institution of the Morale Services Division in the Pacific there was a good effort made by Osborn and the War Department to send good, qualified officers, but where would the subordinate officers and enlisted men come from? The combat commands would be resistant to sending infantry soldiers to man a typewriter or mimeograph machine in Brisbane. On the other hand, General Byron, now directing the traditional Special Services, and Colonel Frank Kerr, commanding the Army Exchange System, were quite happy to go about their business and not be bothered by disseminating information and educational materials. Basketballs, cold beer, American girls in the USO shows, and a constant supply of American cigarettes were their concerns, and they were handling them well.

General Byron, as director of Special Services, had to deal with certain problems that had festered for some time. The Army Signal Corps claimed that the distribution of motion pictures overseas belonged with them and not the Special Services Division. This was the sort of bureaucratic infighting and turf defending that had so angered Byron when he returned from overseas service after World War I, and the War Department in late 1943 had judged that the movies did belong to the Signal Corps. The procurement of films, screens, and projectors fell to the Signal Corps, but Byron's rejoinder was simple: can you show them to the large numbers of GIs, and do you have the manpower, organization, and expertise to do so? Byron had the forty Special Services companies, each with a movie section trained to show movies to the troops in many environments.[32] There was also confusion over the newly created Morale Services Division. Was it or was it not a part of the Special Services Division? Only time could work that out, particularly since General Marshall had evidenced such an interest in the new educational and information organization.

Of benefit for the soldiers overseas was the fact that both Byron and Colonel Frank Kerr wanted to place an emphasis on the Exchange and Canteen Sections of the Special Services companies' ability to serve the troops with small mobile exchanges. Little did Byron realize that in a year the Special Services Division would become a major organization for travel and GI tourism. Special Services officers had offered limited tours for GIs in North Africa and in Sicily, and in the history of tourism there never had been such eager tourists as those in steel helmets, carrying M1 rifles.

Osborn also had a serious project for the Morale Services. There were hundreds of thousands of German prisoners of war in camps throughout the States. In keeping with the Geneva Conventions, the prisoners worked everywhere from the cotton fields of Mississippi to wood cutting in Colorado, and in accordance with the rules they were well housed and well fed within the restrictions of wartime rationing. What would happen to them once Germany was defeated and they were repatriated? If the goals were to de-Nazify and democratize post-Hitler Germany, then it would be necessary to reach out to the German prisoners and teach them the basics of democracy. As a part of the information mission of Osborn's morale service, there was an emphasis on working with the Germans, providing classes, films, and German-speaking lecturers. There was a general agreement with Roosevelt, Marshall, and others that if Germany was to rise from the ruins of war and become a truly democratic state, a start had to be made. The Morale Services Division could not simply go into the prisoner-of-war camps and begin a far-reaching program. There had to be coordination with the military police who oversaw the security of the camps. There were often disagreements with camp security, but with the support of Marshall and Roosevelt, the program went forward and intensified with the discovery of the extermination camps by Allied troops in Germany in 1945.

The first half of 1944 marked the high point of Special Services with the successes of the Special Services companies, the enlarging of morale-enhancing offerings in the United States and overseas, and the creation of the Morale Services Division under Frederick Osborn. That period also brought General Joseph Byron to the directorship of the division and Colonel Frank Kerr to head the Army Exchange System. The second half of 1944 would be marked by a number of key events such as D-Day at Normandy, the liberation of both Rome and Paris, and continual fighting and victories in the Pacific. On June 22 Franklin D. Roosevelt signed into law the Servicemen's Readjustment Act, better known as the GI Bill, which would have far-reaching implications for GI morale. As the fighting continued on the continent of Europe and on islands in the Pacific, the Special Services, the exchanges, and the Morale Services Division would face greater challenges. What would happen to those organizations when Germany and Japan were defeated?

8

Movies, Doughnuts, and M1 Rifles

From D-Day, June 6, 1944, and well into the late fall of the year, the Special Services had to react to a fluid situation. Special Services companies could not operate in France until Allied troops had cleared the German army to the Seine River. What the troops did have was the Special Services radio, and often it was the only touch of home they had. Technical Sergeant Charles Linzy of the 459th Mobile Anti-Aircraft Battalion had crossed Omaha Beach on the second day of the invasion and spent two weeks under fire. His battalion stopped for a rest, a hot meal, and a little time to write home. Linzy told his wife that he had not had time to pen a letter because he had been under "very adverse circumstances," even though he was serving on battalion headquarters staff. The battalion had a radio, and Linzy and his comrades heard the *Bob Hope Show*. Corporal Kenneth K. Gowen's field artillery battalion had landed in southern France in June 1944 and enjoyed the reaction of the French population to seeing the Germans driven out of their towns. Despite those enjoyable moments, Gowen and his buddies eagerly listened to the American Armed Forces Radio. Later Gowen recalled that the Special Services that provided the morale-lifting popular radio programs deserved the highest praise, and "their contribution [to the war effort] was tremendous." Private Eugene Mazza of the 338th Infantry Regiment wrote to his sister back in Brooklyn, New York, that he had been to the rest area in Rome "and have seen all the historic sights that my Italian teacher told us about back in school."[1]

In India Master Sergeant Elmer Franzman of the 329th Service Group had adjusted to his new surroundings. Franzman had acclimated so well to life near Assam that he was known as a "Red Cross Commando" because of his frequent visits to a local Red Cross Club where there were a number of cute American girl volunteers. The Special Services and USO camp shows toured India, and Franzman enjoyed one featuring the famous movie actor Pat O'Brien and the singer Jinx Falkenburg, plus other singers and a band. "After the show they visited our [service] club and signed autographs, shot the bull and Jinx played and won several ping pong games." Franzman and his comrades were fortunate in being served by the 18th Special Services Company, the one company assigned to the China-Burma-India theater of operations in 1944. Considered one of the best-organized and most aggressive of all the forty companies, the 18th's commander and the theater Special Services officer coordinated the USO camp shows that entertained troops in the theater. The 18th also put together a popular GI show called *Monsoon Madness* that toured bases in the theater. The show was well received because the Red Cross allowed two talented American women to be part of the cast. The production brought in a deluge of letters of commendation from every base. Typical of the letters, the commander of the 823rd Engineer Aviation Battalion wrote, "Special appreciation is expressed to the American Red Cross for having allowed the two talented young ladies to participate. They were a welcome feature, a refreshing departure from the usually all-male Army production."[2] American girls were always appreciated by GIs serving in any overseas theater.

Mid-1944 was a good year for Corporal Thomas R. St. George, who had been serving in New Guinea fighting insects, heat and humidity, and occasional Japanese air raids. His work had attracted those who wrote for *Yank*, and, after much string-pulling, he was ordered to Australia, assigned to the Southwest Pacific Area Services Publications. After New Guinea, St. George was more than willing to become what was known as a "Service of Supply Commando," a soldier who had a room with a real bed, hot running water, and hot chow every day. The Services Publications' headquarters was in Townsville, or Tville, a small city close to Brisbane, where relations between Australians and Americans were strained. One American soldier told St. George, "It's that there's been so damned many Yanks here for so damn long the town has plain give up."[3] Army Exchange System and Special Services had expanded in the Brisbane-Townsville area, but due to lengthy supply lines and the sinking of ships, the PX offerings and the Special Services could not consistently supply the large number of troops in that part of Australia. The ever-thirsty GIs flocked to civilian pubs, restaurants, and movie theaters, and they danced with and dated every willing Australian woman in sight.

The Special Services companies serving in the Pacific theater were strung along a series of islands, and they had few dealings with the sprawling exchange and Special Services facilities in the Brisbane area. The 8th Special Services Company had all four platoons dedicated to serving GIs on the many islands, and seldom was the entire company in one place for any length of time. The company headquarters and one platoon were stationed on the island of Espiritu Santo, where almost every soldier was engaged in assisting exchange operations and showing movies.[4] In the late fall of 1944 the 8th Company was informed that it would be one of the first Special Services companies to follow the troops in the invasion of the Philippine Islands.

Every Special Services company experienced the same problems that had not been foreseen when the companies were formed. When *Field Manual 28-105* governing the companies was published, there was a balance between recreation and athletics, entertainment in the field, canteen-exchange services, and education and information, including libraries and movies. With the formation of the Morale Services Division under General Osborn, a portion of the Information Section left the Special Services Division. The publication of camp and unit newspapers remained with the companies, because the newspapers dealt with the specific events in the camp or the unit. There were a large number of complex tasks to be accomplished, even with Osborn taking over a portion of the Information and Education Sections. Of particular irritation to the company commanders was the operation of the Exchange Section that existed in each platoon.

The Quartermaster Department had decided to include cigarettes in the combat rations. The combat rations (known to World War II GIs as the C ration, K ration, or the 10-1 rations) had cigarettes included. The introduction of the combat ration in November 1939 was an attempt to overcome consistent problems in feeding troops in combat and was, despite the universal complaints by GIs, a major reform in subsistence. When free "PX supplies" were issued to the troops, cigarettes, chewing gum, and candy were included.[5] Chewing gum, candy, and cigarettes were among the most popular items sold by the Exchange Section of the Special Services companies. In rest camps and replacement depots, the Canteen-Exchange Sections functioned as envisioned, supplying standard PX items such as toothpaste, shaving creams, candy, cigarettes, crackers, small cakes, and chewing gum. The Canteen Section served cooked hamburgers, hot coffee, and cold (when possible) soft drinks at the rest camps and replacement depots. At the front, however, the Canteen-Exchange Sections could not function because of the proximity of enemy artillery and small arms. For example, the 4th Special Services Company operated full services while in England, but when deployed to France the commander found the Canteen-Exchange Sections ceased to operate as envisioned by *FM 28-105*. He stated that the Exchange Section should be eliminated because of the issuance of cigarettes with rations and with the "PX supplies" that also included candy, chewing gum, writing paper, razor blades, and shaving cream.[6] The 18th Company serving in the China-Burma-India theater of operations also recommended the elimination of the Exchange Section because the PX system served the needs of the troops.[7] The 22nd Company, which served in the Pacific theater, also expressed the same sentiments.

In the United States the PX operated beer halls serving the 3.2 army beer, and those establishments were popular, well attended, and quite profitable. Exchange beer halls were maintained in England and in Australia, and they were welcomed because most GIs did not care for the local beer. On the other hand, a visit to an English or Australian pub did offer the possibility of meeting local women. It was clear, despite reports from the Special Services companies, that there would be no major changes in the structure and missions of the companies. In late 1944 General Eisenhower and General Patton urged the creation of more Special Services companies to serve the troops in the European theater of operations.[8] However, the number of companies would be held at forty until the creation and deployment of the all-WAC company in 1945. Also, the War Department thought that once victory over Germany and Japan had been achieved, the Special Services companies would be demobilized as quickly as the troops came home. They were wrong.

In late 1944 and well into 1945, the Special Services Division was helped by the continuation of civilian organizations providing for the troops. Byron had $30.5 million for the 1944 fiscal year, and Congress would appropriate $42.5 million for fiscal year 1945.[9] The costs of expanding publications for recreation and entertainment and the rising cost for recreational items such as balls, games, and the like were a concern for the Special Services Division. The efforts by civilian agencies such as the Red Cross and the USO were vitally important for expanding morale activities, and they raised their own funds. Other church and community organizations continued to provide for the troops.

New York City became important as troops poured into camps near the city to await transportation to Europe, where they would be replacements for units that had suffered losses in battle. The New York City Defense Recreation Committee, the city's official organization, promised to do everything possible to provide entertainment and places of rest and quiet in the premier city of the United States. The mission of the committee was to make available to service personnel the best of what New York City had to offer in the most wholesome atmosphere possible, steering military personnel away from the

seamy side of the city's life. A number of organizations of theater owners offered free tickets to service personnel in uniform, giving them the opportunity to see the best of American stage shows. Movie theater organizations also
gave free tickets to events at the famed Madison Square Garden. Museums
and churches opened their doors, and even the New York Public Library set
aside reading rooms. Restaurants offered discounts.[10] Private Harry Wilson
of the US Army Air Force Weather Service was on orders to go overseas, and
he went to New York City. There he visited the Public Center for the Armed
Forces near Times Square, where service personnel in uniform could make
a telephone call at a greatly reduced cost. He called his wife in Los Angeles,
California, and told her that he loved her and would be leaving for his assignment soon. He then sat in the well-appointed lounge and composed a letter
recounting their brief conversation and his feelings for her upon his departure.[11] These facilities offered by New York City, Philadelphia (which boasted a large, well-attended Stage Door Canteen), Los Angeles, and many other
cities greatly assisted the work of the Special Services Division, which could
never have afforded such opportunities.

By the summer of 1944, finances became a problem for Byron and the Special Services Division. The difficulty arose with the nature of Special Services
publications. Prior to the outbreak of the war in 1941, the army had produced training, technical, and field manuals in an accepted format and established a definite procedure for distribution of the material. The number of
manuals increased as the army expanded after 1940 and really exploded after
America's entry into the global conflict. Special Services literature did not
conform to accepted standards. It was found that "Special Services literature
[was] published in all sorts of formats, printed by the Government Printing
Office, and also by various private concerns, purchased out of various types of
funds and distributed by various means."[12] In October 1943, the War Department issued a pamphlet that recognized the problem and tried to introduce
a standardization in Special Services Division publications. However, many
publications had begun as civilian-donated material and then carried on by
the Special Services. For example, in 1943 a number of well-known Broadway
playwrights sponsored a contest for GI-written one-act plays, the first prize
being one hundred dollars. One hundred and sixteen submissions sent to the
Special Services officer of the Second Service Command were then given to
the playwrights, who judged them. The top-five winning plays were presented
on the Broadway stage in June and August, with all box-office receipts going to various funds for soldiers. The plays, combined into one booklet, *The
Army Play by Play,* were then published by the *Infantry Journal,* a private, well-
respected military publication, but the Special Services Division was respon-

sible for armywide distribution. The booklet was the eleventh volume in a series that included such titles as *Take It or Leave It: A Humorous Quiz Book* (1943) and *Comedy Acts and Minstrel Show Material* (1943), all distributed by Special Services. When the Publications Section of the entertainment branch was established in 1942, it consisted of one officer and three enlisted men, and by the end of 1944 there were three officers and nine enlisted men. Byron was in the process of trying to enlarge the section because of the expense and magnitude of publication distribution.

An area of entertainment that was not discussed at Special Services officers' conferences in 1942 and 1943 was that of hospital entertainment and morale activities for patients. The heavy combat in Europe and the Pacific produced a flood of wounded in hospitals in the United States and overseas. Traditionally, the American Red Cross had worked in the hospitals distributing reading material, candies, cigarettes, and the like, and while they continued to do so, the workload was heavy. The Special Services Division had to be involved in the hospitals because nowhere in the army was morale needed more than on the wards with the wounded. The Special Services published five basic guides to hospital entertainment based on the nature of the wards to be visited. It was one thing to provide for ambulatory and wheelchair-bound patients in large halls with bands, small USO camp shows, and theatrics, but it was difficult to go into the wards with the amputees, the blind, and the severely wounded. Before the entry of the United States in the war, the American Medical Association tied medical services to army morale, but no one could have expected the expansion of the Special Services' involvement with medical morale issues.[13]

The Special Services Division and the army hospitals had to work together to provide what was needed to do two things: have an ongoing recreational program that depended on the abilities of the soldier to participate and maintain the normal offerings of Special Services, including movie theaters, PXs, and Service Clubs. At the Welch Convalescent Hospital, in Daytona Beach, Florida, the commander of the hospital told each incoming convalescent GI, "Regardless of where you are headed, back to duty or civilian life, you're going to work hard while you're here—you're going to get back into soldier ways—and you're going to have fun, too."[14] At Welch the Special Services maintained a Service Club with a recreational hostess in charge who managed a soft-drink bar and a cafeteria and organized dances. There was also a movie theater and three PXs, one of which was an "infirmary PX" for those unable to walk to the exchanges. Brooke Army Hospital, in Fort Sam Houston, Texas, housed a large occupational therapy department that opened in January 1944 and an art department in the hospital's Convalescent Rehabilitation Training

Program. The departments dealt with combat-wounded GIs who were amputees and those who had lost use of limbs. Brooke Hospital also had a growing army medical technicians' school, which meant that Special Services had
to deal with healthy students, army doctors and nurses, as well as patients,
many of whom were in need of ongoing recreational and other Special Services offerings. The post Special Services maintained theaters as well as first-
run "ward" movies and in conjunction with the USO camp shows organized
smaller shows for those on wards who were unable to attend the larger shows
at the post's theater.[15] Hospitals in the European and Pacific theaters also had
a close relationship with Special Services, stressing GI shows, movies, recreational activities (which depended on the physical abilities of the wounded soldiers), USO shows, and dances. In the European theater hospitals, the
Special Services organized "novelty entertainment" that consisted of carnivals
"complete with everything but a shell game" that featured GI, French, British,
or Italian entertainers.[16]

The music branch of the Special Services Division became involved in music as a feature of "reconditioning" wounded GIs. The demand for music necessitated the creation of a hospital section within the music section, with
Lieutenant Guy Marriner as its chief. What Marriner did was to build on what
the Red Cross had been doing for several years, but he added a military di-
mension, stressing the building of morale for those who faced postwar civilian life as an amputee or as a severely disabled or neuropsychiatric veteran.
Music, Marriner reckoned, could also help prepare the healed soldier who was
physically capable of returning to military duties.[17]

With ever-increasing demands, the Special Services Division had to be
careful of exceeding the budget, and Byron resisted the temptation to pri-
oritize missions. Every section received an equal distribution of funds and
support. General Eisenhower had requested an increase in the number of
Special Services companies. General Mark Clark wanted the rest camps and
Special Services facilities in Rome expanded, and in 1945 General MacArthur insisted that Special Services be established in the liberated capital of
the Philippines. After D-Day, June 6, 1944, and the liberation of Rome only
two days before, the Special Services in the European theater turned its attention to getting the Special Services companies to France. In August 1944,
the liberation of Paris added an extra burden for Special Services and the
Army Exchange System because the city would become a magnet for GIs
who were lucky enough to be in rest areas and get a pass to visit the city.

Special Services companies crossed the English Channel a few weeks after
the Normandy beachhead was secured. They serviced the rest areas near the
beaches as best as they could, supplying recreational items, showing movies

when buildings were found that could house troops, and playing music for the troops. The companies were tied down while the fighting grew in intensity. On July 3 the First Army began a series of attacks through the infamous Normandy hedgerows. On July 18 Saint-Lô was taken, and Operation Cobra, the breakout offensive, began seven days later. By August 13 Allied forces commenced the offensive to close the Falaise-Argentan pocket, capturing a vast number of German troops. Paris was liberated on August 25, and the Special Services companies moved into the city a few days later to reorganize, resupply, and plan for future moves that depended on the pace of combat.

The Third Army, under the flamboyant and aggressive General George S. Patton, became operational and began rapid and successful attacks on August 1 toward the Franco-German border. The Special Services companies realized quickly that they could not keep pace with Patton's tanks. Every offensive operation, however, came to a halt on the first of September due to a lack of gasoline and basic supplies.

In England the remaining companies found that they were welcomed at the bases where the 82nd and 101st Airborne Divisions were stationed. Movies were shown to large crowds of tight-lipped paratroopers, and GI bands played constantly. Sergeant Don Malarkey of the 506th Parachute Infantry recalled that just before the paratroopers were assembled and restricted to their bases, he attended a concert by Major Glenn Miller's Army Air Force band. For decades after, Malarkey remembered this Special Services–sponsored concert before he and his buddies jumped into Holland on September 17.[18] The PXs moved in and set up beer bars for the soldiers waiting to load up into the C4 aircraft that would take them to drop zones in Holland. The main mission of Operation Market-Garden, the jump into Holland, and the attack by the British 30th Armed Corps, failed because the ultimate objective of taking the bridge across the Rhine River at Arnhem, Holland, itself failed due to the presence of two SS panzer divisions that quickly attacked, isolated the British paratroopers, and literally destroyed the British force in and near Arnhem. As late fall descended on Europe, the tempo of battle slowed down, and the Special Services companies could begin to serve the troops again.

The most popular of all Special Services activities was the constant showing of first-run Hollywood movies. Every unit in rest areas requested recreational equipment, especially footballs and decks of cards. A number of Special Services companies deployed to France, and each had a different set of circumstances. It is possible to follow two of the best-trained and most active of the companies: the 2nd and the 13th, both of which had training and seen service in England prior to D-Day, and both of which would be caught up in the great German Ardennes offensive of December 1944. The Special Services Division and the manuals that governed the companies stressed that the members of the companies had been trained as infantry, and often, until the surrender of Germany in May 1945, they came under enemy artillery and small-arms fire. The 13th company, activated at Fort Meade, Maryland, claimed to be the father of many of the Special Services companies—the 8th, 18th, 23rd, 24th, 25th, and 26th.[19] Between December 1942 and April 1943, the 13th sent more than five hundred soldiers to those companies; they became known as the companies that had the best-trained Special Services soldiers who also excelled at infantry skills. In England the company recognized early that theatrics, USO camp shows, recreational activities, and especially movies were what the GIs wanted. The PXs provided for comfort needs and set up beer halls. Only when troops were on extended training exercises did the Canteen-Exchange Sections function. For example, when airborne units began their tactical exercises, they parachuted onto drop zones (as they would do in Normandy and then Holland) far away from an established PX. There the Canteen-Exchange Sections would function. The same was true for those seaborne infantry units that moved to training areas along the English coast.

Once the Allies had secured the Normandy area, the 2nd and 13th deployed to France, where they served in the rest camps. There the personnel oversaw the distribution of balls, games, and decks of cards. The Exchange Section and the Library Section were the least productive, due to the quick establishment of the PX and the small number of books available. During the late-summer and fall campaigns of 1944, the weather was wet, slowly changing to cold and snow. Books did not fare well in such conditions, and only when the 13th found a permanent location in Belgium could the Library Section function to meet the GIs' heavy demand for books. The company also discovered that when near a US Army Air Force facility, the library needs were taken care of by the American Red Cross. The company commander stated that there were too many jobs within a company, and consequently those Library and Exchange Section soldiers should be cross-trained in other fields. The exchange soldiers were quickly grabbed up by the movie projectionists, or, if competent, they would become drivers. "The librarian, it turned out had nothing to do except be the leading stage technician, scenic designer and builder, costume creator, Platoon Artist, and featured performer in the shows," the company commander reported. It was not that GIs were anti-intellectual or illiterate. The average soldier carried his knapsack, a musette bag, a web belt with canteen first-aid pouch, bayonet, and ammunition pouches. He also had an M1 rifle or submachine gun and other weapons, and there was little room for anything else. Also, books would become badly damaged in the rain and snows.

In late 1944 the company arrived in Belgium, hoping for a permanent location to have a building for movies and theatrical shows. On the bitterly
cold morning of December 16, word reached the company that the Germans
had launched a major offensive in the Ardennes Forest. There was no time
for movies or musical shows as the German army smashed across the Allied
front. The 13th Company, which had proudly proclaimed its proficiency in
combat infantry skills, had their chance to prove it. Like many other Special
Services companies in northern Europe, the company manned outposts and
roadblocks. By 1945 the 13th Company would be established in a permanent
facility in a liberated town in Belgium.

The 2nd Special Services Company remained in the Normandy area longer
than the 13th, but as the armies pressed their attacks to the East, the company moved into Belgium, where it set up a recreational center in November.
Its location was south of the small town of Herve, near the city of Liège. Like
the 13th, the company began to organize recreational activities and athletic
games and set up an ongoing movie schedule. Just to the south of the company's location was the town of St. Vith, where the untested 106th Infantry
Division was located. The area to be covered by the 2nd Company was considered a "quiet area" where newly arrived American troops could acclimate
to the harsh winter climate in the Ardennes Forest and learn the duties of a
combat infantry division. In the region covered by the 2nd Company was the
99th Infantry Division, which had seen limited combat action. Northeast of
Herve was the town of Eupen, where the 13th Company had its headquarters
and most of its equipment. The Special Services companies in early December looked forward to the Christmas season in a quiet sector, and rumors
abounded that offensive combat operations might begin again in late February or March 1945. On the night of December 15, 1944, there were heavy
clouds, a light snowfall, and falling temperatures, and on the German side in
the dense Ardennes the officers and noncommissioned officers of the 6th SS
Panzer Army and the 5th Panzer Army finished final checks in preparation for
action at dawn, December 16.

Without warning the quiet sector became a major combat zone when the
Germans launched their offensive. The 106th Infantry was totally surprised,
and it collapsed as a combat division. Two regiments, 7,500 GIs, surrendered.
All along the line there was confusion, and as historian Stephen E. Ambrose
wrote, "It was every man for himself." Not every unit fell apart. The 2nd Infantry Division entered the line just prior to December 16 and fought well
and skillfully, and on December 19 the 101st Airborne marched into immor-
tality when it entered the major crossroads town of Bastogne, which it would
defend against massive, but uncoordinated, German attacks.

The Special Services companies had made a point of being trained as combat infantry as well as movie projectionists, band members, or USO camp show coordinators. December 16, 1944, was the time to prove it. The 2nd Company's 5 officers and 105 enlisted men were now infantrymen. Fifteen men occupied a roadblock with rifles and a machine gun. More soldiers formed a reserve, protecting the headquarters of the 5th Army Corps. On December 21, First Lieutenant Ronald J. Fraser was awarded the Purple Heart for wounds received in combat. The 2nd Company sent eleven trucks and a platoon to evacuate a ration and petrol dump to keep vital supplies from falling into the hands of the advancing panzers. Staff Sergeant Philip A. Pegnato, a motor sergeant, was awarded the Bronze Star Medal.[20]

Every Special Services soldier was expected to function as an infantryman. The 15th Special Services Company was in Holland with the headquarters of the Ninth Army on December 16, and though not directly involved with the Ardennes offensive, the 15th was part of the defensive plan of the army.[21] When the Special Services companies were being formed, General Byron stressed that when needed, the companies would put aside basketballs and shut down movie projectors, pick up M1 rifles and grenades, and fight. The Ardennes offensive proved that the concept was correct and those Special Services GIs would fight.

It was obvious that the war in Europe and Japan would go on well into 1945. The 12th Special Services Company began service on New Guinea, and as fighting ended there and on other islands, the company increased its activities. The main enemy was no longer the Japanese; it was now the torrential rains. By early May the company was unified in one camp and was attached to the Sixth Army headquarters for further combat operations. For several weeks the 12th Company inventoried and inspected personal and unit equipment, finding that the tropical heat, rains, and insects had taken their toll. Of primary importance was the condition of the movie projectors, screens, and generators because there were urgent requests for movies to be shown. This also necessitated an inspection of the films received from the United States to see if the transportation across the Pacific or the conditions on New Guinea had damaged the films. There were requests from units to begin softball- and baseball-league competition. The athletic technicians were tasked with coordinating with local engineer units for the building of several ball fields. The engineers were more than happy to oblige, and within a week games between units could begin. A softball league was established, and the first game pitted the 12th Company against the 98th Medical Battalion, with the 12th winning the game.

While the mission of the 12th Company to provide for the troops was being accomplished, the company began to experience a serious problem with the health of its own soldiers. On May 9 the first 12th Company GI was admitted to the hospital with dengue fever, and by May 12 six soldiers from the company were in the hospital with the same disease. On May 15 two platoons were alerted for deployment to other islands needing Special Services activities. One platoon went to New Britain and the other to the Admiralty Islands. The 12th Company was again split up and separated by hundreds of miles, a problem that affected every Special Services company in the Pacific theater. In the European theater the platoons of the Special Services companies were separated by a few miles, and they had established paved roads to move equipment. This would not be the case in the Pacific. No one in the 12th Company knew that their assignment to the Sixth Army would have important consequences, because the army would soon be relieved of duty in New Guinea and begin preparations for the invasion of the Philippine Islands. When conditions allowed, the 12th Company would be reunited in the Philippines. On October 30, 1944, American troops landed on Leyte. General MacArthur waded ashore with cameras rolling to tell the people of the Philippines, who had suffered terribly under Japanese occupation, that he had returned.

Duty for the 12th Company had become routine, with platoons rotating among the various islands, furnishing movies; coordinating for an army show, *Stars and Gripes,* which had, much to the distress of the GIs, no American girls; and providing dinner music for various units on New Guinea. A fairly well-stocked PX was opened, and men from the company assisted the exchange personnel as stockmen and clerks. The 3rd platoon, stationed on New Britain, worked with the 40th Infantry Division and helped the PX to provide ongoing ice cream sales. The 3rd platoon had problems because high winds kept aircraft carrying new movies from landing at a nearby airfield. A recreational center was built near the division headquarters, where enlisted men congregated in large numbers every night. On September 12 a beer ration of three cans or bottles per soldier was issued. The most interesting incident to occur for the platoon was when Private First Class Mc-Caigue was carried to the hospital unconscious. The medics realized that the soon-to-be Private McCaigue was simply drunk and not entitled to be listed as sick in the line of duty. So severe was his intoxication that it was decided to evacuate the patient. The other platoons of the company experienced much the same routine.

Toward the end of October it was obvious that major operations were near, and the 12th Company was to be replaced on New Guinea by the 6th Special Services Company. The 71st Evacuation Hospital and the Red Cross agreed to take over the work of the 12th until the 6th arrived in force. The 12th Special Services Company would be one of the first Special Services companies to go into the Philippines. On Christmas Day the companies, plus some WACs and soldiers from the 6th Ranger Battalion, formed a choir to entertain wounded GIs at the 78th and 165th Station Hospitals. The day-to-day tedium of New Guinea was certainly over as the campaign to liberate the Philippines had begun, and Special Services companies would play their role.

In the European theater, conditions were fluid as Allied forces recovered from the German attack in the Ardennes. Work in the large replacement camps went on at a rapid pace as soldiers poured into France to await orders that would assign the bulk of the troops to combat divisions. Special Services companies had to recover the equipment that was secured during the German Ardennes offensive and prepare to serve the troops in any way they could. Of great importance were the programs in the evacuation hospitals in France and the general hospitals in England. But there was an issue that would be difficult to resolve, and that centered on the city of Paris. The Special Services, Red Cross, and USO saw in the city a place where GIs could go when they were given leave from the rest camps. From experience it was clear that Paris would be a magnet for GIs, just as London had been, and in Rome there was a full menu of Special Services activities and tours. Paris, however, would be different. The problem rested with a major decision by Eisenhower's quartermaster general, John C. H. Lee, who commanded the Service of Supply for the European theater. Eisenhower was uncomfortable with Lee, and General Somervell did not like him at all because he was a pompous and pious man. His own troops, looking at the initials "J. C. H." Lee, said that his name was really "Jesus Christ Himself." In planning for the liberation of Europe, Eisenhower decided to bypass Paris and then surrounded it, allowing the German garrison there to simply wither on the vine until they surrendered. The planning was based on the number of troops required to liberate and occupy the city, and the amount of food and fuel required to supply civilians. By mid-August it was clear that fuel for the combat troops was in short supply and would possibly bring the Allied advance to a halt. The liberation of Paris was, then, not part of Eisenhower's plans, but in late August the French Resistance in the city attacked the German garrison, and a full-scale battle was at hand. Word had reached Allied headquarters that Hitler expected German forces to put down the insurrection with all severity and then literally reduce Paris to a smoldering heap of ruins. Eisenhower had to scrap his plans to bypass Paris, and he sent French and American troops into the city. The German commander had decided to ignore Hitler's orders to destroy the city, and consequently there was little damage. A few weeks after the liberation, General Lee decided to move the Service of Supply into the city without consulting Eisenhower, who simply could not afford the fuel to move it out of the city.

The Special Services, Red Cross, and USO found it difficult to obtain hotel rooms for the number of GIs who wanted to visit the city. As it was the headquarters of the Service of Supply, there were masses of supplies, including the cigarettes, candies, soaps, and the like that were the mainstays of the Special Services, exchanges, and the "PX supplies." A massive black market for pilfered goods sprang up in Paris. Also irritating was the appearance that supply troops stationed in Paris had the pick of exchange supplies. The most popular cigarette brands stayed in Paris, while the combat GIs got the unpopular off-brands. It was not a good situation for the Special Services and their civilian Allied organizations. Adding to the situation was the unwillingness of General Lee to work with the Special Services, the exchanges, and the newly formed Information and Education Division under General Osborn. General Somervell, as chief of the Army Service Forces, became highly irritated with Lee and continually admonished him to accept the morale-building organizations.[22] Somervell was greatly disturbed with the Service of Supply in Paris because he quickly realized the impact of quartermaster officers and enlisted men occupying 167 hotels in the city. Eisenhower and Somervell understood that the image of supply soldiers living in hotels, sleeping between clean sheets, drinking good wine, and smoking only the top-of-the-line cigarettes would have a detrimental effect on the GIs in muddy, cold foxholes who faced death every minute of the day.[23]

With the liberation of Paris, Osborn's division prepared for the troops a basic tourist guide to the city: "You'll find that the real Paris is not the Paris of night life and wild women. Instead, you will probably find it a city of great beauty and culture."[24] At no point did the guide address the availability of food or shelter in Paris, nor did it discuss sex and venereal disease. Prior to the invasion, American troops were given a guide to France that was explicit about prostitution and disease, as it was about shortages of food and soap.[25] Unfortunately, the decision to move the Service of Supply into Paris with its mass of supplies bred the conditions that led to increases in criminal activities (both GI and French) and prostitution. There were shortages in hotel rooms and dormitory space for GIs on leave from the front. To make matters worse, PX supplies would soon dry up for the troops in combat; many items such as cigarettes, shaving cream, and soap were stolen by the case from the army trucks carrying them to the East. These conditions would continue to exist after the conclusion of the war in Europe in 1945.

Sometimes things went well for the combat GIs and the Special Services. Corporal Kenneth K. Gowen's 69th Armored Field Artillery Battalion had been attached to the 14th Armored Division and in mid-December was brought off the line for rest and refitting before being attached to the 103rd Infantry Division in locations near Strasbourg, France. An unusual event occurred on December 18, when the commander of a nearby field hospital agreed with his nurses to hold a dance for the enlisted GIs of the 69th. It was after much thought that he allowed the dance to take place. The Special Services provided a loudspeaker system and current phonograph records and even found a jukebox to play music. Small food items were served, and the nurses decorated a small basketball court for the dance. Most of the nurses had civilian dresses and used perfume. Gowen, who never thought himself to be a good dancer, remembered the dance as one of the best moments of the war—dancing with an American girl. On Christmas Day the 69th was back in combat, but all Gowen could think about was the three-hour dance.[26] Very few combat GIs were that lucky, however. Technical Sergeant Charles Linzy received a Christmas package from a cousin in Little Rock. In it were several bars of soap and a carton of Lucky Strike cigarettes, a top-of-the-line brand. He wrote to his wife that the gift, which arrived two days before the Ardennes offensive, was greatly appreciated, especially because soap and top-brand cigarettes disappeared from the PX rations.[27]

An example of the folly of occupying Paris by the Service of Supply can be seen in the experience of Corporal Keith Winston of the 100th Infantry Division. The division was attached to the Seventh US Army in late October 1944 and was quickly sent into combat in the Vosges Mountains. The Service of Supply had established depots away from the city of Marseilles, which was known for criminal gangs. Inevitably, there was a black market in the city, but never on the scale of Paris. It took less than a week for PX rations to reach the troops, and the PX ration for one soldier was one pack of cigarettes and a candy bar per day. Winton told his wife that it had been five days between issues, and in one day he received five packs of cigarettes (a mix of brand and off-brand smokes) and five candy bars plus chewing gum, soap, tooth powder, and shaving cream. Corporal Winston wrote, "Knowing of the cigarette shortage back home, the boys joke about sending them back to the states."[28] Soldiers serving in northern France, Belgium, and Holland, dependent on supplies going through Paris, would not have joked about their situation.

The troops now fighting to liberate the Philippines would not be short of Special Services. The 12th Special Services Company was alerted for a major move, and all company activities were turned over to the Special Services officers who would continue to serve troops on New Guinea. On November 12 the company arrived at Leyte and set up a temporary camp near the town of San Jose. Within three days the company was established, with unit tents raised and a mess hall in operation. A volleyball court was started, and a large tent was designated as a recreational center. On the night of November 15 the company showed the first movie, but during the show an alert was sounded, a blackout was ordered, and an air raid by Japanese planes occurred. For the remainder of November the company had to contend with heavy tropical rains that curtailed all outside recreational activities. Like their Special Services brothers in the European theater, the 12th Company pitched in and helped organize and distribute PX rations to the troops engaged in combat against a staunch Japanese defense.

The 3rd platoon was attached to the 96th Infantry Division to provide Special Services. On November 24 the platoon was helping unload supplies when they came under heavy attack by Japanese aircraft. The next day the 3rd platoon moved twenty miles to begin work with the Special Services officer of the 96th Division. At the division headquarters they found, "[The] mess accommodations at the 96th is so bad that we decided to set up our own, so we went into headquarters for more rations and a stove."[29] The platoon had trained and experienced Canteen-Exchange Sections, and they had cooks available to make palatable meals. On the night of November 27 all units in the vicinity of headquarters were under alert because of the presence of Japanese infantry patrols in the area. The Special Services soldiers of the 3rd platoon shut down their movie projector, picked up their M1 rifles, and became combat infantrymen ready to fight. The early emphasis on infantry training and the continuation of that training paid off in the Pacific theater as it did in the European theater.

The value of the Special Services company had been proven overseas in the combat areas. In the United States, the Special Services Division had to adjust to a change from supporting units in training to replacement training, and the needs for the GIs were quite different. Such units as an infantry division formed in the United States and then sent overseas already had knowledge of their officers and NCOs, which one of their buddies was a chow hound or a heavy drinker, and were also bonded by common memories such as the beer party that the men of the 69th Infantry Division had at Camp Shelby, Mississippi, the day before the division left for their port of embarkation and then to combat in France and Germany. The replacement training camps by 1944 were filled with soldiers who had no real idea what unit they would go to once in the combat theaters. They would not go, for example, as a member of a rifle squad that had been together since the first day of training. The building of morale was difficult, and this placed a great deal of pressure on the offerings of Special Services such as the enlargement of Service Clubs, PXs, cafeterias,

and the like. The activities of the off-post civilian organizations were of ines-
timable value to Byron and the Special Services Division.

Meghan K. Winchell, in her study of the USO in World War II, wrote, "uso
[*sic*] hostessing and maintaining morale was gendered emotional work because as the uso understood, while hostesses inhabited uso space, they would
remind soldiers of their hometown 'girl' or wife." At no time was this as important as it was in late 1944 into 1945 when soldiers were not a part of a distinct unit. A vast number of civilian volunteers worked with the army to raise
morale. At the University of Wisconsin, Mary Ann Reed majored in speech
and theater and decided to volunteer to help at Truax Army Air Field Hospital near Madison, Wisconsin. She felt that her university major would be
of value in entertaining the sick and recovering wounded, and volunteering
would also present a good opportunity to meet soldiers. There were service-
club dances, and there were times when she visited the wards where many of
the troops were in wheelchairs. "The wheelchair patients just wanted some-
one to sit and talk," she recalled. For Mary Ann Reed, the war was no longer
just a matter of ration stamps, war-bond drives, and few male students at the
university. She remembered, "I did not realize before I arrived in the Truax
area just how wounded some of the audience would be."[30] Being a speech and
theater major, she participated in the USO show featuring the famed movie
actor Edmond O'Brien. Given the demands on the Special Services by mid- to
late 1944, the work provided by a university-trained, intelligent volunteer was
valuable beyond measure.

Volunteering knew no sectional boundaries. While Mary Ann Reed worked
at Truax Field in Wisconsin, Maralyn Howell was a student at the University of Mississippi in Oxford. The university is in the northern part of the
state, and Memphis, Tennessee, the closest city, was more than seventy miles
away over crude two-lane roads at that time. There was a large number of
Army Specialized Training Program students at the university in 1944. Maralyn Howell, its first female student-body president, gave serious effort to providing for the morale of the ASTP soldiers. In conjunction with the dean of
women, she convinced a wary university administration that the ASTP GIs
should be considered part of the university. Dances were organized and held
in the gymnasium under the football field's bleachers. The soldiers became a
part of the university, and since football had been suspended for the war, they
organized football teams based on their companies and played against each
other wearing the red and blue colors of the University of Mississippi. Morale
was maintained for the ASTP troops, who hailed from every section of the
nation. It was thought that the ASTP students would be sent to the technical
branches of the army, and when the army began phasing out the program, it

was believed that the soldiers would go into the engineer branch. The regular students and most of the ASTP did not know that the vast majority would be assigned to the combat infantry. While they were at the university, the morale of the ASTP students was maintained without the presence of a Special Services officer.[31]

General Byron of the Special Services Division and Colonel Frank Kerr of the Army Exchange System had to be pleased with the progress made by their respective activities. The concept of the Special Services companies proved to be a great contribution to the war effort by providing for the troops and, when the situation demanded, by picking up their weapons and manning outposts, often under enemy fire. Several Special Services soldiers were decorated with the Bronze Star. Some things looked good in the field manual, such as the Canteen-Exchange Sections of the company. They functioned in training areas in the United States, but proved unworkable in combat, especially since the army decided on sending free "PX supplies" to the troops. The companies were so well thought of that General Eisenhower strongly suggested that more companies be formed. Special Services reacted well to the change from unit training to replacement training, and also the consolidation of training on a select number of posts, which meant enlarging the number of Special Services hostesses and expanding Service Clubs, gymnasiums, guesthouses, and cafeterias on those posts. The year 1945 would provide new challenges for the Special Services Division and the Army Exchange System.

9

Aftermath, 1945–48

On February 24, 1945, two enlisted men from the 2nd Special Services Company joined the 112th Infantry Regiment of the 28th Infantry Division to show movies to the troops resting from heavy combat. The Special Services officer told Technician Fourth Class Backmurski that the troops would welcome movies and the two GIs should find a place to show them. Near the village of Schoneseiften they found a wrecked barn that would provide some shelter and a wall against which they would put their screen. They went to work setting up their generator and telling the troops that there would be a first-run movie that night. What they did not know was that several hundred yards away were German artillery forward observers. The movie started, and German artillery fired on the barn, causing casualties and shaking up two Special Services soldiers. Two days later another projection team found another barn, and the Germans fired mortars at that barn while mortars of the 112th Infantry fired at the Germans, who were about five hundred yards away. At the 2nd Company headquarters at Eupen, Belgium, it became clear that the enemy realized that when the Special Services team arrived with generators, there would be a concentration of American GIs, a tempting target for an enemy that was yet to be beaten.[1]

The commander of 2nd Company recorded that from March 14 to March 16, the projectionists showed movies to units of the 2nd Infantry Division at Breisig, Germany. The company was the first Special Services unit to show movies on both sides of the Rhine River. A few days later Technician Fourth Class Raymond A. Reinhart was awarded the Bronze Star for his actions during the Ardennes offensive in December 1944. In the monthly report for the

160

2nd Company, the commander noted that a million movies had been shown to GIs from the Normandy area to Germany. A few men had been wounded, and several had been decorated for their service.[2]

In the Pacific the 12th Special Services Company continued its work on Leyte and had the experience of having the four platoons of the company about twenty miles apart. That was a new feeling because in the islands they were often hundreds of miles away from each other. On Luzon, however, the company was in proximity to Japanese infantry and sustained enemy air raids. There was a feeling that Manila was an objective that would eventually be taken, and it would take many more battles to defeat the Japanese. On the other hand, in Europe the troops felt that one more offensive would end Hitler's Thousand-Year Reich.

The 18th Company in the China-Burma-India theater was in need of assistance because of the magnitude of the workload and the distances to be covered between platoons. The Library Section of the platoons had great difficulty distributing books and decided to combine their efforts with the troops organizing PX rations that were scheduled to be distributed to outlying areas once a month. The main base and the headquarters of the 18th Company were stationed at Assam, India, and served the units building the Ledo Road into China. Platoons operated 175 to 245 miles from headquarters. The theatrical sections put together a GI show that toured the Ledo Road and put on forty shows in forty-eight days. At the headquarters the company operated a popular radio station that featured big band music, "hillbilly" music, and American comedy and drama shows. The unit coordinated with the Red Cross to provide shows for army hospitals. It was a heavy schedule for the company. Assistance came when the 36th Special Services Company arrived in the theater of operations and began to work more than a 300-mile stretch of the Ledo Road. The 18th Company had arrived in India in mid-1943, and the 36th deployed to the China-Burma-India theater in March 1944.

An activity report from the 18th Company indicated that conditions on the Ledo Road were difficult. Captain Richard W. Conway, commanding, stated, "The need for Special Services is great. At no place along the entire road are living conditions themselves conducive to high morale. The road itself is cut out of the jungle and out of the mountains." Conway went on to report that "rations of necessities" left Calcutta, but were hijacked or simply left by the roadside. Cigarettes were limited to one carton per month. The Canteen-Exchange Sections ceased to function, and those soldiers went to work for the main PX. Captain Conway was informed when shipments were ready to depart from Calcutta, and he sent an armed section to guard the items for the base exchange and the PX supplies for the troops working along the Ledo

Road. At the end of his report Conway informed the Special Services Division that the exchange and Special Services were acting as one unit and that the Ledo Road operation was so vast that one company could not supply special activities to even a minority of the troops.[3] Master Sergeant Elmer Franzman of the 329th Service Group stationed at Assam base expressed his frustration when he wrote to his parents in Indiana that he needed razor blades, toothpaste, and Vaseline oil. As he wrote, the PX had none of these items.[4] If Franzman at the main camp at Assam had serious shortages, one can only imagine the needs of the troops working on the Ledo Road. Finally, the 36th Special Services Company arrived in India, and a good deal of the stress was taken off the 18th Company. Even with two Special Services companies in the China-Burma-India theater, their efforts and the work of the exchanges were not enough to support all of the troops.

The work of the Special Services Division by late 1944 and well into 1945 cost a great deal of money, a fact not lost on General Byron and the War Department. The vast majority of Special Services' efforts were focused on the three major theaters of operations, but funds were also allocated for service in smaller posts in West Africa, the Pacific Islands, and elsewhere.

A good example of what was expected outside of the three major theaters was the two air bases in Brazil. The United States Air Forces South Atlantic demanded Special Services. This meant, for the permanent troops, the Service Club with recreational activities and equipment, movie theaters, and cafeterias. For transient troops there also had to be facilities because it was never certain when aircraft would be available to transport them to their new post or back home. Transient troops were required to remain on the bases, and Special Services had to be available. The Service Club, cafeterias, and movies were available, and at Belem Air Base the movies were free to transients. The Post Exchange described itself: "Even on its quiet days, [the PX] looks like Macy's basement on bargain day." The base guide stated that American cigarettes were rationed, but there was a large selection of Brazilian cigars available. Calfskin wallets and handbags, dolls, jewelry with semiprecious stones, and Brazilian silk stockings were on sale. The Army Exchange System operated an establishment on a par with any modern airport duty-free store.[5] The PX was a profit-making organization that made the exchange self-supporting. The Special Services activities were not profit making and were dependent on what funds the Special Services Division could allocate.

For the fiscal year of 1945 the Special Services Division had a budget of $42.5 million, and Congress saw fit to raise that sum for fiscal year 1946 to a record $49 million. The cost of supplies, however, was rising, especially for the three theaters of war. The consolidation of training bases in the United

States in 1944 meant that Special Services had to be enlarged at the replacement training centers, but that could be offset by downsizing the Special Services activities at training bases that were now much smaller or scheduled for closure. The Special Services Officers Training School at San Luis Obispo, California, was also closed, and all training shifted to the school at Washington and Lee University in Virginia. The problem of costs continued, and some programs had to be canceled. One such program was the V Disk, a small plastic disk that would record a soldier's thoughts and then be sent to loved ones back home. In mid-1944 the V Disk program was discontinued because of cost and the need for plastics for other war manufacturing. General Byron agreed to its discontinuation.

To better facilitate the missions of the Special Services Division, the 1944 War Department issued Memorandum W 35-44, *Basis of Issue of Special Services Items Supplied on Overseas Requisitions,* which regularized the shipment of equipment for the Special Services activities. First, overseas theater commanders had to ensure that equipment such as balls, movie projectors, generators, and the like be used only for the morale and welfare of the enlisted troops. The theater commander's staff officers, especially the Special Services officers, had to consolidate what was needed by the fiscal quarters and estimate how much it would cost. Those requisitions had to be submitted sixty days in advance of the following quarter. The War Department informed the theater G1 and Special Services officer how much money was available, and the consolidated requisition had to stay within that allocation. Movie projectors, generators, and films had to be requested from the Signal Corps, a situation disliked by General Byron, although it took some pressure off the Special Services Division budget.[6]

Also of help was the nonprofit organization Editions for the Armed Services, Inc. They produced paperback books, known as "council books," with thirty titles being published per month. They were shipped overseas, and one set of thirty books was issued for every 150 enlisted men and one set for each large hospital ward. The cheaply produced council books were a great success and were eagerly sought by the troops because they were lightweight and easy to carry, and, being paperback, no one worried much if they were damaged by the elements. Magazines such as *Life* and others like *Time* and detective or movie magazines were not included and had to be purchased through the exchange system.[7]

The War Department memorandum then addressed the costs of the most requested recreational items to be purchased for overseas use. For example, an archery set cost $8.00, boxing gloves (one of the most requested items) cost $6.00 per set, and fishing equipment ran $10.00 for a set (such equipment for troops in the United States had to be personally purchased or rented). The most requested items were footballs ($3.70 each), baseballs ($4.40 per six), and baseball mitts ($3.25 each). Artists' materials were limited, with most going to hospitals, and theatrical scenic and lighting equipment was restricted.[8]

War Department Memorandum W 35-44 went into effect on May 6, 1944, one month before D-Day in Europe. This was followed up by War Department guidance (Circular 344, dated August 22, 1944) that stated that no recreational equipment could be sent to colleges or universities where the Army Specialized Training Program would soon end. The Special Services Division would coordinate with the major service commands in the United States for recreational materials for the training camps and the permanent parties stationed at the camps. Overseeing this was the Kansas City Quartermaster Depot, which furnished to the services commands and the Special Services Division what funds were used and what moneys were available. What happened to the recreational equipment used on a training base that was now to be closed due to the consolidation of training at a few replacement centers? The circular required that units being reassigned to the new bases inventory, pack up, and transport recreational equipment. That which could not be transported would be turned over to the service command for redistribution.[9] These publications caused the Special Services Division to designate a chief of the supply, and in turn the chief had three subsections—plans, distribution, and contracts. *Cost-effectiveness* and *economy* became watchwords for the Special Services. By late 1944 the main question at General Byron's headquarters was basically whether the Special Services Division could stay within its budget.

Going into 1945 it appeared obvious that the war in Europe would probably end before the war in the Pacific. The disciplined German army could inflict casualties and defend positions with skill, but after the Ardennes offensive of December 1944 failed, with heavy losses in armor and infantry, the ability of the Wehrmacht to mount a serious counterattack was gone. Fighting continued throughout January 1945, and in February Allied forces were poised to cross the Rhine River into the heartland of the Third Reich. On February 23 the Ninth Army attacked across the Roer River toward the Rhine, and on March 9 their 9th US Armored Division seized a bridge across the Rhine at Remagen. The stage was then set for major operations across the Rhine with an assault across the river with an airdrop of the British 6th Airborne Division and the American 17th Airborne Division called Operation Varsity, on March 24. This was followed by the crossing of the river by the Seventh US Army near Worms and the crossing of the Third US Army on March 27 near the city of Oppenheim.

The speed of the Allied armies in moving across Germany had its effect on the Special Services. Each company had its own allocation of trucks and other motor vehicles, and they had to compete for gasoline and oil with the combat units. Priority went to those units in battle. To their credit, most of the companies obtained what fuel and rations were needed to carry on their missions, and when combat units rested, the companies set up movies in buildings, if any remained usable, or in barns. The 13th Special Services Company was everywhere it could be, despite the possibility of attack by local Hitler Youth or the Volkssturm, the local last-ditch militia. Mainly, the companies discarded the idea of the Canteen-Exchange Sections, and those soldiers helped the exchange officers and quartermasters put together the PX supplies. There was no need to even unpack the theatrical equipment, but if in a location for several days, there were impromptu bands put together. In a two-week period the 13th Special Services Company showed movies to units such as the 167th Chemical Smoke Company, 122nd Evacuation Hospital, 49th Medical Battalion, 4032 Quartermaster Truck Company, units of the 94th Infantry Division, plus many other units that they could reach with projectors, screens, and generators.[10] There was an overwhelming demand for the popular council books, and the 13th Company recorded that in a period of two weeks to a month in May 1945, it distributed twenty-five thousand such books.

On April 29 the German forces in Italy surrendered, and the next day the Seventh US Army captured the city of Munich, the birthplace of the Nazi Party. General George Patton's Third US Army occupied Pilsen, Czechoslovakia, on May 6; just three days later the war in Europe ended. Immediately, the Special Services companies moved to locations to support the combat troops. Throughout the European theater of operations the great question was "Now what?" That question had great impact on the morale of the troops throughout the ETO from Germany to Italy, and it also meant that the Special Services companies and the Special Services and exchange officers at every level of command had to be innovative and aggressive in their morale-maintaining mission.

PFC Keith Winston, a combat medic in the 100th Division, wrote to his wife, "All the boys are conjecturing—some say it means occupation, others say CBI [China-Burma-India]; still others, the states. We'll see." Sergeant Don Malarkey, Company E, 506th Parachute Infantry Regiment of the 101st Airborne Division, was in Belgium recovering from a wound when the news came that the German army had surrendered, and in his mind was the worry that the division would be sent to fight against Japan. The Screaming Eagles of the 101st had been alerted to go to the Pacific theater of operations. Tech Sergeant Charles B. Linzy of the 459th Mobile Anti-Aircraft Battalion had been at Normandy, entered Paris with the French 2nd Armored Division, fought in the Battle of the Bulge, was awarded the Bronze Star, and at the end of the war was in Lauterbach, Germany. He wrote to his wife, "I hope that I am not in the bunch that has to go on over to the Pacific area." Four days later Linzy wrote to his wife that the Special Services put on a show starring Mickey Rooney and other entertainers. He thought it was good entertainment for the troops.[11] Rooney, a famous Hollywood star, was a GI himself, serving in the 3rd Special Services Company. The "Now what?" question weighed on the minds of the GIs in Europe.

When it became apparent that Nazi Germany was near the end, discussions began in the War Department and the Special Services Division about the future of the Special Services company. There were two possible courses of action: the companies assigned to Europe could be brought back to the United States and demobilized, or they could be brought back to the United States, given monthlong furloughs, and then reassigned to the Pacific theater of operations. It would be necessary to leave a few companies in Germany to serve the troops as they prepared to return home. The army had occupied portions of Germany on the west bank of the Rhine River from 1918 to 1923, but that experience offered few lessons learned. In May 1945 the destruction in Germany was immense; many great cities were masses of rubble and their populations without food, water, or shelter. The political infrastructure was tied to the Nazi Party and was certainly suspect. Farm fields were littered with the aftermath of heavy combat, and it was late in the season to plant crops in the fields not touched by combat. To complicate the situation, the sector of Germany under Allied control was overrun by refugees fleeing from the Soviet onslaught and by released camp inmates, most of them without official papers of identification. Many of the American combat units found themselves peacekeepers in Germany and Austria, a mission for which they were ill-prepared. This placed the Special Services and exchanges in a difficult situation because there was a dire need for entertainment for the troops and a demand for PX items. A carton of cigarettes could be traded for cash, sex, or valuables, and although the exchanges introduced a strict rationing system, an active black market existed.

The number of Special Services companies had been restricted to forty. In 1945, however, the Special Services finally decided to activate the first all-female Special Services company. On June 6, 1944, the WAC director in the European theater approved a plan to activate a company, but the conditions of heavy combat after D-Day pushed the authorization to the back burner. Captain Ruby Jane Douglas was selected to command what would become the 1st WAC Special Services Company. The idea of the company came to the attention of Ovita Culp Hobby, director of the Women's Army Corps in the War Department, who added her energy and political connections to the formation of the company. With everyone's agreement, the plan was approved and in January 1945 was passed on to Lieutenant Colonel Anna W. Wilson, WAC director in the European theater.[12] Captain Douglas was then tasked with selecting the 5 officers and 109 women for the company. The process of selection was a long one, consisting of background checks, proof of proficiency in the area in which the soldier would work, and, last, an in-depth interview in London. There were a few male officers at the headquarters of the Supreme Allied Command who did not like the idea of an all-female unit, but the British, in their dire need, utilized a large number of females, and, frankly, the ETO was in real need of more entertainment and recreation in peacetime Europe. It had always been known that soldiers with too much time on their hands and the availability of alcohol could present serious discipline problems. This was the observation that Raymond Fosdick made in World War I, and it was just as true in Germany and Austria in 1945.

The War Department decided that the twenty Special Services companies would be reduced to five after VE Day. The WAC Special Services company, however, was retained for the ETO because it would replace one that would be redeployed to the Pacific. "The purpose of the First WAC Special Services Company [is] . . . to benefit mutually the WAC and the EM of the Armies of Occupation." This first all-female company was a pilot project "to test the feasibility of activating additional WAC Special Service Companies."[13] On September 15, 1945, the company was assigned to Headquarters, Third United States Army Special Orders Number 256, by order of General George S. Patton. The headquarters of the WAC company was first at Bad Tolz in Bavaria and then assigned to Salzburg, Austria. With a full roster of officers and enlisted women, the sections of the company could go to work. First Lieutenant Geneva H. Fober, a graduate of the Special Services School at Washington and Lee University, was selected as the first commander of the unit.

The Third Army had jurisdiction over an area of Germany and Austria that was scenic and had picturesque towns and villages untouched by the ravages of war. The Special Services officer and his staff at the Third Army became a major tourist organization. Tours offered to GIs included Munich, Garmisch, Linderhof (King Ludwig II's castle), Oberammergau (site of a famed Passion play), Chiemsee (lakes), Dachau (concentration camp), Bad Reichenhall (famed mineral baths and scenery), and other places in Bavaria and Austria.[14] The Special Services officers of the subordinate corps had to submit a complete roster of the troops taking the tours and would provide rations for their own soldiers. The Special Services officer of the Twentieth Corps operated a hotel in the Garmisch area where soldiers could find overnight billets. (Incidentally, the United States Army still maintains a vacation facility in the area today.)

Tourism was not restricted to Germany. In southern France the Special Services worked in conjunction with the American Express Company to offer tours to Nice, Cannes, Grasse, Cap d'Antibes, and other vacation areas.[15] Paris, however, remained the most visited tourist sight in France. The official guide, written by General Osborn's Information Division, stated, "You'll find that the real Paris is not the Paris of night life and wild women."[16] That was fine for the academically influenced Information Division, but it was not reality. For example, the "Allied Troops Night-Club Coliseum, for Enlisted Personnel in Uniform Only" sounded official, but in reality it was a nightclub opened by enterprising Frenchmen and offered champagne by the bottle and cognac by the drink.[17] By August 1945 a tourist weekly magazine, *Parisian Weekly Information,* was distributed free of charge to the hotels and Special Services offices throughout Paris. This well-printed English-language magazine told GIs where museums and theaters were and what they offered. There was a section that advertised famed Parisian cabarets.[18] To bring some focus to Paris, the Seine Section, European theater of operations, Advanced Base, published a booklet for visiting soldiers that indicated what was available for them, especially a major PX system featuring such items as perfumes, novelty jewelry, and "ladies accessories." In September 1945, there were fourteen clubs for GIs and ten thousand beds for visiting soldiers. The Special Services officer had a fairly large staff to organize beds, tours, and meals for GIs. Interestingly, the well-printed color guide had a drawing of the Coliseum GI Night Club.[19] By the fall of 1945 the Red Cross and the USO had opened facilities and clubs for the visiting GIs. With the emphasis on providing for soldiers in the ETO, it was slowly becoming clear that troops might not be redeployed to the United States as quickly as the War Department believed.

The United States Forces Austria, under the command of General Mark Clark, would not be outdone by Special Services in France or Germany. In 1945 Special Services, USFA, published a color booklet called *Rest Resorts All over Austria.* "Officers and men of the United States Forces in Austria they're yours! Austria's most famous resorts: Hotels, Castles and Villas, located in the most choice spots midst Austria's scenic beauty. . . . It is my personal wish that each and every one of you have an opportunity to visit one of these fine USFA Rest Resorts." The Special Services took over many of the ski resorts in Austria and offered cheap rooms and meals. Each resort had the standard movies, exchanges, and all aspects of recreational activities, from the ski slopes and horseback riding to dances. The jewel of the USFA resorts was the famous ski resort of Kitzbühel. For those not interested in ski slopes, there were tours of Vienna with local expert guides.[20] It appeared that American soldiers had nothing better to do than visit German or Austrian resorts or Parisian cabarets. These were troops with too much time on their hands, too easy access to liquor, and far too many willing women. The PXs had precious commodities such as cigarettes, candy, soap, and other items that had vanished from store shelves in France, Germany, and Austria. This situation was dangerous to civilian laws and military discipline, and the more the Special Services could offer, the better for occupation forces.

Most of Paris, southern Bavaria, and Austria had escaped the ravages of war, and few of their buildings had been destroyed. The same, however, could not have been said about Manila. Captain William Hurt, a medical officer with the 33rd Infantry Division, wrote to his parents in Tennessee, "I drove down to Manila. . . . It looks just like it does in the pictures you have seen and it will take several years for them to clean up the place. To sum up my impression it's just a big, smelly, pile of twisted steel and rubble of what was once a beautiful city. . . . I didn't buy a single souvenir: everything is terribly high and the things I liked I couldn't possibly reach." After his trip Hurt and several other doctors went to a Special Services showing of the movie *A Song to Remember*. Hurt never returned to the city of Manila. It had been a hard and bloody road for the GIs to reach Manila. Corporal Jack Binnion of the 128th Infantry regiment had fought in New Guinea and now was in combat in the Philippines. The Special Services company with the 128th continually tried to show movies, but he wrote to his sweetheart in Kentucky, "More air raids tonight last night to prevent us from having movies."[21]

On February 13, 1945, the First Cavalry Division entered the ruined city of Manila. Three days later there was an airborne and an amphibious assault on Corregidor Island. It would take almost another three months before General MacArthur could declare Luzon secured by American troops. Special Services and the exchanges gravitated to Manila, searching for intact buildings to open PXs and Service Clubs. The Special Services opened Coca Cola and Hamburger Bar Number 1 in short order, and it was filled to capacity by GIs and WACs every day. For more than a year First Lieutenant Margaret Katherine Hisgen had requested overseas duty with the US Army Air Forces, and in the spring of 1945 she was on a transport ship off the shores of the Philippine Islands. As an American girl she had every opportunity to dance and found, as she called him, a cute naval lieutenant junior grade to visit the sites with. Hisgen was disappointed that Manila was so destroyed, offering little nightlife except for the Special Services dances for officers. At any rate, she was overseas in a theater of operations.[22] The Special Services dances for enlisted men had a large number of well-chaperoned Philippine girls who enjoyed the selection of snacks and sandwiches as much as they did the music of American big bands provided by the music sections of the Special Services company. The Special Services worked with the exchanges to provide free PX goods to released American prisoners of war.

For the troops in the Philippines, the most feared three words were *invasion of Japan*. The infantry had faced the Japanese fighters in clearing the islands, and word of US Marine casualties at Iwo Jima and Okinawa filtered through the islands. Reorganization, refitting, integrating replacements into units, and training for battle occupied their time. On August 14, 1945, word quickly passed through the ranks that after two atomic bombs had been dropped on Hiroshima and Nagasaki, Japan had surrendered, and VJ Day was celebrated. The question the troops asked constantly was when they would go home. The 11th Airborne Division moved quickly as an occupation force, followed by the First Cavalry Division. The 5th and 6th Special Services Companies were alerted to deploy to Japan once security was established. The 5th was located at Nagoya and the 6th near Tokyo.

By the end of 1945 the 5th Company had set up a film service for their movie sections that repaired projectors and sound systems. The commander of the 5th requisitioned the Nagoya public hall for a movie theater and the athletic stadium for baseball and football games. The company supplied a qualified football coach to the 98th Infantry Division to prepare for a game between the Nagoya base camp and the division on Christmas Day 1945. The first platoon sent members to the Sixth Army athletic training school at Osaka.[23] The 6th Special Services Company remained near Tokyo and performed the same duties as the 5th Company. The 6th Company would remain in Japan until 1948, when Special Services began to phase out the companies and bring in civilians to run the Special Services under the control of the Special Services officer.

In Europe, meanwhile, there was uncertainty about the fate of the Special Services companies. The plan was to reduce the number of companies from about twenty to five companies to serve the troops in Germany, Austria, and Italy. The occupation of those areas would prove to be more difficult than the War Department had believed; the requirements of rebuilding a shattered Germany and the threat of all of Europe collapsing into political anarchy was very real. The problem of organizing the vast number of displaced persons (DPs) would take years to solve. In Germany and Austria there was great difficulty in vetting the population and searching for war criminals who had simply melted into the general populations. There was no precedent for what the army had to do.

The 3rd Special Services Company, for example, began its ETO assignments in Iceland in August 1942, was sent to England, and crossed into France in July 1944. On VE Day the 3rd Company was in Schwalbach, Germany. It had been awarded three campaign stars: Ardennes, Normandy, and Central Europe. In July 1945 the company moved to a new headquarters in Pilsen, Czechoslovakia. After a brief attachment to the Third US Army, the company was ordered to report to the 7729th Special Services Entertainment Center "to provide enlisted personnel for the production and administration of all Soldier Shows in the European Command." The company then set up auditions for soldiers who claimed to have talent. By June 1947 the company was authorized to hire DPs and Germans to assist in putting on soldier shows. On June 20, 1948, the 3rd Company was inactivated—the last of the Special Services companies of World War II. In listing its accomplishments, Captain Edwin H. McDowell, the last commander, recounted the building of an officers' club and a club for enlisted men that provided dances. a cafeteria, and floor shows. The Army Exchange System worked with the company in constructing a good PX using civilian personnel. Of interest, the 3rd Company established a German Youth Activities Center in Assmannshausen, with baseball, soccer, boxing, and boating programs. The center also taught German youth the benefits of a democratic political system, hoping to wipe away what was taught to those who lived under Nazism. The last movie was shown on June 21, 1948.[24]

With the deterioration of relations between the United States and its Allies and the Soviet Union, it was clear that American troops would remain in Europe, and the Special Services would continue to be of service to American troops in the United States and overseas. The wartime Special Services Division and the Army Exchange System had far exceeded 1941 expectations, but what had happened to General Frederick Osborn? In a postwar interview Osborn made it clear that his interests were in education and information rather than recreation. General Somervell was unhappy with the pace of the development of recreational programs for the troops, and he proposed to Osborn that the Morale Services Division be divided into two parts. General Byron would direct the newly created Special Services Division, and Osborn would direct the Information and Education Division. Somervell's decision was a wise one, because Byron, the businessman, had created a successful worldwide system of GI stores that all soldiers and airmen relied on. Osborn revealed that his staff was upset over the split, but there was work to do. Simply put, Osborn, a brilliant academic, was a fish out of water in dealing with the realities of an army engaged in a global war. There was a small Education Section that offered correspondence courses for GIs, but Osborn wanted the program expanded. Osborn convinced Professor Francis Trow Spaulding, dean of Harvard University's School of Education, to accept the rank of colonel and direct the United States Armed Forces Institute (USAFI), basically a correspondence-course school.[25] Spaulding reached an agreement with the University of Wisconsin to be the center of USAFI, offering at first sixty-four correspondence courses ranging from basic English grammar to history, science, business, mathematics, and more.[26] The courses were written for soldiers. For example, the textbook *English Grammar: A Self-Teaching Course* presented this sentence that the soldier had to correct: "Any Soldier which has ever gone to Fort Bragg knows what the horse cavalry does to help the flowers around the barracks."[27] USAFI was a great success and expanded as the war ended.

Osborn was especially proud of *Yank,* which reached a circulation of about 2.5 million copies bought by GIs. He brought to Washington the filmmaker Frank Capra and gave him the responsibility of producing films, the most notable being *Why We Fight* and *Our Ally England.* In 1944 Secretary of War Henry Stimson worked closely with Osborn to ensure that there was no political influence in any army publications. This suited Osborn, because as he later put it, "There wouldn't have been any politics anyway, because I wasn't interested." In 1944 Osborn was greatly pleased to see Congress pass the Servicemen's Readjustment Act, better known as the GI Bill. General Osborn's Information Section printed and distributed millions of guides to the bill and what benefits veterans could expect after their discharge. Osborn had pushed for more information for the troops, and by 1944 there was a Troop Information and Education (TI&E) program for troops who were not in direct combat. The information office sent out to units material for lectures or discussions, including ball scores, current events, and selected military information about the progress in the theaters of operation.[28] While Osborn was pleased with the TI&E program, success depended on the emphasis command put on it and the enthusiasm of the presenter.

After World War I, American soldiers attended French and British universities on an individual basis. GI education would follow that example when practical, but there was a need to consolidate soldier education. In 1945 the education branch founded the Biarritz American University on the Bay of Biscay, away from the distractions of Paris or the French Riviera. The army and Special Services had already established the United States Riviera Recreational Area with headquarters in Nice under the command of Brigadier General Riley P. Ennis. The area covered Nice, Cannes, Cap d'Antibes, and Grasse, all of which were internationally known as vacation areas with beautiful beaches and fine cuisine. The area, known as USRRA, was strictly controlled and patrolled by the American military police. Enlisted personnel were quartered in Nice, while Cannes was reserved for officers. Leaves to the USRRA were restricted to seven days, and the army provided mess facilities for the troops. A GI bar was established in Nice, and the American Red Cross offered a large number of sightseeing tours as well as operating a large club and cafeteria for enlisted men. The exchange system established a huge PX at the Palais des Fêtes, offering a large selection of local gifts, and the PX included a beer bar, cafeteria, perfume shop, and barbershops. USRRA was fertile ground for the Special Services, exchange system, Red Cross, and even the Education Division, which maintained an active USAFI center.[29]

The selection of Biarritz was a wise one. The city was known worldwide for its beaches, casinos, and beautiful spacious public buildings. Osborn's Information and Education Division arranged for three army universities in Europe, one in England and two on the Continent. Biarritz was the largest of the three, enrolling four thousand GIs for terms of three months. Two officers were responsible for education in Europe: Brigadier General Paul H. Thompson, chief of the Information and Education Division in Europe (directly responsible to General Osborn), and Brigadier General Samuel L. McCroskey, who located the army university at Biarritz after close communication with city officials. Within three months the Biarritz American University opened its doors to male and female students in August, a remarkable accomplishment because McCroskey had to find buildings for living accommodations, classrooms, and Special Services and exchange operations.[30] There were more than 260 instructors in the academic division, and like an American college or university, the division was administered by a director and a dean. Courses from agriculture to commerce and from engineering to the liberal arts were offered and well attended.

The troops wore their uniforms, and the instructors, many of them civilians, wore a uniform with a special shoulder insignia and were treated as officers. The students had the use of all Special Services and exchange facilities, including beaches, sporting events, exchange beer halls, and cafeterias.[31] Unlike in USRRA, the GIs in Biarritz were encouraged to mix with the French population and attend French cultural and recreational events. Many GIs earned their first college credits through the university, which remained open until 1947, when the army negotiated with the University of Maryland to offer college-level courses through post educational facilities. Establishing the American universities in Europe begun by Osborn's Information and Education Division was a major accomplishment and fitted in with General Osborn's interest in education as a large factor in the evolution and improvement of American society.

Most GIs in Europe and Asia could not have cared one whit about Osborn's thoughts; they just wanted to go home. Tech Sergeant Charles Linzy listened to speeches by Eisenhower, Bradley, Truman, and Churchill on the Armed

Forces Radio about the end of the war. He wrote to his wife, "I hate to think about sitting over here doing only military government work, it will be worse than being in combat. In fact honey, I only want one thing at present time and that is to come home." A few days later Linzy told his wife, "We will do military government work and educational work." While waiting for word about his unit's future, Linzy took several courses offered by information-education officers or NCOs. PFC Keith Winston of the 100th Infantry Division wrote to his wife, "The final defeat of Germany didn't seem to make a whole lot of difference here. The boys have no way of celebrating, no place to go and they're still in the same war set up—no closer to home." Private Gene Mazza of the 1st Battalion, 133rd Infantry, in Italy, knew that he would not be going home soon, but his mind was on the opportunity to go to Milan to see a USO show featuring fellow Italian American Frank Sinatra. In July 1945 Mazza, who had studied Italian in Brooklyn, New York, found out that the education-information officer would send him to the University of Florence for a three-month session. Corporal Jack Binnion of the 128th Infantry Regiment had fought in New Guinea and the Philippines and served on occupation duty in Honshu, Japan. He wanted to go home to Kentucky, and on October 29, 1945, he was told that he would be on a troop ship soon that would sail to the east. Special Services continued to function for the troops in the Philippines. Staff Sergeant Robert Tuttle of the 499th Heavy Equipment Engineers knew he would be on Luzon for a while as they cleared the wreckage from the fighting in Manila. Every night he saw another first-run movie. They were so new he continually asked his fiancée back in Marion, Ohio, if she had seen them yet.[32]

The mission of the United States Army in Europe was changing at a time when the country demanded a rapid demobilization of the troops. The war had been won, but the United States had agreed to administer Germany with the British and then with the French. By 1948 the army had been reduced to only ten active divisions, but there was a growing Soviet threat in Eastern Europe and in their occupied zone in East Germany. The troops that remained in Europe were in need of exchanges and Special Services. By 1947 the needs of military dependents began to appear in the offerings of the exchanges. With supplies for the exchanges and Special Services (which continued to operate cafeterias and distribute free cigarettes for prizes and the like) came the possibility of exchange goods finding their way into the expanding black market. There was a rationing system with cards showing monthly allocations of candy, tobacco, coffee, and American alcohol.

On July 1, 1946, the United States Constabulary was activated in Germany and Austria, with a squadron of the 4th Regiment being stationed in Berlin. This new force had mobility and flexibility that allowed the constabulary to cover large areas with fewer troops. They could function as police and border guards and had horse platoons consisting of thirty mounts that operated in difficult terrain. Initially, the constabulary had a force of thirty-five thousand troops, organized into three brigades operating in the American Zone in West Germany. There were morale problems in the constabulary and in the permanent military personnel who administered Germany. There was a continual rapid personnel turnover within the constabulary regiments. Germany remained a nation of rubble and unemployment that offered few recreational opportunities to soldiers or dependents. German civilians who had been investigated and found to have no Nazi Party affiliations were employed as janitors and in other menial jobs. The Special Services companies that remained in Germany had major tasks in providing for troops and dependents. By 1946 Special Services activities were consolidated into battalions providing for the three constabulary brigades and the GIs working at the ports and in supply units.

Tech Sergeant Charles Linzy found peacetime boring, but he enrolled in a mechanical drawing course. As a senior NCO working at 459th Anti-Aircraft Battalion headquarters, he "found out what we pay the Heinie Frauleins that work for us. They serve our table, clean the rooms and do our laundry. The government pays them 100 marks a month and their eats. A mark is worth 10 cents. So that means $10.00 per month for them. [N]ot very much but better than making slaves of them as the Germans did in the countries that they overran." Linzy had been in combat for a year, from Normandy to the Ardennes and then into Germany, and he was scheduled for a weeklong leave to the Riviera. He listed the Special Services movies he saw almost every night and enjoyed the American beer now on sale in the exchange. He commented to his wife in Little Rock, "I can't understand these darn Heinie girls they are really crazy about the Yanks. Lots of the boys go with them and there is also a large percent that do not indulge."[33] A month later, after a restful leave on the Mediterranean, Linzy was assigned to finding SS men, looking for the telltale SS tattoo on their arms.

By 1946 Special Services, the Red Cross, exchange system, and military command had prepared booklets for the German cities where major headquarters were established. For example, the city of Wiesbaden, which would remain an American military center for more than a half century, required a GI guide. The city suffered a bombing raid on February 2, 1945, that destroyed a quarter of the city. The American command, however, had the necessary facilities for a command center with space for recreational activities. The Kurhaus, a prewar social and exhibition center, served as the Eagle Club, a Service Club, cafeteria, and Red Cross club. The military government took over most movie theaters and allowed closely monitored German-owned nightclubs to open. With caution the military command encouraged GIs to visit German bars and sample the local beers, which were a far cry from the 3.2 army beer once offered by the PX beer hall.[34] The war was certainly over, and the occupation had begun.

In November Major General Frederick Osborn left the army, returning to civilian life. Brigadier General Joseph Byron also decided to leave the army, but he would do so in the spring of 1946. They were two different men, coming from two different areas of prewar American life. Osborn was the intellectual educated at Princeton University, whereas Byron was a West Point graduate who turned his hand to business after resigning from the army. Osborn and Byron owed their important positions in World War II to two men: General George C. Marshall and General Brehon Somervell. Marshall was experienced in war and knew soldiers and what their expectations were. It was inherent in the draft of 1940 that the men called to service by lot numbers were the products of a changed society based on mass consumption and advertising. They were not the Doughboys of 1917–18, who were in many ways closer to the soldiers of the American Civil War. The Doughboys complained about the quality of their food, the lack of recreation, and the inability to get those small comforts such as a candy bar or a pack of cigarettes. When discharged from the army, what awaited them in civilian life? Many World War I soldiers got forty dollars to buy a suit of clothes and a pair of shoes, but many did not. Their jobs had been taken when they were called up for service, and bitterness felt by so many boiled over in the Bonus Marchers of the early 1930s. To avoid this, Marshall selected Osborn and Byron to do what was not done in the Great War.

It fell to General Somervell to see that Osborn and Byron did what was needed. Somervell was chief of the Army Service Forces, and his task was monumental. John Kennedy Ohl summed up Somervell's role in World War II: "Somervell was the principal logistical advisor and troubleshooter for War Department Chief of Staff General George C. Marshall. In effect, Somervell was the army's principal logistician."[35] Given the size of the army, the many theaters of war, and the vast distances to be covered, the task facing Somervell was daunting.

Somervell, who was brilliant, graduated from West Point in 1914, and by chance he met John C. H. Lee, who was chief of staff of the 89th Infantry Division. Lee had Somervell assigned as a G3 (operations officer) for the division. A relationship developed between Lee and Somervell that carried both men into World War II, where they would often clash over logistics and transportation. As G3 of the 89th, Somervell showed himself as an officer who learned quickly, but who could also be brusque, with little tolerance for an officer who did not do his job well or be as quick to grasp a situation as Somervell could.[36] In World War II this trait would earn him the enmity of many in the logistical system. When he saw that Osborn as chief of Special Services was not really the man for the job, Somervell created a directorate of information and education for him. Byron, the highly aggressive and successful director of the Army Exchange System, was elevated to be director of the Special Services Division. Osborn and Byron found their positions appropriate and functioned well until the end of the war.

Both Osborn and Byron had a great impact on the army into the twenty-first century. When not engaged in combat, the army has an emphasis on education, especially because of the many extensions of the GI Bill. The Servicemen's Readjustment Act of 1944 has been called the most successful piece of social legislation passed by the US Congress. Osborn's Information and Education Division printed booklets explaining veterans' rights and benefits and how to apply for them. After 1945 countless thousands of men and women trained and went to universities. Thousands of GIs and WACs attended American military universities in Europe. As Osborn later recalled, it was General Somervell who urged him to set up a system that would evaluate soldier morale and attitudes toward a number of critical issues.[37] For decades after the war, units had a Troop Information and Education NCO (this writer was a TI&E NCO).

The Army Exchange System lived on into the twenty-first century as an important part of the soldier's life in the United States and overseas. At the end of the war General Byron could boast that the Army Exchange System was the world's largest and most profitable chain store. The Army Exchange System became the Army Air Force Exchange System when the United States Air Force was created as an independent arm of the US defense system in 1947.

The 112th Infantry Regiment stationed in Germany in 1950 gave to each soldier a well-printed booklet titled *Welcome to the 112th Infantry*. The regiment, part of the 28th Infantry Division, was stationed at Heilbronn. A major part of the booklet was concerned with the offerings of the exchange system, from barbershops to bowling alleys, movies (twenty-five cents per ticket for GIs and their dependents), and a main PX that featured current styles of civilian clothes and the best of German cameras. One section dealt with an education center where a soldier could enroll in USAFI or take college courses offered by qualified instructors and professors from the University of Maryland.[38] The Special Services maintained Service Clubs that offered day-length tours and had special nights devoted to card playing, bingo, and the like. Coffee, soft drinks, popcorn, and cakes were served. The influence of those two civilians-turned-generals in World War II lives on well after they have passed from this world.

Epilogue

The war was over, and GIs marveled at the massive destruction in Germany. The 504th Parachute Infantry Regiment was sent to Berlin, which was well within the Russian zone of control. There really was not much to do except man checkpoints and try to maintain at least correct relations with the Russians who had taken this city. In the Friedenau area of Berlin the officers found an intact building and set up an officers' mess. There was not much extra to eat, but the paratroop officers found a lot to drink. They had rationed and nonrationed drinks. Rye, scotch, and a little bourbon were available, but rum and gin were nonrationed, and the GIs had a choice of such drinks as Alexander's Sister, American Beauty, Cabaret Cocktail, or Champs-Élysées. Of course, German beer was on their "wine list." The 504th did not jump into Berlin, but at least the paratroopers could enjoy their spare time.[1]

Corporal Thomas R. St. George had enough of soldiering in the Pacific and was ready to go back to civilian life, eventually becoming a well-known author and Hollywood screenwriter. Ironically, during his GI days he found a WAC sergeant, fell in love with her, married, and lived in bliss until her death in 1994. Linzy returned to Sybil in Little Rock, Eugene Mazza went back to Brooklyn, and Keith Winston arrived back in Philadelphia with a Bronze Star and a Purple Heart. All of these GIs are now gone, as is Carole Landis. Sergeants Don Malarkey and Bill Guarnere are old soldiers who mourned the passing of their beloved commander, Richard Winters. Their exploits were immortalized in the successful HBO miniseries *Band of Brothers*. Mary Ann Reed Bowen and Maralyn Howell Buillion reside in Oxford, Mississippi, both living active lives and enjoying their friends and their social activities.

Journalist and author Tom Brokaw wrote, "This is the greatest generation any society has produced."[2] One could not contest the truth of Brokaw's judgment about those who served from the call-up of 1940 to the massive buildup of American forces from 1941 to the end of World War II in 1945. Professor

Douglas Brinkley has pointed out that President Ronald Reagan's great speech delivered on the fortieth anniversary of D-Day in 1984, "Boys of Pointe du Hoc," began a reevaluation of the war, and from that time the Second World War became a "good war," noble in its ideals of liberation and democracy. The greatest generation arose because there was forward-looking, solid leadership by dedicated men and women. George C. Marshall as army chief of staff, Brehon Somervell as head of the Army Service Forces, and Ovita Culp Hobby as the head of the WACs serve as examples of that committed and highly motivated leadership. Osborn and Byron accepted the mission of providing for the soldier, building his morale under the difficult circumstances of combat or the confusion that the newly drafted soldier felt. When one considers World War II, the names of Frederick Osborn or Joseph Byron seldom occupy any time. However, without Osborn and Byron, the job of winning the war could have been more difficult. Wilbur Todd, a GI who served in an ordnance unit and saw action in the European theater of operations, including the Battle of the Bulge, recalled, "I could not have survived without the service clubs."[3] Almost every World War II GI interviewed remembered the PX and the Special Services with a favorable attitude. Having first-run movies on a post or in a battered German barn was important, and being able to buy a pack of smokes on a GI's monthly pay of fifty dollars meant a great deal. Both institutions, the PX and Special Services, survived the war and continue to serve the GIs of the twenty-first century.

With the war over, Byron and Osborn left the service with a sense of accomplishment. Osborn resigned in the fall of 1945 and began to take up his work on population, but in 1946 George Marshall called him back to Washington. Marshall convinced Osborn to work with the United Nations' Atomic Energy Commission. He continued his UN work until 1950. In 1954 he helped to found the *Eugenics Quarterly* and expressed concerns with the population explosion in the third world. In January 1981, at the age of ninety-two, Frederick Osborn died.

Byron took off his uniform in 1946 and returned to the business world. As a veteran of the Great War, a successful businessman, a dollar-a-year man prior to December 7, 1941, and then leader of the hectic building of the Army Exchange System and the Special Services Division, Byron was tired. On an extended vacation in April 1951, Joseph Byron fell ill and died. For these two men, history can pronounce the benediction of "well done."

To be fair, the work of the Special Services would not have been as successful had it not been for the USO, USO camp shows, the American Red Cross, and the legions of civic and church groups who provided for the troops. The maintenance of soldier morale was part of the great efforts put forth by the military and civilian sectors.

More than a half century has now passed since the guns of World War II fell silent. Twelve million men and women served in uniform. One of those was Margaret Katherine Hisgen of Albany, New York. She entered the army as a private, but because of her education and motivation, Hisgen was commissioned as a second lieutenant and then promoted to first lieutenant in the US Army Air Force. Hisgen agitated and pushed for an overseas assignment, and she was assigned to the Philippines. As an American girl, her social calendar was filled, but soon she received new orders that would send her home. The ship homeward bound stopped in Guam, and Margaret telegraphed her mother, "Left Manila 10 Nov. Your wayward daughter is on her way home."[4] For Margaret and twelve million GIs, sailors, Marines, and airmen, the war was over and morale was never higher.

Notes

1 The Abnormal Communities

1. Robert H. Ferrell, *A Soldier in World War I: The Diary of Elmer W. Sherwood*, 22.
2. Bruce Catton, *Glory Road*, 221–22.
3. David Kenyon Webster, *Parachute Infantry*, 368.
4. Frederick Palmer, *Newton D. Baker: America at War*, 1:297.
5. Ibid., 299–300.
6. Edward Frank Allen and Raymond B. Fosdick, *Keeping Our Fighters Fit for War and After.*
7. Palmer, *Newton D. Baker,* 1:309–10.
8. CPL Maurice Moser to parents, January 2, 1918, Moser Letters and Diaries.
9. Surgeon General of the Army, *Keeping Fit to Fight,* (1917), 3.
10. Allen and Fosdick, *Keeping Our Fighters Fit,* 7–8.
11. James J. Cooke, *The Rainbow Division in the Great War, 1917–1919,* 18.
12. Sergio Lugo, "The Books We Need When We Want Them," 8–13.
13. Fielder to Parents, May 30, June 3, 1918, SGT Eustace Fielder Letters.
14. Moser to parents, December 17, 1917, Moser Letters and Diaries.
15. For a detailed study of American logistics in World War I, see Phyllis A. Zimmerman, *The Neck of the Bottle.*
16. For a detailed look at Pershing, see James J. Cooke, *Pershing and His Generals.*
17. Palmer, *Newton D. Baker,* 2:4.
18. Albert M. Ettinger, *A Doughboy with the Fighting 69th,* 175.
19. James J. Cooke, *The All Americans at War,* 52, 92.
20. Erna Risch, *Quartermaster Support of the Army, 1775–1939,* 671–72, 685–87.
21. Entry 25, December 1918, Moser Diaries.

22. Palmer, *Newton D. Baker*, 2:206–7.
23. Allen and Fosdick, *Keeping Our Fighters Fit*, 51, 95–96.
24. CPL Harold H. Sherman Diary.
25. James J. Cooke, *The U.S. Air Service in the Great War, 1917–1919*, 203–4.
26. James J. Cooke, "The Americans," 142–56.
27. Palmer, *Newton D. Baker*, 2:404–6.
28. Ferrell, *A Soldier in World War I*, 152.

2 American Beer and American Girls

1. Risch, *Quartermaster Support of the Army*, 689–98.
2. Frederick H. Osborn, "Eugenics and National Defense," 203–4.
3. Frederick Osborn, oral history interview, Harry S. Truman Library and Museum.
4. Ibid.
5. Memorandum from Byron to General Somervell, May 25, 1943, Army Service Forces Records, Records Group 160, Entry 1, Carton 13.
6. Meghan K. Winchell, *Good Girls, Good Food, Good Fun: The Story of USO Hostesses during World War II*, 7.
7. Osborn, oral history interview, Truman Library.
8. Office of the Chief of Military History, *History of the Special Service Division*, Special Services Division Records.
9. *Special Services Handbook* (draft copy), 1942, ibid.
10. Office of the Chief of Military History, *Historical Record of the First Special Services Unit*, Adjutant General's Office files, Special Services Division Records.
11. Transcript, Morale Officers' Conference, January 19–23, 1942, Army Service Forces Records, Records Group 160, Entry 196A, Carton 445.
12. For a comprehensive study of Somervell's command of the Army Service Forces, see John Kennedy Ohl, *Supplying the Troops: General Somervell and American Logistics in WW II*.
13. See James J. Cooke, *Chewing Gum, Candy Bars, and Beer: The Army PX in World War II*.
14. Information Chart, ca. 1943, Army Service Forces Records, Records Group 160, Entry 1, Carton 13.
15. Enclosure from Lawrence, contained in a letter from Somervell to Osborn, June 14, 1942, Army Service Forces Records, Records Group 160, Entry 1, Carton 13.
16. Ibid.
Office of the Chief of Military History, *Historical Record of the First Special*

Services Unit, Adjutant General's Office files, Special Services Division Records.

18. Carole Landis, *Four Jills in a Jeep,* 1–9.

3 1943: Consolidation

1. Sarah Winston, ed., *V-Mail: Letters of a World War II Combat Medic,* 10–11.
2. PVT Arthur F. Jacklewski to sister, June 23, 1943, Jacklewski Letters.
3. Memorandum for Osborn, August 19, 1942, Army Service Forces Records, Records Group 160, Entry 1, Carton 73.
4. James J. Cooke, "The Songs behind the Stars and Stripes," 60–63.
5. Frederick H. Osborn, "Recreation, Welfare, and Morale of the American Soldier," 50–51.
6. *History of the Financial Services Branch,* Center of Military History, Special Services Division Records.
7. See Cooke, *Chewing Gum, Candy Bars, and Beer,* for a discussion of the civilian efforts.
8. Report to board, June 6, 1943, President's War Relief Board Records, Records Group 220, Entry 32055, Carton 196.
9. *Souvenir Menu,* the American Center Canteen, Melbourne, Australia, December 25, 1943, James J. Cooke World War II Morale Collection of Documents and Publications (military, civilian, and home front).
10. OWI release, December 30, 1942, American Red Cross Records, Records Group 200, Carton 660.
11. Tech SGT Charles B. Linzy to wife, November 11, 1943, Linzy Letters and Diary.
12. *Pocket Guide to North Africa,* 1942, Cooke Collection.
13. *Welcome to Casablanca: Passenger Information,* 1943, ibid.
14. *Pocket Guide to West Africa,* 1943, ibid.
15. *Pocket Guide to India,* 1943, ibid.
16. *Pocket Guide to Australia,* 1943, ibid.
17. *Transcript of Major Hart's Comments,* January 19, 1942, Center of Military History, Special Services Division Records.
18. Osborn to Somervell, June 15, 1942, Army Service Forces Records, Records Group 160, Entry 1, Carton 13.
19. Marshall to Roosevelt, October 8, 1942, ibid., Carton 22.
20. Bill Mauldin, *Willie and Joe: The WW II Years,* 1:15.
21. Somervell to Osborn, November 12, 1942, Army Service Forces Records, Records Group 160, Entry 1, Carton 22.
22. Memorandum, Army Services Forces, July 10, 1943, ibid., Carton 123.

23. SGT Robert D. Tuttle to sister, December 28, 1943, Tuttle Letters.

24. CPL Thomas R. St. George, *C/o Postmaster,* 40–41, 68.

25. LT Margaret Katherine Hisgen to parents, July 20, 1942, Hisgen Letters.

26. Proceedings of the Overseas Special Services and Exchange Officers, May 16–19, 1944, Lexington, VA, Army Service Forces Records, Records Group 160, Entry 196A, Carton 445.

27. History of the First WAC Special Services Company, ibid., Carton 451.

28. *V . . . , Fort Lewis,* Washington, 1943, Cooke Collection.

29. *Camp Joseph T. Robinson Pocket Guide,* 1944, ibid.

30. *Camp Crowder,* 1943, ibid.

31. MSGT Elmer Franzman to parents, December 21, 1943, Franzman Letters.

32. SSGT Wilbur R. Dunbar to Clara Belle Edwards, May 20, 1943, Dunbar Letters.

33. *New York Times,* May 28, 1943, Army Service Forces Records, Records Group 160, Entry 196A, Carton 241.

34. Hugh K. Wiltsire to PVT Jack Wilson, October 14, 1943, Wiltshire Letters.

4 Picadilly Lilly

1. *Entertainment News* (Louisville, KY), May 8–14, 1943, Cooke Collection.

2. *Greater Boston Soldiers and Sailors Committee,* 1943, ibid.

3. Salem Defense Recreation Committee, *Service Men's Guide to Salem,* 1943, ibid.

4. Winchell, *Good Girls, Good Food, Good Fun,* 19.

5. Thomas Edward Oblinger, *The Old Man from the Repple Depple,* 37.

6. Linzy to wife, March 1, 1943, Linzy Letters and Diary.

7. Ibid., September 5, 1943.

8. St. George, *C/o Postmaster,* 70–71.

9. William Guarnere, Edward Heffron, and Robyn Post, *Brothers in Battle, Best of Friends,* 84.

10. Russell M. Jones and John H. Swanson, *Dear Helen: Wartime Letters from a Londoner to Her American Pen Pal,* 207.

11. Linzy to wife, April 25, 1944, Linzy Letters and Diary.

12. Ibid., November 11, 1943.

13. SGT Don Malarkey and Bob Welch, *Easy Company Soldier,* 69.

14. GHQ, SWPA, *Chronology of the War in the Southwest Pacific, 1941–1945,* 1–3.

15. 32nd Division, *13,000 Hours: Combat History of the 32nd Infantry Division,* 4–6.

16. St. George, *C/o Postmaster,* 97.

17. SGT William E. George to mother and sister, April 14, 1943, George Letters.

18. HQ, Army Air Forces, *Assignment to Britain.*
19. Special Services Division, *A Short Guide to Great Britain,* Cooke Collection.
20. Guarnere, Heffron, and Post, *Brothers in Battle,* 94.
21. *History of the Special Services Division,* Center of Military History, Special Services Division Records, Carton 104.
22. Stephen Budiansky, "The Dancing Master Sergeant," 23.
23. *We're All in It, Let's Win It,* program, 1942, Cooke Collection.
24. La Guardia to Osborn, October 1, 1942, Army Service Forces Records, Records Group 160, Entry 1, Carton 73.
25. *The Soldier's Guide Book: Trinidad,* 1943, Cooke Collection.
26. Functional Chart, ca. 1943, Army Service Forces Records, Records Group 160, Entry 1, Carton 13.
27. Memorandum for Osborn, August 19, 1942, ibid., Carton 73.
28. Functional Chart, ca. 1943, ibid., Carton 13.
29. Byron to Somervell (and Osborn), May 21, 1943, ibid., Carton 22.
30. Byron to Somervell, May 21, 1943, ibid., Carton 13.
31. Ibid., May 25, 1943.
32. Styer to Osborn, January 18, 1943, ibid., Carton 22.
33. Memo from LTC William Beveridge, August 7, 1943, ibid., Carton 13.
34. Somervell to Osborn, February 20, 1943, ibid., Carton 22.
35. Somervell to Marshall, February 27, 1943, ibid.
36. Memorandum by Marshall, August 26, 1943, ibid.
37. Styer to Osborn, August 28, 1943, ibid.
38. Styer to Osborn, July 20, 1943, ibid.
39. Styer to Osborn, July 25, 1943, ibid.
40. Osborn to Styer, March 24, 1943, ibid.
41. *Welcome to Casablanca,* 1943, Cooke Collection.
42. Tuttle to May Hannegan, January 1, 1944, Tuttle Letters.
43. Jacklewski to parents, April 2, 1943, Jacklewski Letters.
44. *King Post* 1, no. 25 (1943), Cooke Collection.

5 A One-Man Band

1. *The 87th Division Acorn,* September 1943.
2. *The 87th Division Acorn,* April 1943.
3. *FM 28-105: The Special Services Company* (Washington: GPO, 1944).
4. Shelby L. Stanton, *World War II Order of Battle,* 13–14.
5. *History of the Special Services Division,* Center of Military History, Special Services Division Records, Carton 104.
6. *Organization of the 2nd Special Services Unit,* 1942, ibid.

7. *History of the Third Special Services Unit,* 1943, ibid.

8. Ibid.

9. *History of the 4th Special Services Unit,* 1943, ibid.

10. Memorandum for Somervell, August 23, 1943, Army Service Forces Records, Records Group 160, Entry 196A, Carton 233.

11. *8th Special Services Company, after Action Report,* October 3, 1943, Center of Military History, Special Services Division Records, Carton 104.

12. Memorandum, War Department, April 18, 1942, 9th Special Services Company Files, ibid.

13. Persian Gulf Command, 1944, Cooke Collection.

14. 7th Special Services Company Report, June 20, 1943, Army Service Forces Records, Records Group 160, Entry 196A, Carton 233.

15. *History of the 18th Special Services Company,* 1945, Center of Military History, Special Services Division Records, Carton 104.

16. Inspection Report, 23rd Special Services Company, November 16, 1943, Army Service Forces Records, Records Group 160, Entry 196A, Carton 233.

17. Inspection Report, 27th Special Services Company, November 12, 1943, ibid.

18. Policy for the Desert Training Center, 1943, ibid.

19. Ibid.

20. Report, 22nd Special Services Company, July 27, 1943, ibid.

21. Memorandum, Special Services Division, October 4, 1943, ibid.

22. Memorandum, Army Service Forces, July 19, 1943, ibid.

23. Memorandum, Special Services Division, June 29, 1943, ibid.

24. Obituary, August 15, 1945, PVT Gerald S. Hirshberg Letters and Papers.

25. PVT Tom A. Molley to friend, March 20, 1944, Molley Letters.

26. Tuttle to friend, December 24, 1943, Tuttle Letters.

27. Ibid., December 10, 1943.

28. Linzy to wife, December 24, 1943, Linzy Letters and Diary.

29. Final Report, 13th Special Services Company, 1945, Center of Military History, Special Services Division Records.

30. Ibid.

31. Franzman to parents, August 1, 1943, Franzman Letters.

32. George to parents, July 13, 1943, George Letters.

6 1944: Invasions and Frustrations

1. Thomas R. St. George, *Proceed without Delay,* 6.

2. Tuttle to May Hennigan, January 18, 1944, Tuttle Letters.

3. George to parents, April 11, 1944, George Letters.

4. *Supplementary History of Training Special Service Units and Companies,* 1945, Army Service Forces Records, Records Group 160, Entry 196A, Carton 450.

5. *Proceedings of the Special Services and Exchange Officers Conference, 1944,* ibid.

6. Ibid.

7. Kenneth K. Gowen, *Granddaddy, Tell Us about the War,* 61–62.

8. *History of the 1st Special Services Company,* 1945, Center of Military History, Special Services Division Records, Carton 104.

9. See Cooke, *Chewing Gum, Candy Bars, and Beer,* for a complete study of the PX system both in the United States and overseas.

10. PVT Harry G. Wilson to wife, May 8, 1944, Wilson Letters.

11. *History of the 1st Special Services Company,* 1945, Center of Military History, Special Services Division Records, Carton 104.

12. *History of the 3rd Special Services Company,* 1945, ibid.

13. *History of the 15th Special Services Company,* 1945, ibid.

14. *Memorandum from Control Division,* War Department to Director, Special Services Division, December 9, 1943, Army Service Forces Records, Records Group 160, Entry 1, Carton 22.

15. *Proceedings of the Special Services and Exchange Officers' Conference, 1944,* Army Service Forces Records, Records Group 160, Entry 196A, Carton 445.

16. Ibid.

17. Hisgen to parents, July 17, 1943, Hisgen Letters.

18. *Colonel Frank Kerr's Briefing, June, 1944,* Army Service Forces Records, Records Group 160, Entry 131, Carton 41.

19. *Proceedings of the Special Services and Exchange Officers' Conference, 1944,* Army Service Forces Records, Records Group 160.

20. Malarkey and Welch, *Easy Company Soldier,* 83.

21. Wilson to wife, June 8, 1944, Wilson Letters.

22. Don Kurzman, *The Race for Rome,* xxviii.

23. *Colonel Frank Kerr's Briefing, June, 1944,* Army Service Forces Records, Records Group 160, Entry 131, Carton 41.

24. Ibid.

25. Morale Services NATO USA, *A Soldier's Guide to Rome, 1944,* Cooke Collection.

26. Gowen, *Granddaddy,* 150–51.

27. Wiltshire to Corporal Jack Wilson, February 26, 1944, Wiltshire Letters.

28. Byron to Somervell, June 22, 1944, Army Service Forces Records, Records Group 160, Entry 1, Carton 13.

29. *Allied Swimming Championships, Rome, 1944,* program, Cooke Collection.

30. Gowen, *Granddaddy,* 158–59.
31. Franzman to parents, June 9, 11, 13, 1944, Franzman Letters.
32. Special Services Division, *Special Services for Fighting Yanks,* 1944, Center of Military History, Special Services Division Records.
33. Ibid.
34. *History of the Fiscal Branch* (Athletics and Recreation), 1946, ibid.
35. Special Services Officer, ed., *Pass in Review.*
36. Winston, *V-Mail,* 11.

7 "Unnecessarily Unsatisfactory"

1. Bob Hope, *I Never Left Home,* 56.
2. George to parents, August 10, 1943, George Letters.
3. Ibid., August 13, 1943.
4. Memorandum for the Director, Special Services Division, November 13, 1942, Army Service Forces Records, Records Group 160, Entry 1, Carton 22.
5. Ibid.
6. Transcript of a Special Services and Exchange Officers Conference, May 16–19, 1944, ibid., Entry 196A, Carton 445.
7. Memorandum for Somervell, May 20, 1943, ibid., Carton 233.
8. Memorandum for Osborn, August 23, 1943, ibid.
9. Memorandum by Special Services Division, August 26, 1943, ibid.
10. *History of the Fiscal Branch,* 1945, Center of Military History, Special Services Division Records.
11. Memorandum by Major General W. D. Styer, June 13, 1944, Army Service Forces Records, Records Group 160, Entry 1, Carton 22.
12. *MR 1-10 Morale,* Section III, 27–28.
13. *A Guide to the Field Artillery Replacement Training Center,* Fort Bragg, March 1944, 11–12, Cooke Collection.
14. *Camp Crowder,* 1943, 3–4, ibid.
15. *Camp Joseph T. Robinson Pocket Guide,* 1944, ibid.
16. *Fort Lewis, Washington,* 1943, ibid.
17. These surveys are found in Army Service Forces Records, Records Group 160, Entry 1, Carton 13.
18. Ibid.
19. Memorandum by Somervell, February 29, 1944, ibid.
20. Osborn, oral history interview, 1974, Truman Library.
21. Ibid.
22. Memorandum for General Somervell from Major Monroe Leaf, May 11, 1944, ibid.
23. Osborn, oral history interview, 1974, Truman Library.

24. War Department Memorandum for Byron and Osborn, August 12, 1944, Army Service Forces Records, Records Group 160, Entry 1, Carton 13.

25. Memorandum by Somervell, April 13, 1943, ibid.

26. Osborn, oral history interview, 1974, Truman Library.

27. Memorandum by Marshall to Somervell, February 25, 1944, Army Service Forces Records, Records Group 160, Entry 6, Carton 4.

28. Memorandum by McNarney, ca. February 25, 1944, ibid.

29. Memorandum from General Thomas Handy to Somervell, ca. February 27, 1944, ibid.

30. Memorandum by Styer, ca. February 28, 1944, ibid.

31. Cablegram from Marshall to MacArthur, ca. March 1944, ibid.

32. *History of the Special Services Division,* Center for Military History, Special Services Division, Carton 104.

8 Movies, Doughnuts, and M1 Rifles

1. Linzy to wife, June 21, 1944, Linzy Letters and Diary; Gowen, *Granddaddy,* 195–96; PFC Eugene Mazza to sister, July 11, 1944, Mazza Letters.

2. Franzman to parents, December 10, 1944, Franzman Letters; *Letters of Commendation to the 18th Special Services Company,* December 1943, Special Services Files, Center of Military History, Special Services Division Records.

3. St. George, *Proceed without Delay,* 76.

4. *History of the 8th Special Services Company,* 1946, Special Services Files, Center of Military History, Special Services Division Records.

5. See Cooke, *Chewing Gum, Candy Bars, and Beer.*

6. *After Action Report,* ca. 1945, Army Service Forces Records, Records Group 160, Entry 196A, Carton 450.

7. *After Action Report,* ca. 1945, ibid.

8. *Supplementary History of Training,* Special Services Units and Companies, ca. 1946, ibid.

9. *A Brief History of Special Services Publications,* ca. 1947, Special Services Files, Center of Military History, Special Services Division Records.

10. *What to Do in New York,* 1944–45; Public Telephone Center, *For Members of the Armed Forces in New York City,* 1944, Cooke Collection.

11. Wilson to wife, March 31, 1944, Wilson Letters.

12. *A Brief History of Special Services Publications,* ca. 1947, Special Services Files, Center of Military History, Special Services Division Records.

13. American Medical Association, *Army Morale and the Medical Reserve Corps,* November 1941, Cooke Collection.

14. *Welch Convalescent Hospital Guide,* 1944, ibid.

15. *Brooke Bluebonnet Broadcast* 1, no. 20 (1945), ibid.

16. Information Branch, ETO, *The Story of Rehabilitation,* 1945, ibid.

17. LT Guy Marriner, "Music in Reconditioning in Army Service Forces Hospitals."

18. Malarkey and Welch, *Easy Company Soldier,* 119.

19. *After Action Report,* 13th Special Services Company, ca. 1946, Special Services Files, Center of Military History, Special Services Division Records.

20. *After Action Report,* 2nd Special Services Company, ca. 1946, ibid.

21. *Historical Files,* 15th Special Services Company, ca. 1945, ibid.

22. Somervell to Lee, July 18, 1944, Army Service Forces Records, Records Group 160, Entry 1, Carton 13.

23. Ohl, *Supplying the Troops,* 235.

24. *Pocket Guide to Paris and the Cities of Northern France,* ca. 1944, Cooke Collection.

25. *Pocket Guide to France,* ca. 1944, ibid.

26. Gowen, *Granddaddy,* 229–31.

27. Linzy to wife, December 14, 1944, Linzy Letters and Diary.

28. Winston, *V-Mail,* 132.

29. *Platoon After Action Reports,* 12th Special Services Company, ca. 1945, Special Services Files, Center of Military History, Special Services Division Records.

30. Winchell, *Good Girls, Good Food, Good Fun,* 88; Mary Ann Reed Bowen, interview and statement, April 5, 2011, Cooke Collection.

31. Maralyn Howell Buillion, interview and statement, March 31, 2011, ibid.

9 Aftermath, 1945–48

1. *After Action Reports,* 2nd Special Services Company, ca. 1946, Special Services Files, Center of Military History, Special Services Division Records.

2. *Special Services Company Overseas Activities,* ca. 1945, Army Service Forces Records, Records Group 160, Entry 196A, Carton 450.

3. *After Action Reports,* Captain Richard W. Conway, January 6, 1944, Special Services Files, Center of Military History, Special Services Division Records.

4. Franzman to parents, July 16, 1944, Franzman Letters.

5. *Guide: Homeward Bound, Brazil,* 1945, Cooke Collection.

6. *War Department Memorandum,* W 35-44, May 6, 1944.

7. Ibid.

8. Ibid.

9. *War Department Circular, 344,* August 22, 1944.

10. *After Action Reports,* 13th Special Services Company, May, 1945, Special

Services Files, Center of Military History, Special Services Division Records.

11. Winston to wife, May 5, 1944, in *V-Mail,* edited by Winston, 233; Malarkey and Welch, *Easy Company Soldier,* 15; Linzy to wife, May 13, 17, 1945, Linzy Letters and Diary.

12. *History of the First WAC Special Services Company,* ca. 1946, Army Service Forces Records, Records Group 160, Entry 196A, Carton 451.

13. Ibid.

14. Third Army Special Services, *Tours in Austria and Bavaria* and *Here Is the Third Army's Tour for You,* Cooke Collection.

15. Special Services, *Excursion to Grasse,* ca. 1945, ibid.

16. *Paris and the Cities of Northern France* (Washington, DC: GPO, 1944), 1, ibid.

17. Advertising card, ca. 1945–46, ibid.

18. *Parisian Weekly Information (22–29 August 1945),* ibid.

19. *Seine Section, Paris, France,* 23.

20. Special Services, USFA, *Rest Resorts All over Austria: Salzburg,* ca. 1945, ibid.

21. William Hurt to parents, June 21, 1945, Hurt Letters; Jack Binnion to girlfriend, December 26, 1944, Binnion Letters.

22. Hisgen to parents, September 22, 1945, Hisgen Letters.

23. *After Action Reports,* 5th Special Services Company, 1945–1947, Special Services Files, Center of Military History, Special Services Division Records.

24. *Final Report,* 3rd Special Services Company, July 1948, ibid.

25. Osborn, oral history interview, July 1974, Truman Library.

26. "Education: Dear Old USAFI."

27. USAFI, *English Grammar: A Self-Teaching Course,* 1943, 1, Cooke Collection.

28. Osborn, oral history interview, July 1974, Truman Library.

29. USRRA, *Welcome to the Riviera,* 1945, Cooke Collection.

30. Biarritz American University, *BAU Beacon* (yearbook), 1945, ibid.

31. Ibid.

32. Linzy to wife, May 8, 20, 1945, Linzy Letters and Diary; Winston to wife, May 8, 1945, in *V-Mail,* edited by Winston, 240; Mazza to parents, June 23, 1944, Mazza Letters; Mazza to a friend, July 29, 1945, Mazza Letters; Binnion to his sweetheart, October 29, 1945, Binnion Letters; Tuttle to May Hannegan, September 2, 28, 30, 1945, Tuttle Letters.

33. Linzy to wife, June 6, 10, 1945, Linzy Letters and Diary.

34. *Views and Facts of Wiesbaden, as Seen through the Eyes of the American Soldier,* Wiesbaden, 1946, Cooke Collection.

35. Ohl, *Supplying the Troops,* 3.

36. Ibid., 13–14.
37. Osborn, oral history interview, July 1974, Truman Library.
38. *Welcome to the 112th Infantry,* Heilborn, Germany, 1950, Cooke Collection.

Epilogue

1. Wine List, 504th Parachute Regiment Officers Mess, ca. 1945, Cooke Collection.
2. Tom Brokaw, *The Greatest Generation,* xxx.
3. Wilbur Todd, interview with the author, May 4, 2011, Cooke Collection.
4. Hisgen to mother, telegram, November 27, 1945, Hisgen Letters.

Bibliography

Archival and Personal Sources

American Red Cross. Records. Records Group 200, National Archives II, College Park, MD.

Army Service Forces. Records. Records Group 160, National Archives II, College Park, MD.

Cooke, James J. World War II Morale Collection of Documents and Publications (military, civilian, and home front). Oxford, MS.

Harry S. Truman Library and Museum. Independence, MO.

Letters and Diaries (author's private collection)

PVT Jack Binnion Letters, 1943–45.

SSGT Wilbur R. Dunbar Letters, 1942–44.

SGT Eustace Fielder Letters, 1918–19, courtesy of Mrs. Gail Fielder Andrews.

MSGT Elmer Franzman Letters, 1942–45.

SGT William E. George Letters, 1942–45.

PVT Gerald S. Hirshberg Letters and Papers, 1943–44, now housed in the Archives of the Second World War Experience Centre in the United Kingdom.

LT Margaret Katherine Hisgen Letters, 1942–45.

CPL William Hurt Letters, 1942–45.

PVT Arthur F. Jacklewski Letters, 1943–45.

MSG Will C. Johnson Letters, 1943–45.

Tech SGT Charles B. Linzy Letters and Diary, 1942–45.

PFC Eugene Mazza Letters, 1944–46.

PVT Robert Molley Letters, 1943–45.

CPL Maurice Moser Letters and Diaries, 1917–19.

CPL Harold J. Sherman Diary, 1917–19.

PVT Vernon Startman Letters, 1943–44.

SGT Robert D. Tuttle Letters, 1943–45.

PVT Harry G. Wilson Letters, 1943–44.

PFC Hugh K. Wiltshire Letters, 1943–45.

President's War Relief Board. Records. Records Group 220, National Archives II, College Park, MD.

Special Services Division. Records. Office of the Chief of Military History, Washington, DC.

Primary Sources

26th Infantry Division. *History of World War II.* Druck, Belarus: Buch und Kunstdrucker, 1945.

32nd Division. *13,000 Hours: Combat History of the 32nd Infantry Division.* Philippine Islands: Printed by the 273rd Engineers, 1945.

The Thirty-Eighth Division, Camp Shelby, 1941. Atlanta: Army-Navy Publishers, 1941.

The 87th Division, Acorn. N.p., 1943.

Allen, Frank, and Raymond B. Fosdick. *Keeping Our Fighters Fit for War and After.* New York: Century, 1918.

Blood and Fire: 63rd Infantry Division. N.p.: HQ, 63rd Division, 1945.

Burgett, Donald R. *Seven Roads to Hell: A Screaming Eagle at Bastogne.* New York: Dell, 1999.

"Education: Dear Old USAFI." *Time,* June 7, 1943.

Ettinger, Albert M. *A Doughboy with the Fighting 69th.* Edited by A. Churchill Ettinger. Shippensburg, PA: White Mane, 1992.

Ferrell, Robert H. *In the Company of Generals: The World War I Diary of Pierpont L. Stackpole.* Columbia: University of Missouri Press, 2009.

——, ed. *A Soldier in World War I: The Diary of Elmer W. Sherwood.* Indianapolis: Indiana Historical Society Press, 2004.

Ganter, Raymond. *Roll Me Over: An Infantryman's World War I.* New York: Ballantine, 1997.

GHQ, SWPA. *Chronology of the Occupation, 1945–1946.* Manila: Historical Division, G3, 1946.

——. *Chronology of the War in the Southwest Pacific, 1941–1945.* Manila: Historical Division, G3, 1945.

Gowen, Kenneth K. *Granddaddy, Tell Us about the War.* Oxford, MS: Kay-Dot, 1998.

Guarnere, William, Edward Heffron, and Robyn Post. *Brothers in Battle, Best of Friends.* New York: Berkley, 2007.

——. *History of a Combat Regiment: 104th Infantry.* [Germany]: n.p., 1945.

Hope, Bob. *I Never Left Home.* New York: Simon and Schuster, 1944.

HQ, Army Air Forces. *Assignment to Britain.* Washington, DC: GPO, 1942.

Landis, Carole. *Four Jills in a Jeep.* New York: World, 1944.

LeRoy, Trooper Bob. *From My Foxhole to Tokyo.* Boring, OR: CPA, 1992.

Malarkey, SGT Don, and Bob Welch. *Easy Company Soldier.* New York: St. Martin's Press, 2008.

Marriner, LT Guy. "Music in Reconditioning in Army Service Forces Hospitals." *Music Library Association Notes* 2, no. 3 (1945).

MR 1-10 Morale. June 12, 1942 edition. Washington, DC: War Department.

Ninturno to the Appennines: 85th Infantry Division. N.p.: Information Section, 85th Division, 1944.

Oblinger, Thomas Edward. *The Old Man from the Repple Depple.* [Bloomington, IN]: Xlibris, 2007.

The Officers' Guide. Harrisburg, PA: Military Service Publishing, 1943.

Osborn, Frederick H. "Eugenics and the National Defense." *Journal of Heredity* 32 (1941).

———. "Recreation, Welfare, and Morale of the American Soldier." *Annals of the American Academy of Political and Social Science* 220 (March 1942).

Regimental Historical Committee. *History of the 376th Infantry Regiment.* Wuppertal, Germany: Carl Weddigen, 1945.

Report by the Supreme Commander to the Combined Chiefs of Staff on the Operations in Europe of the Allied Expeditionary Force, 6 June 1944 to 8 May 1945. Washington, DC: GPO, 1945.

Seine Section, Paris, France. Paris: 660th Engineer Base Topographical Battalion, 1945.

Special Services Division. *A Short Guide to Great Britain.* Washington: GPO, 1943.

Special Services Officer, ed. *Pass in Review.* N.p., 1944.

St. George, CPL Thomas R. *C/o Postmaster.* New York: Thomas Y. Crowell, 1943.

———. *Proceed without Delay.* New York: Thomas Y. Crowell, 1945.

Surgeon General of the Army. *Keeping Fit to Fight.* Washington, DC: GPO, 1917.

To Bizerte with the II Corps. Washington, DC: GPO, 1944.

Webster, Davis Kenyon. *Parachute Infantry.* New York: Dell, 2002.

Winston, Sarah, ed. *V-Mail: Letters of a World War II Combat Medic.* Chapel Hill, NC: Algonquin Books, 1985.

Secondary Sources

Ambrose, Stephen E. *Band of Brothers.* New York: Simon and Schuster, 2001.

———. *Citizen Soldiers.* New York: Simon and Schuster, 1997.

——. *D-Day: June 6, 1944.* New York: Simon and Schuster, 1994.

Bell, William Gardner. *Commanding Generals and Chiefs of Staff, 1775–1983.* Washington, DC: Center of Military History, 1983.

Bourne, John, Peter Liddle, and Ian Whitehead. *The Great World War, 1914–1945.* 2 vols. London: HarperCollins, 2001.

Brokaw, Tom. *The Greatest Generation.* New York: Random House, 1998.

Budiansky, Stephen. "The Army's Choreographer." *World War II* (January 2011).

——. "The Dancing Master Sergeant." *World War II* (January 2011).

Camfield, Thomas M. "Will to Win: The U.S. Army Troop Morale Program of World War I." *Military Affairs* 41, no. 3 (1977).

Catton, Bruce. *Glory Road.* New York: Doubleday, 1952.

Coffey, Frank. *50 Years of the USO: Always Home.* New York: Brassey's, 1991.

Collins, Clella R. *The Army Woman's Handbook.* New York: Whittles House, 1942.

Cooke, James J. *The All Americans at War.* Westport, CT: Praeger, 1999.

——. "The Americans." In *At the Eleventh Hour,* edited by Hugh Cecil and Peter H. Liddle. London: Leo Cooper, 1998.

——. *Chewing Gum, Candy Bars, and Beer: The Army PX in World War II.* Columbia: University of Missouri Press, 2009.

——. *Pershing and His Generals.* Westport, CT: Praeger, 1997.

——. *The Rainbow Division in the Great War, 1917–1919.* Westport, CT: Praeger, 1994.

——. "The Songs behind the Stars and Stripes." *Everyone's War,* no. 6 (Autumn–Winter 2004).

——. *The U.S. Air Service in the Great War, 1917–1919.* Westport, CT: Praeger, 1996.

D'Este, Carlo. *Fatal Decisions.* New York: HarperCollins, 1991.

Freidel, Frank. *Over There.* New York: McGraw-Hill, 1990.

Friedman, Barbara G. *From Battlefield to the Bridal Suite: Media Coverage of British War Brides.* Columbia: University of Missouri Press, 2007.

Gavin, James M. *On to Berlin.* New York: Viking, 1978.

Hendrickson, Robin, ed. *World War II Memories.* Jackson: University Press of Mississippi, 2001.

Higonnet, Margaret Randolph, et al. *Behind the Lines: Gender and the Two World Wars.* New Haven, CT: Yale University Press, 1987.

Jackson, W. G. F. *The Battle for Rome.* New York: Bonanza Books, 1969.

Jeffers, H. Paul. *Taking Command.* New York: New American Library, 2009.

Jones, Russell M., and John H. Swanson. *Dear Helen: Wartime Letters from a Londoner to Her American Pen Pal.* Columbia: University of Missouri Press, 2009.

Kennedy, David M. *Over Here: The First World War and American Society.* New York: Oxford University Press, 1982.

Kurzman, Dan. *The Race for Rome.* New York: Doubleday, 1975.

Lugo, Sergio. "The Books We Need When We Want Them." *Relevance* (2008).

Mauldin, Bill. *Willie and Joe: The WW II Years.* 2 vols. Seattle: Fantagraphic Books, 2008.

Nichol, John, and Tony Rennell. *Tail-End Charlies.* New York: St. Martin's Press, 2006.

Ohl, John Kennedy. *Supplying the Troops: General Somervell and American Logistics in WW II.* DeKalb: Northern Illinois University Press, 1994.

Palmer, Frederick. *Newton D. Baker: America at War.* 2 vols. New York: Dodd, Mead, 1931.

Pogue, Forrest C. *George C. Marshall: Ordeal and Hope, 1939–1942.* New York: Viking, 1966.

Risch, Erna. *Quartermaster Support of the Army, 1775–1939.* Washington, DC: Center of Military History, 1989.

Sherman, Nancy. *The Untold War.* New York: W. W. Norton, 2010.

Stanton, Shelby L. *World War II Order of Battle.* New York: Galahad Books, 1991.

Titus, James, ed. *The Home Front and War in the Twentieth Century.* Washington, DC: Office of Air Force History, 1982.

Waller, Maureen. *London 1945: Life in the Debris of War.* New York: St. Martin's Press, 2004.

Weingartner, Steven, ed. *A Weekend with the Great War.* Cantigny Military History Series. Shippensburg, PA: White Mane, 1996.

Winchell, Meghan K. *Good Girls, Good Food, Good Fun: The Story of USO Hostesses during World War II.* Chapel Hill: University of North Carolina Press, 2008.

Zabecki, David T. *World War II in Europe: An Encyclopedia.* 2 vols. New York: Garland, 1999.

Zimmerman, Phyllis A. *The Neck of the Bottle.* College Station: Texas A&M University Press, 1992.

Index

The USO, USO Camp Shows, the American Red Cross, and the Salvation Army do not appear in the index because the Army Exchange System (AES) and the Special Services Division (SSD) worked very closely with those organizations, and they appear so often in the text that to track their appearance would make the index unduly cluttered and quite long. The AES and the SSD were successful, but those army organizations could not have accomplished their mission without the coordination with the civilian organizations which were very active in the war effort to build and maintain GI morale.

Pearl Harbor, 26, 32, 36, 64
Pershing, John J., 1, 4, 5, 9, 14, 15, 21, 63
Persia, 67
Persian Gulf Command, 98–99
Phenix City, AL, 35, 45
Philippine Islands, 2, 8, 113, 125, 131, 156, 169
Power, William H., 97–98
Prisoners of War in the US, 140–41

Raye, Martha, 23, 39
Raycroft, Joseph E., 18
Reed, Mary Ann, 158, 179
Reinhart, Raymond A., 160
Remagen Bridge, 164
Reykjavik, Iceland, 95
Rome, 112, 113, 118, 120, 121, 122
Rooney, Mickey, 166
Roosevelt, Franklin D., 29, 96, 121, 141

Saint-Mihiel campaign, 1
Salem (OR) Defense Recreation Committee, 55
San Obispo School, 163
Send 'Em Smokes, 43
Servicemen's Readjustment Act (GI Bill), 126, 141, 172, 177
729th Special Services Entertainment Center, 171
Sharpe, Henry G., 13
Shaw, Artie, 3, 58
Sherwood, Elmer, 5, 14, 22
Sidney, Harper, 44
Smokes for Yanks, 43
Solomon Islands, 102
Somervell, Brehon: Army Exchange Service, 49–50, 65; chief, Army Service Forces, 33, 49–50; concern over morale in the PTO, 139, 171; concern over political surveys, 136; concern over slow shipment of PX supplies (PTO), 69; Eisenhower informs Somervell of the need for much more recreational equipment (ETO), 70; and George C. Marshall, 33–34, 126; John C.

H. Lee, 154, 155, 176; and Joseph Byron, 67, 69, 119; relations with Osborn, 37, 51, 124, 136, 171; support for athletic events (Rome, ETO), 122, 126
Spaatz, Carl, 36
Spaulding, Francis Trow, 171
Special Services Companies: 1st, 37–38, 51, 91, 93, 113, 115; 2nd, 93, 94–95, 149, 150, 151, 152, 160–61; 3rd, 94, 115, 171; 4th, 95–96, 144–45; 5th, 170; 6th, 153–54, 170; 7th, 99; 8th, 97, 150; 9th, 98; 12th, 100, 152, 153, 156–57; 13th, 107–8, 116, 149, 150, 151, 165; 15th, 102, 104, 152; 17th, 111; 18th, 99–100, 143, 145, 150, 161–62; 22nd, 102; 23rd, 101, 150; 24th, 150; 25th, 150; 26th, 150; 27th, 102; 28th, 73; 29th, 111; 31st, 102; 1st WAC, 145, 166–67
Special Services Plays, 146–47
Stage Door Canteen, 43, 44, 64, 146
Stars and Stripes, 47–48, 123
St. George, Thomas R., 57, 60, 110, 143, 179
Stimson, Henry L., 25, 62, 172
St. Vith, Belgium, 151
Styer, W. D., 70, 71
Sullivan, Ed, 63
Supplee, H. Clay, 63
Sutlers, 6–7
Swallow, Betty, 58
Sweeny, Mary, 16
Sweeny, Sunshine, 16

Third (3rd) US Army, 149, 164–65; occupation of Germany, 1918–1923, 4, 17, 21, 24; 1945–1952, 167–68, 171
Todd, Wilbur, 180
Torquay, England, 95
Training Circular 87 (1942), 124
Transportation Corps Training Center, 73
Trinidad, 64–65
Troop Information and Education (TI&E), 172, 173, 177
Truax Army Air Hospital, 158
Tuttle, Robert, D., 50, 71, 107, 111, 174

About the Author

The late James J. Cooke was a Professor Emeritus of History at the University of Mississippi. He was the author of many books, including *Chewing Gum, Candy Bars, and Beer: The Army PX in World War II* (University of Missouri Press).